English Pronunciation in Use

Advanced

Self-study and classroom use

Martin Hewings

CAMBRIDGE UNIVERSITY PRESS

Cambridge, New York, Melbourne, Madrid, Cape Town, Singapore,
São Paulo, New Delhi

Cambridge University Press
c/o Cambridge University Press India Pvt. Ltd.
Cambridge House
4381/4, Ansari Road, Daryaganj
New Delhi 110002
India

www.cambridge.org
Information on this title: www.cambridge.org/9780521619561

First published 2007
First South Asian edition 2009

This South Asian edition is based on Martin Hewings / English Pronunciation in Use: Advanced / 9780521693769 / 2007

Printed in India at Replika Press Pvt. Ltd.

A catalogue record for this publication is available from the British Library

ISBN-13 978-0-521-75745-4 (Paperback)
ISBN-13 978-0-521-73641-1 (Paperback + CD-ROM+ Audio CDs)

Contents

Organising information in conversation

Intonation in telling, asking and answering

Intonation in managing conversation

Section D Pronunciation in formal settings

Section E Reference

Acknowledgements

I would like to thank Frances Amrani for guiding the project, and Roslyn Henderson and Alyson Maskell for their invaluable suggestions and their attention to detail in editing the material.
I also wish to thank the following reviewers for their suggestions in the early stages of writing:
Barbara Bradford, Kent, UK
Ian Chitty, Melbourn, UK
David Deterding, Singapore
Amanda Lloyd, Cambridge, UK
Andrea Paul, Melbourne, Australia
Dolores Ramirez Verdugo, Madrid, Spain

A number of people have provided inspiration and information, and also specific advice on the pronunciation of non-native English speakers. Thanks in particular to Richard Cauldwell, Frances Hotimsky, Philip King, Gerard O'Grady and Dorota Pacek. I have drawn extensively for information and ideas on a wide variety of teaching materials and reference works, and I acknowledge the part they have played in shaping the book. In particular, I wish to acknowledge Hahn, L. D. & Dickerson, W. B. (1999) *Speechcraft: Workbook for academic discourse.* Ann Arbor: University of Michigan Press (Units 40 & 41) for the analysis of stress adapted for Unit 12.

At home, thanks to Ann, Suzanne, and David for their support and willingness to listen.

Martin Hewings 2007

The author and publishers are grateful to the following for permission to reproduce copyrighted material in *English Pronunciation in Use Advanced.*

Jones, D. (2006) *Cambridge English Pronouncing Dictionary*, 17th edn. Edited by P. Roach, J. Setter and J. Hartman. Cambridge: Cambridge University Press.

Cambridge Advanced Learner's Dictionary (2005), 2nd edn. Cambridge: Cambridge University Press.

Development of this publication has made use of the Cambridge International Corpus (CIC). The CIC is a computerized database of contemporary spoken and written English, which currently stands at 1 billion words. It includes British English, American English and other varieties of English. It also includes the Cambridge Learner Corpus, developed in collaboration with the University of Cambridge ESOL Examinations. Cambridge University Press has built up the CIC to provide evidence about language use that helps to produce better language teaching materials.

Audio recording by James Richardson, AVP studios, London.

Illustrations by Jo Blake, Mark Draisey, Julian Mosedale and David Shenton.

Cover design by Dale Tomlinson.

Designed and typeset by Kamae Design, Oxford.

About this book

English Pronunciation in Use Advanced gives students of English practice in pronunciation to help improve both speaking and listening. Although it has been written so that it can be used for self-study, it will work equally well in a class situation with a teacher.

It will be particularly useful for students whose English is adequate for most social, professional or educational purposes, but who want to work further on pronunciation to improve their understanding and ensure that they are easily understood both by native and non-native English speakers. The focus is primarily on improving pronunciation in communication rather than practising individual sounds or words.

Organisation

There are 60 units in the book. Each unit looks at a different point of pronunciation. Each unit has two pages. The page on the left has explanations and examples, and the page on the right has exercises. The 60 units are divided into four sections.

- Section A introduces accents in different varieties of English, resources for independent study of pronunciation and differences between pronunciation in slow and fast speech.
- Section B is about pronunciation in words and phrases, including consonant clusters and stressed and unstressed syllables, and pronunciation of foreign words.
- Section C is about pronunciation in conversation, including how intonation contributes to meaning.
- Section D is about pronunciation in formal settings, including professional contexts such as giving business or conference presentations.

After the 60 units there is a fifth section, Section E, which contains the following:

- Exercises to practise the phonemic alphabet
- Further practice of consonant clusters
- Further practice of word stress
- Glossary
- Further reading

At the end of the book there is a Key with answers.

To accompany the book, there is a set of five CDs, available separately or as part of a pack.

A CD-ROM is also available for use on a computer. On the CD-ROM additional practice exercises are provided on all of the units (different from those in the book). The CD-ROM can be bought separately or as part of a pack.

Additional equipment needed

A CD player is needed to listen to the recorded material that goes with this book.
It will also be useful for students to have equipment to record their own voices.
The symbol (A1) indicates the CD track number for recorded material, i.e. CD A, track 1.

English Pronunciation in Use Intermediate and *English Pronunciation in Use Advanced*

It is not necessary to have worked on *English Pronunciation in Use Intermediate* (see Section E5 *Further reading*) before using this book. However, to practise pronunciation of particular letters and sounds, it is recommended that students use *English Pronunciation in Use Intermediate*, where additional practice of stress and intonation can also be found. Both books have the same format of explanations and examples on the left page and exercises on the right page in each unit.

Using the book

There is no fixed order in which the units should be worked through. However, it will be useful to do the units in Section A *Getting started* first to provide some background to later units. In addition, it will be useful to study the basic units on intonation (Units 32–34 on breaking speech into units and highlighting information, and Unit 39 on falling and rising tones) before doing later units which focus on intonation.

Phonemic symbols

It is not necessary to understand phonemic symbols to use this book. Where phonemic symbols are used, example words are given and/or the words are found on the recording. However, being able to understand phonemic symbols is a useful skill to have in order to make use of the information about pronunciation in dictionaries. The phonemic symbols used in this book are listed on page 192 and there are exercises to practise the phonemic alphabet in Section E1.

Pronunciation in speaking and listening

Although the focus of the book is pronunciation in speaking, it also gives the opportunity to practise listening to speech at conversational speed and in a variety of English accents. Where an explanation refers to a feature of pronunciation that is particularly relevant to understanding English, rather than one that students should necessarily try to include in their own speech, this is shown with the sign "Important for listening". Where an explanation is particularly relevant for developing advanced fluency, this is shown with the sign .

Accents of English used in the recording

For a model of pronunciation to copy when speaking, we have used the accent of English sometimes referred to as 'BBC English'. However, in work or travel a wide range of English accents might be heard. To help prepare for this, a number of accents are found on the recording. These include both native-speaker varieties of English (from the United States, Canada, Australia, South Africa, Jamaica, India and various parts of Britain) and non-native speaker varieties of English (from China, Spain, Poland and Japan). In the Key, information can be found about where speakers come from on the recordings for the exercises.

More about BBC English and other varieties of English can be found in Units 1 and 2.

Using the further practice material

After working through Units 7, 8 and 9 on consonant clusters, further practice can be found in Section E2 *Consonant clusters*. After working through Units 11, 12 and 13 on suffixes and word stress, further practice can be found in Section E3 *Word Stress*.

The glossary

In Section E4 *Glossary*, explanations can be found of terms used in this book. Most of these are specific to the subject of pronunciation.

Using the recording

When working with the recording, a track should be played as often as necessary. When doing an exercise, it may be necessary to press 'pause' after each sentence to give time to think or write an answer. When instructed to repeat single words, there is space on the recording to do so, but to repeat whole sentences the recording will have to be paused each time. In some exercises, special instructions are given on how to use the recording.

To help you further improve your pronunciation and understanding of spoken English, it is important to listen to as much English as you can. The internet provides access to a wide range of sources of spoken English, and in Unit 4 you can find suggestions on some that you might find useful.

1 Accents (1): Varieties of English

A Although we commonly talk about 'English pronunciation' (including in the title of this book), obviously not all speakers of English pronounce it in the same way. Even between countries where English is the first language of the majority of the population there are considerable differences, and we can distinguish between the pronunciation of 'British English', 'American English', 'Australian English', 'South African English', and so on.

B A2 Important for listening

Across these varieties of English, there may be differences in how vowels and consonants are pronounced, how words are stressed, and in intonation. For example, listen and notice differences between standard British English (Br) and American English (US) pronunciation in these sentences (you will hear British English first):

That's better.	In US /t/ is 'flapped' so that it sounds like /d/ (and often transcribed in dictionaries as /t̬/) when it comes between two vowels.
I'm picking up the car next Tuesday.	• car = /kɑː/ in Br and /kɑːr/ in US. In Br, /r/ is pronounced only when it is followed by a vowel, while in US it is also pronounced before consonants and at the end of a word. • Tuesday = /tjuː-/ in Br and /tuː-/ in US. The sounds /tj/, /nj/, /dj/, etc. are not used in US.
What's your address?	Some words are stressed differently in Br and US, including a'ddress (Br) and 'address (US).
I went out because I was hot and wanted some fresh air.	Some speakers of US (and also Australian and New Zealand English) use a 'high rising' tone for statements where most speakers of Br would use a falling tone.

C A3 Important for listening

Within Britain and the US there are also many regional accents. For example, listen and notice differences in pronunciation in these sentences, said first by a speaker of 'BBC English' (see Unit 2) and then by a speaker from the city of Birmingham in England (you will hear BBC English first):

See you tonight.	The second vowel in 'tonight' is pronounced /aɪ/ in BBC English but /ɔɪ/ (as in 'boy') in a Birmingham accent.
Are those your brother's?	The vowel in 'those' is pronounced /əʊ/ in BBC English but more like /aʊ/ (as in 'now') in a Birmingham accent. The first vowel in 'brother's' is pronounced /ʌ/ (as in 'but') in BBC English but /ʊ/ (as in 'would') in a Birmingham accent.
She was smoking.	The last sound in *-ing* words is /ŋ/ in BBC English, but /ŋg/ in a Birmingham accent, i.e. the *-g* is pronounced.

Section E5 *Further reading* gives suggestions on where you can find more information about pronunciation in national and regional varieties of English.

Exercises

1.1 (A4) Listen. You will hear speakers from Britain, the USA, Canada, Australia and South Africa talking about what they enjoy doing in their spare time.

Which of these accents are you most familiar with? Is there one you find easier to understand than the others?

1.2 (A5) Here is a text read aloud first by a British English speaker and then an American English speaker. Listen as many times as you need and note differences in pronunciation that you observe, focusing on the underlined words. A few are done for you. (It is not necessary to use phonemic symbols in this exercise, but a list can be found on page 192 if you want to refer to it.)

I was reading in a <u>magazine</u> the other day about how <u>common obesity</u> is now. Some <u>new research</u> has found that <u>over</u> <u>forty</u> percent of the population is <u>overweight</u>. Most people in the <u>survey</u> said <u>they'd rather</u> drive than <u>walk</u>, and that it's <u>better</u> to spend <u>leisure</u> time at home than outside. That's <u>understandable</u> in the winter, I guess, but <u>surely</u> everyone can build some <u>exercise</u> into their daily <u>schedule</u>?

- common: the first vowel is more 'open' in US
- new: said 'nyoo' (/njuː/) in Br and 'noo' (/nuː/) in US
- rather: the first vowel is different – /ɑː/ (like 'car') in Br and /æ/ (like 'hat') in US
- surely: the first vowel is different – /ɔː/ (like 'or') in Br and /ʊ/ (like 'put') in US; also the 'r' is pronounced in US

1.3 (A6) You will hear four more people talking about what they enjoy doing in their spare time. They are from northern England, Scotland, Wales and Northern Ireland. Listen as many times as you need and write brief notes about what they say.

northern England: ....

....

Scotland: ....

....

Wales: ....

....

Northern Ireland: ....

....

Now read the transcripts in the Key. Are there particular features of their pronunciation that you had problems understanding? In what ways is their pronunciation different from BBC English – that is, British English spoken *without* a regional accent (see Unit 2)?

Follow up: Record yourself reading one of the extracts in exercise 1.1. (These are written down in the Key.) Compare your reading and the version on the recording. What are the main differences in pronunciation that you notice?

2 Accents (2): English as an international language

A

In this book...	
... you will use British English as a model for pronunciation.	In particular, you will use the variety that has come to be known as 'BBC English'. BBC English is the pronunciation used by speakers such as newsreaders and announcers on television and radio, including the World Service. Some of these speakers have regional accents from the United Kingdom, such as Scottish, Welsh or Northern Irish accents, but the accent you will hear in this book is typical of those with an English accent. This accent is taken as the 'model' because it is a widely broadcast and respected variety, and for most people is easily understood.
... you will hear a wide variety of English accents.	Recorded material used mainly for listening includes speakers with different English accents. Some have English as their first language (e.g. from Australia and the United States), while others have English as a second or foreign language (e.g. from Japan and Poland). This will help prepare you to understand different pronunciations of English. Information about where speakers come from is given in the Key.

B

Important for listening

The use of English has spread far beyond those countries where it is used as a first language. In some countries, such as India, Malawi, the Philippines and Singapore, English is an important second language for many speakers, and has often become the language used in official contexts such as courts, parliament and higher education. More recently, many other countries, such as Brazil, China, Thailand and Russia, have recognised the importance of English as an international language of communication, and encouraged its teaching in schools and colleges. In each country, the English spoken is influenced by other languages widely used there, and each variety is different in features of its grammar, vocabulary and pronunciation.

The widespread use of English as an international language means that much of the interaction in English that now goes on around the world is between speakers who don't have English as a first language. For example, when German and Spanish politicians meet to discuss policies of the European Union, their chosen language of communication might well be English. The same might apply when Saudi Arabian and Japanese people meet to do business.

C

Important for listening

The consequence of this is that there is an enormous variety of accents of English in addition to those of 'British English', 'American English', 'Australian English' and so on, and you may be more likely to speak to people with 'Indian English', 'Singaporean English' or 'Russian English' pronunciation.

It would be impossible, however, to learn to 'switch' your pronunciation each time you were talking to a speaker with a variety of English different from your own – to use an Australian English pronunciation with an Australian, or Chinese English pronunciation with a Chinese person. Consequently, it is useful to 'model' your pronunciation on one variety – but also recognise that this is just one of many equally acceptable varieties.

Exercises

2.1 You will hear speakers with international accents of English from five countries talking about their families. Where do you think they are from? Listen and write the name of the country in the space.

A7

Speaker 1 is from ....
Speaker 2 is from ....
Speaker 3 is from ....
Speaker 4 is from ....
Speaker 5 is from ....

Poland   Japan   China   India   Spain

Now check your answers in the Key. Which of these accents do you find easiest to understand and which most difficult? Can you say why? Which of these English accents is closest to your own?

2.2 Listen. You will hear the same text read three times: first by a speaker of BBC English, second by a speaker of Jamaican English, and third by a Polish speaker of English. They are talking about moving into a new house and some of the things they have had to buy.

A8

Here are some notes on how the pronunciation in part of the reading by the speaker of Jamaican English is different from that in the reading by the speaker of BBC English.

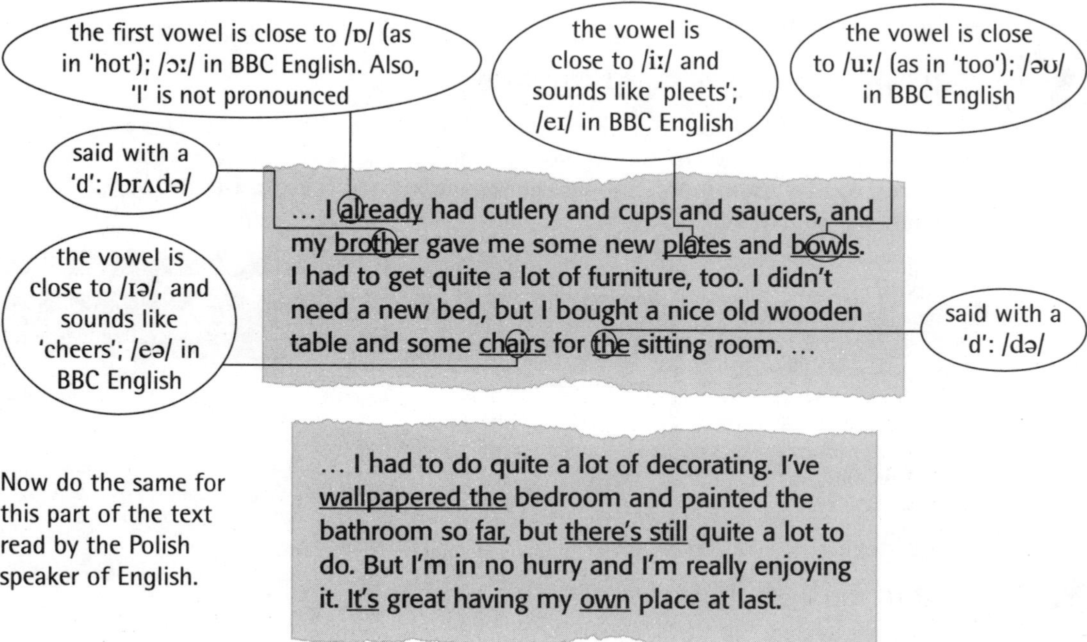

Now do the same for this part of the text read by the Polish speaker of English.

2.3 Are there any accents of English that are of particular interest or importance to you? Practise listening to people with these accents as much as possible. If you have access to the internet, you could regularly listen to English language broadcasts where you will hear these accents. For example, for New Zealand accents, try http://www.radionz.co.nz/; for Swedish accents of English, Radio Stockholm has a weekly English news broadcast (at http://www.sr.se/rs/red/ind_eng.html) where many of the speakers are Swedish. (For more information, see Unit 4.)

Follow up: Record yourself reading the text in exercise 2.2. Practise a few times before recording. Then write out the text again, and make notes on it, highlighting differences between your pronunciation and that of the speaker of BBC English. (Alternatively, you could get a friend or teacher to make notes for you.)

3 Finding out about pronunciation (1): dictionaries

A Dictionaries

Many dictionaries represent pronunciation using the symbols of the International Phonetic Alphabet (IPA), or a similar system. From this you can find out about the sounds that make up a word and how it is stressed. For example, the *Cambridge Advanced Learner's Dictionary (CALD)* gives the pronunciations of 'lemon', 'lemonade' and 'lemon sole' (a type of fish) as shown here.

It is useful to spend some time learning the IPA symbols so that you can make use of pronunciations shown in dictionaries. A full list of phonemic symbols used in this book, and in many dictionaries, is given on page 192. Section E1 also includes some exercises to help you learn the symbols.

/ˈlem.ən/
The word has 2 syllables with stress on the first syllable.

/ˌlem.əˈneɪd/
The word has 3 syllables with primary (main) stress on the third syllable and secondary stress on the first.

ˌlemon ˈsole
Since this is a compound, no separate IPA pronunciation is shown, as this is given at 'lemon' and 'sole'. In this compound, primary stress is on the second part and secondary stress is on the first syllable of the first part.

B Talking dictionaries and CD-ROMs

If you don't have time to learn phonemic symbols, 'talking dictionaries' are available which will read aloud words and definitions to you. In addition, some dictionaries come with a CD-ROM on which you can hear words spoken. For example, *CALD* has a CD-ROM, including the entry for 'kimono' shown here.

Clicking on 'UK ◀)) ' gives the British English pronunciation, and on 'US ◀)) ' gives the American English pronunciation. If your computer has a microphone, you can also practise your pronunciation by clicking on the microphone icon.

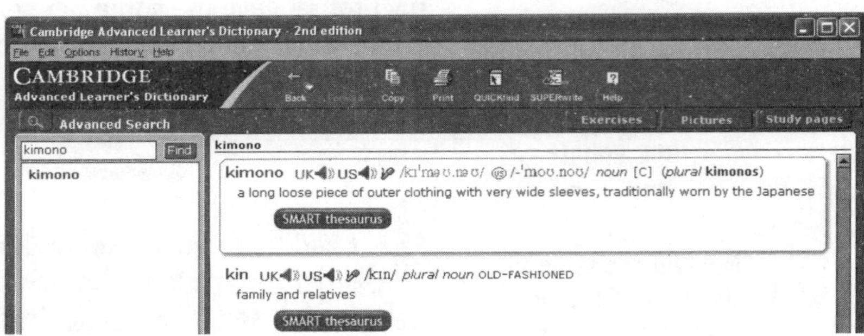

C Pronunciation dictionaries

Pronunciation dictionaries usually include more words than general dictionaries and so can be particularly useful for finding out how to pronounce place names, family names, brand names and technical terms. They also give more information about variation in pronunciation. For example, compare the information about the pronunciation of 'kimono' from *CALD* given in B with this entry from the *Cambridge English Pronouncing Dictionary, 17th edition (CEPD)*.

Both *CALD* and *CEPD* give British and American English pronunciations. *CEPD* shows also that in American English the last vowel is usually pronounced /ə/ but can also be pronounced /oʊ/. It also shows that the plural '-s' is pronounced /z/.

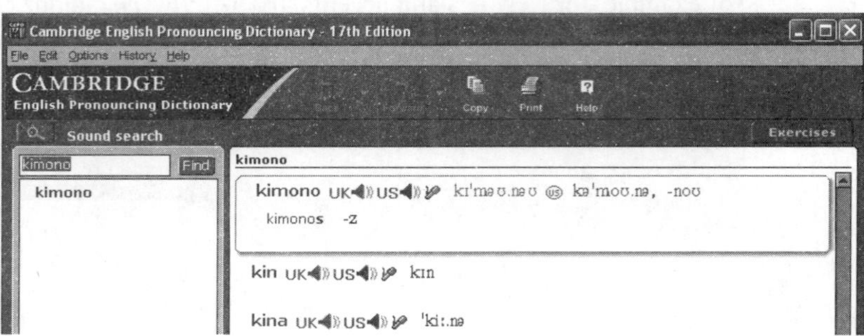

Exercises

3.1 Use a dictionary with IPA to help you match the words with their pronunciations.

EXAMPLE a flier — ii /flaɪə/; b flower — i /flaʊə/

1 a stock	i /stɔːk/	7 a sand	i /sænd/	13 a bear	i /beə/
b stalk	ii /stɒk/	b send	ii /send/	b buyer	ii /baɪə/
2 a here	i /hɪə/	8 a far	i /fɑː/	14 a should	i /ʃʊd/
b hair	ii /heə/	b fear	ii /fɪə/	b showed	ii /ʃəʊd/
3 a stand	i /stʌnd/	9 a leak	i /leɪk/	15 a chin	i /tʃɪn/
b stunned	ii /stænd/	b lake	ii /liːk/	b chain	ii /tʃeɪn/
4 a tour	i /taʊə/	10 a voice	i /vɔɪs/	16 a full	i /fuːl/
b tower	ii /tʊə/	b vice	ii /vaɪs/	b fool	ii /fʊl/
5 a turn	i /tɜːn/	11 a geese	i /ges/	17 a order	i /əʊdə/
b ton	ii /tʌn/	b guess	ii /giːs/	b odour	ii /ɔːdə/
6 a learn	i /laɪn/	12 a oil	i /ɔɪl/	18 a pond	i /paʊnd/
b line	ii /lɜːn/	b owl	ii /aʊl/	b pound	ii /pɒnd/

3.2 Underline the syllable in these words and compounds which you think has main stress. Check your answers in a dictionary. (For more practice, see exercise 10.1.)

EXAMPLE re<u>pu</u>diate

1 tortuous
2 methylated spirits
3 flabbergasted
4 symbiosis
5 subterranean
6 decompression chamber
7 pistachio
8 glitterati
9 debutante
10 repetitive strain injury
11 rotisserie
12 idiolect

(A9) Which of these are you not sure how to pronounce? Use the pronunciation given in your dictionary to try to work out how to say them. You can hear the words pronounced on the recording.

3.3 For this exercise you need to use a dictionary CD-ROM, such as the one that comes with *CALD*. Write down a list of sounds you find difficult to pronounce, and then use the dictionary CD-ROM to find words with this sound and practise them. Here is an example of what you might do.

If you have problems pronouncing the consonant cluster /sk/, first think about how it might be spelt. The most common way is 'sc'. In the 'Search' box type 'sc*'. This will give you all the words beginning with this letter combination, as you can see here. Then listen, repeat, and, if you have a microphone, record yourself. Then do the same with '*sc*', which will give you all the words with this letter combination *within* the word. (Note that 'sc*' and '*sc*' are not always pronounced /sk/.)

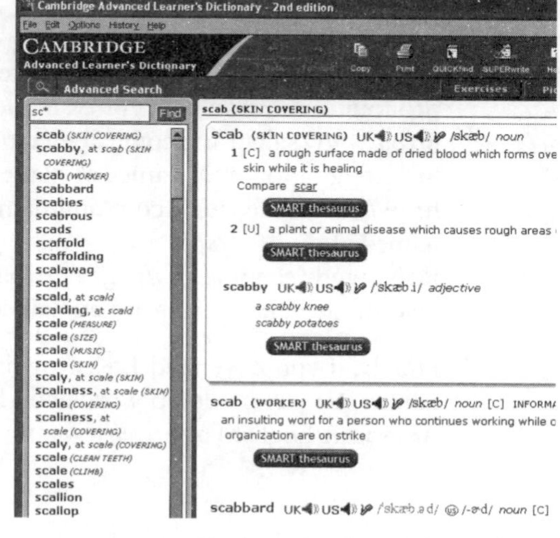

(A10) **Follow up:** What do you think are the most common pronunciations in British English of the following family names (Beauchamp, McFadzean), British place names (Mousehole, Towcester), and technical terms (isogloss, ozokerite)? If you are not sure, use a pronunciation dictionary, such as *CEPD*, to find out. Some of the pronunciations may surprise you! You can hear the words pronounced on the recording.

4 Finding out about pronunciation (2): online resources

There are many sites on the internet where you can listen to accents of English from around the world, find examples of particular styles of speech, or find out how words are pronounced. This unit gives just a few examples which you could explore.

A

Some countries broadcast radio online. If you listen to news reports, for example, you are likely to hear the 'standard' pronunciation from that country. Try, for instance:
http://www.bbc.co.uk/radio/ from the BBC (British Broadcasting Corporation)
http://www.abc.net.au/streaming/ from the ABC (Australian Broadcasting Corporation)
http://www.rte.ie/ from RTÉ (Radio Telefís Éireann) in Ireland
http://www.rsi.sg/english from Radio Singapore

The website http://www.penguinradio.com/ gives links to many radio stations from around the world that broadcast online.

On some of these radio station websites, transcripts of certain recordings are available. These might help you to understand broadcasts. Type 'transcript' into the site search box and follow links.

B

You can listen to examples of British regional accents either at the BBC's http://www.bbc.co.uk/voices/ or the British Library's http://www.bl.uk/collections/sound-archive/accents.html

C

A number of sites allow you to listen to samples of particular styles of speech.
For example:
at http://www.historyplace.com/speeches/ you can hear some famous political speeches;
at http://www.lsa.umich.edu/eli/micase/audio/ you can hear speech in a variety of academic contexts (lectures, seminars, meetings, student presentations, etc.) from the Michigan Corpus of Academic Spoken English (MICASE).

D

Some online dictionaries show the pronunciation of words using the International Phonetic Alphabet (IPA) or some other system. These include the *Cambridge Advanced Learner's Dictionary* and the *Cambridge Dictionary of American English* at http://dictionary.cambridge.org/. The Miriam-Webster Online Dictionary also allows you to hear words pronounced in North American English, at http://www.m-w.com/.

If you have a specialist area of interest or study, you may be able to find websites to help you pronounce terminology. For example:
http://www.saltspring.com/capewest/pron.htm gives rules on how to pronounce Biological Latin, including taxonomic names of plants and animals;
http://www.dinosauria.com/dml/names/aeto.htm has sound files with the pronunciation of the names of dinosaurs;
http://www.genome.gov/page.cfm?pageID=10002096 is a 'talking glossary' of terms from the field of Genetics. Terms are explained and you will also hear how they are pronounced.

Finally, if you have read J. K. Rowling's *Harry Potter* books and are unsure how to pronounce names and the made-up words you find, you can hear how to pronounce them (in North American English) at http://www.scholastic.com/harrypotter/reference/.

Exercises

These exercises depend on you having internet access. It may be that you have to download free software to listen to some of the material.

4.1 Visit the websites of two English-language internet radio stations from different countries. You could take two of the four given in A or look for others. (The website http://www.penguinradio.com/ can help you find them.) Find one recent news story that you are familiar with that is reported on both stations and listen carefully to the broadcast on the first radio station. Write down a few of the key words you hear. Now listen in detail to the story on the second radio station and notice whether these key words are pronounced in the same or a different way. What differences do you notice?

4.2 Go to http://www.bbc.co.uk/voices/. Follow links to 'Voices Recordings'. Here you can listen to voices from many parts of the UK. Choose one of the recordings by clicking on a dot on the map, and then do the following:

1 Click on the name of one of the speakers under 'More clips from this interview'.
2 Read 'About the interviewee'.
3 Read the transcript. Check in a dictionary any words you don't understand.
4 Listen to the recording and follow the transcript.
5 Some clips have a section on 'More about the speech in this clip'. Read this, focusing in particular on information about pronunciation. Some dialect words, which you may not find in the dictionary, are explained here.
6 Do the same with any other 'More clips from this interview'.
7 Go back and listen to the 'Voice clip(s)'. These don't have transcripts. How much of them do you understand? Do you notice features of pronunciation you observed and read about earlier?
8 Do the same with accents from other parts of the UK by clicking on other dots on the map.

4.3 Go to http://dictionary.cambridge.org/ and look up the following words in the *Cambridge Advanced Learner's Dictionary*:

belligerent charade continuum felafel precinct sepia
vitamin wrath

Is the usual British and American pronunciation the same or different for each? Try to work out from the phonemic symbols how each is pronounced. (See Section E1 for advice, if necessary.) If you want to hear how these words are pronounced in North American English, go to http://www.m-w.com/. Notice that where more than one pronunciation is given, the most common one comes first.

4.4 Go to http://www.genome.gov/page.cfm?pageID=10002096 and look up the following words:

centromere monosomy nucleotide

Listen to the explanations and find out how they are pronounced. Say the words after the recording.

Follow up: Use your search engine (such as *Google*) to try to find one other website that gives information about the pronunciation of terms in a specialist area. Use the search words 'pronunciation guide [specialist area]'.

5 Pronunciation in slow and fast speech (1)

A

Important for listening

In different contexts we change the speed at which we speak.

We are likely to speak more slowly, for example, ...	... when we are carefully explaining to someone what we want them to do, when we are talking to a large audience, or when we are talking about an unfamiliar or difficult topic.
We are likely to speak more quickly, for example, ...	... in conversation, when we are talking to friends or relatives, or when we are talking about routine or familiar topics.

In Units 5 and 6 we will introduce some of the changes in pronunciation that take place in fast speech when compared with slow, careful speech. These include linking sounds, leaving out sounds and changing sounds. These changes are looked at in more detail in Units 26 to 31.

B

A11

Important for listening

Speech is broken up into units, often with a pause between them. Within these *speech units*, words are linked together smoothly. (For more on speech units, see Unit 32.) In fast speech in particular, these units may be quite long and the words spoken quickly. Compare the units (marked with // below) in these examples of slow and fast speech:

Slow speech: A nurse is explaining how to make a sling:
// this goes under the arm// and then over the shoulder// all the time// make sure you support the arm// talk to the patient// and find out what position// is most comfortable for them//

Fast speech: Three friends are in a Chinese restaurant:

A: // is anyone having a starter or not// or are we going straight to the main course//
B: // I'm going to go straight to the main course//
C: // yeah//
B: // but I might have an extra portion of something// you never know//
A: // do they do nice sweets here//
C: // I think it's just lychees//
A: // what's lychees//
B: // they're the funny little white ones// aren't they//
C: // that's right// I'm not terribly keen on them//

Listen again to some of the long units from the restaurant conversation. Notice how the words are run together:

// or are we going straight to the main course//
// but I might have an extra portion of something//

C

A12

Important for listening

Because words within units are run together, it can sometimes be difficult to understand them. However, one or more word in each unit is emphasised and may be said more clearly than others (see also Units 33 and 34). It is important to focus on these, as they usually carry the most important information in the unit. Listen to these speech units from the restaurant conversation and notice how the words with syllables in large capital letters are emphasised:

//I'm going to go STRAIGHT to the MAIN course//
// I think it's just lyCHEES//
// they're the FUNny little WHITE ones//
// that's RIGHT//

Exercises

5.1 In which three of these situations is slow speech more likely?

1 A lecturer is giving details of timetable changes to a group of university students.
2 Two friends are discussing what they might do at the weekend.
3 You are giving directions to a stranger who has asked how to get to a local hospital.
4 A witness in a trial is explaining to a jury what she saw when a robbery was taking place.
5 A hairdresser and a customer are talking about their recent summer holidays.
6 Members of a family are having dinner and talking about what they have been doing during the day.

5.2 (A13) Here are some long speech units taken from fast speech. Listen to each just once and try to write down what you hear.

EXAMPLE What are you doing tomorrow about half past twelve?

1 I .... not.
2 She .... before.
3 They .... well.
4 As .... late.
5 We .... hours.

If you had difficulties, listen again as many times as you need, and then check your answers in the Key.

5.3 (A14) First, listen to an extract from a business meeting. Then repeat six single speech units taken from the discussion. If possible, repeat them without looking at the units written out below. Try to run the words in the unit smoothly together.

1 // so why did you go for Jensens//
2 // and we've done business with them before//
3 // and they've still got a pretty good reputation//
4 // that the product isn't up to scratch//
5 // they've been pretty poor//
6 // shall I contact the lawyers about it//

5.4 (A15) Listen to these speech units taken from the same conversation. Underline the one word, or sometimes two words, that are emphasised in these units.

EXAMPLE // to <u>supply</u> the machines//

1 // but that was years ago//
2 // but the management hasn't changed at all//
3 // to be honest//
4 // we ought to be looking for a different supplier//
5 // we'll leave that to you//

Now check your answers in the Key and then say the speech units aloud. Try to run the words in the unit smoothly together and emphasise the underlined words.

Follow up: Record yourself reading all parts of the business meeting extract used in exercises 5.3 and 5.4 (or act it out in a group of three). Try to divide it into speech units as in the recording, making sure you run the words in the units smoothly together. In the Key you will find the extract with the speech units marked.

6 Pronunciation in slow and fast speech (2)

A

A16 Important for listening

In fast speech, sounds that are found in words spoken slowly may be missed out. Listen and notice how the highlighted sounds are missed out in this conversation extract:

It occurred to me that Terry hadn't been in touch for ages, so I thought I ought to phone him. Well, just then there was a ring on the front door and there he was.

/d/ is missed out

the two /t/ sounds merge into one

/h/ is missed out

/t/ is missed out

/t/ is missed out

/h/ is missed out

For more details, see Units 8, 9, 29 and 30.

B

A17 Important for listening

As well as sounds, syllables or whole words that we would expect to hear in slow speech may be reduced or missed out in fast speech. Listen and notice how the highlighted parts are reduced or missed out in this conversation:

A: Come on, it's time to go. What are you looking for?
B: I don't suppose you've seen my glasses?
A: Have you lost them again?
B: You'd better carry on. I can't go without my glasses.

'it's' is reduced to /s/

'are' is missed out

'I' is missed out

the vowel /ə/ is missed out and the word is said with one syllable

'Have' is reduced to /v/

'd' is missed out

'I' is missed out

For more details, see Units 27–30.

C

A18 Important for listening

Sounds in words may also change in fast speech compared with how they are said in slow speech or how they are represented in dictionaries. Listen and notice how the sound /t/ changes in the highlighted parts of this conversation:

A: I want you to paint my kitchen.
B: What colour?
A: A light green.
B: Right.

/t/ + /j/ ('y') is said /tʃ/ ('ch')

/n/ is missed out and /t/ is said like /p/ before /m/

/t/ is said as a 'glottal stop' (a sound made by stopping the flow of air by closing the vocal cords)

/t/ is said like /k/ before /g/

For more details, see Units 26 and 29.

It is not essential to make these changes in your own speech in order to be understood, although they can help your speech sound more natural and fluent.

Exercises

6.1 (A19) Listen to these sentences as many times as you need. First you will hear them said slowly and carefully and then at a more normal speed for conversation. Indicate the differences you hear in the 'conversation' versions.

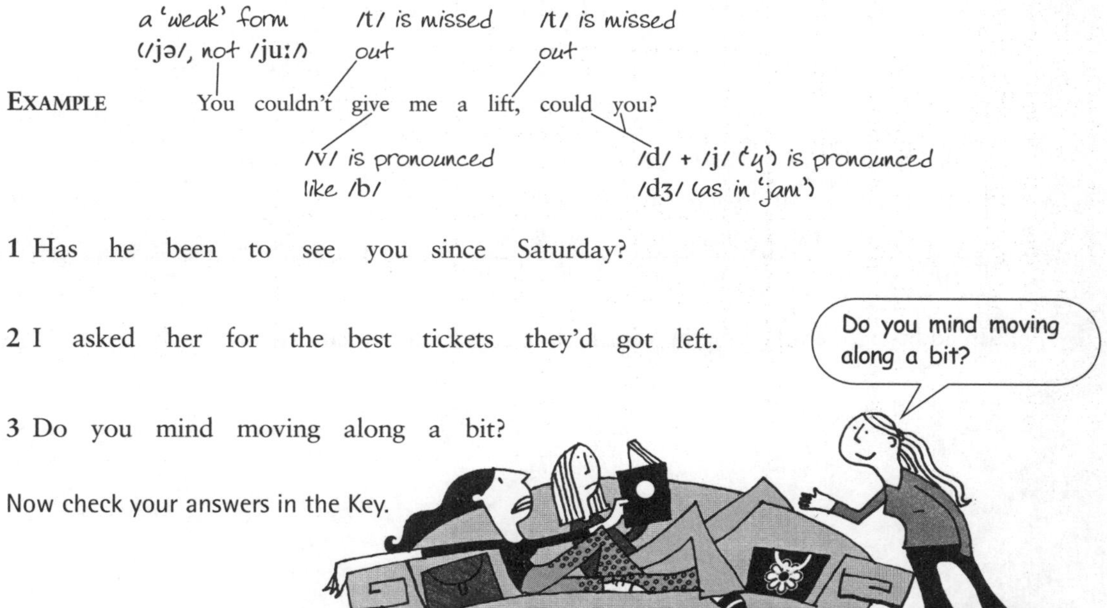

EXAMPLE You couldn't give me a lift, could you?

1 Has he been to see you since Saturday?

2 I asked her for the best tickets they'd got left.

3 Do you mind moving along a bit?

Now check your answers in the Key.

6.2 (A20) Listen to these conversations as many times as you need and fill in the spaces. How is the pronunciation of each missing word different from its slow form?

doesn't — 'n' is said like 'm'

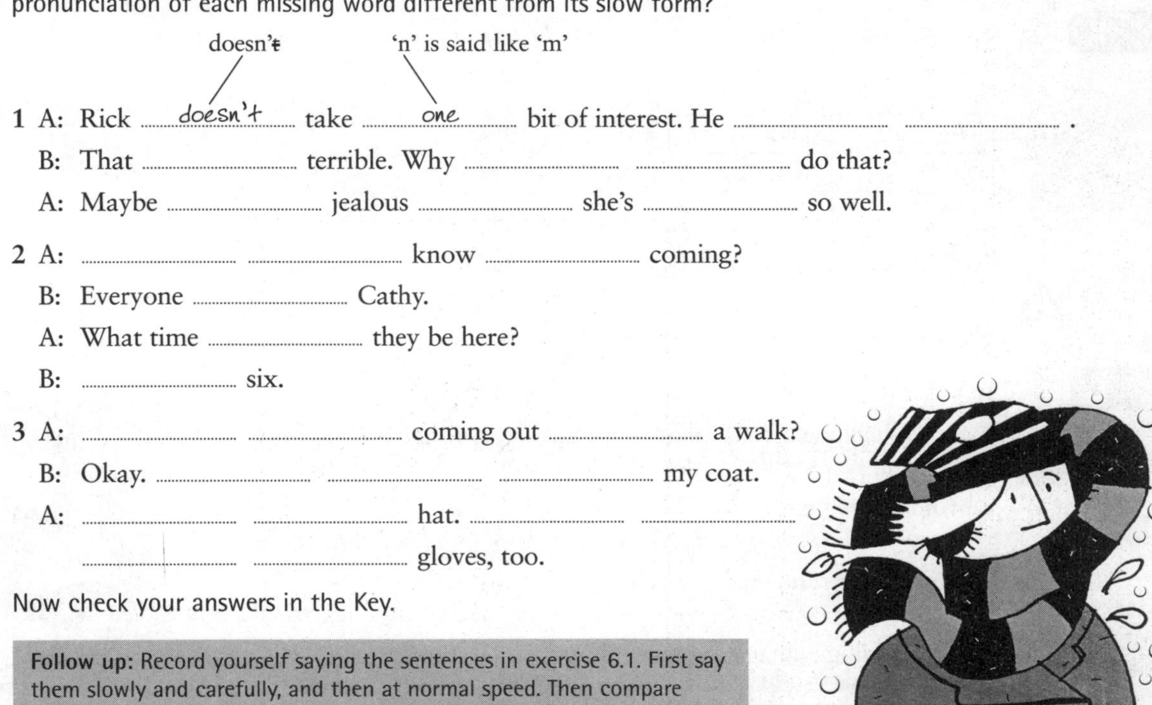

1 A: Rick ....doesn't.... take ....one.... bit of interest. He ....
B: That .... terrible. Why .... do that?
A: Maybe .... jealous .... she's .... so well.

2 A: .... know .... coming?
B: Everyone .... Cathy.
A: What time .... they be here?
B: .... six.

3 A: .... coming out .... a walk?
B: Okay. .... my coat.
A: .... hat. ....
.... gloves, too.

Now check your answers in the Key.

Follow up: Record yourself saying the sentences in exercise 6.1. First say them slowly and carefully, and then at normal speed. Then compare what you said with what you heard in the recording.

7 play, grow, splash
Consonant clusters at the beginning of words

A

A21 Combinations of consonant sounds (*consonant clusters*) can be difficult to pronounce for some learners. English words can start with a vowel, or one, two or three consonant sounds. Compare:

am ram cram scram

Here are the possible *two-consonant clusters* at the start of English words:

	/p/	/t/	/k/	/b/	/d/	/g/	/m/	/n/	/f/	/v/	/θ/	/ʃ/	/h/
+/l/	play	×	class	black	×	glass	×	×	fly	×	×	×	×
+/r/	pray	trip	crime	brown	drop	grow	×	×	fry	×	three	shrink	×
+/w/	×	twins	queen	×	dwell	×	×	×	×	×	×	×	×
+/j/	pure	tube	queue	beauty	due	×	music	news	few	view	×	×	huge

In addition, the following two-consonant clusters are possible with /s/:

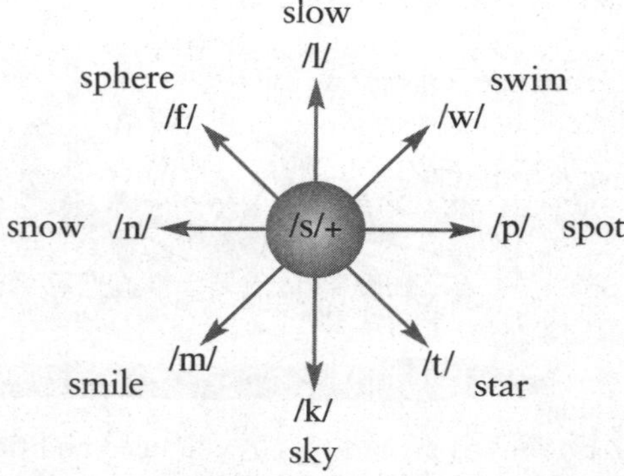

B

A22 Here are the possible *three-consonant clusters* at the start of English words:

	/sp/	/st/	/sk/
+/l/	splash	×	×
+/r/	spray	straw	scream
+/w/	×	×	squeak
+/j/	×	stew	skewer

⚠ **Note:** Some consonant clusters marked × in A and B are used in a few uncommon words, for example *schwa* (the name of the sound /ə/) and people's names.

C

In order to be understood clearly you should –

- avoid changing a consonant in a cluster to a different consonant.
  For example: saying 'present' for 'pleasant' or saying 'queue' for 'crew'
- avoid leaving out one of the consonant sounds.
  For example: saying 'poblem' for 'problem' or saying 'foo' for 'few'
- avoid adding an extra vowel between consonants.
  For example: saying 'tewin' for 'twin' or saying 'faree' for 'free'
- avoid adding an extra vowel at the beginning of the word.
  For example: saying 'estop' for 'stop' or saying 'escream' for 'scream'

You can find more practice of consonant clusters at the beginning of words in Section E2.

Exercises

7.1 A23 You will hear some short definitions. After each definition, press 'pause', tick (✓) the word you think is being defined and say it aloud. When you press 'play' again you will hear the correct answer. Repeat it and then continue in the same way.

EXAMPLE 'to cook in hot oil' fly / fry ✓

1 string / sting	3 strain / stain	5 slum / sum	7 slip / sip	9 scare / square
2 clean / queen	4 Spain / sprain	6 pain / plain	8 kick / quick	10 grass / glass

7.2 A24 You will hear some words. After each word, press 'pause' and underline the correct definition. When you press 'play' again you will hear the correct answer.

EXAMPLE 'stray' to not leave / to move away from the intended route

1 to produce a continuous light / to increase in size
2 to shake with fear / a sweet food
3 to move through water / attractively thin
4 dried stalks of wheat / another word for shop
5 watery liquid in your mouth / to divide into two
6 activity done for enjoyment / to give money for something
7 a border around a picture / burning gas
8 not mixed / not rich

7.3 A25 Listen and underline the sentence you hear.

EXAMPLE The band isn't very popular. / The brand isn't very popular.

1 Just across the road. / Just cross the road.
2 The cat was following its tail. / The cat was following its trail.
3 Before that I had tried a motorbike. / Before that I had to ride a motorbike.
4 It's Michael's twin. / It's Michael's to win.
5 He fell into a deeper sleep. / He fell into a deep sleep.
6 I thought it was a terrible slight (= insult). / I thought it was a terrible sight.
7 Just blow your nose. / Just below your nose.
8 This one is a pear. / This one is spare.

Now check your answers in the Key. Then listen again and repeat the sentences.

7.4 Try building words by adding consonant sounds. Start with a vowel sound, and then add one consonant sound at a time before or after the vowel, in any order, to build new words. (Note: (i) a consonant sound may consist of more than one letter; (ii) don't add any new vowel sounds.) Then say aloud the words you have written. For example:

/eɪ/: ache ⇒ lake ⇒ flake ⇒ flakes (2 consonants before the vowel and 2 after)

/aɪ/: rye ⇒ rife ⇒ rifle ⇒ trifle ⇒ trifles (2 before and 3 after)

/iː/: sea ⇒ seem ⇒ scheme ⇒ scream ⇒ screamed (3 before and 2 after)

Now try with other vowels. You might find it helpful to use a dictionary. (Note: There is a list of vowels on page 192.)

Follow up: Are there any consonant clusters at the beginning of words that you have special problems with? Collect a list of words that start with these, record yourself saying them, and listen. Repeat this often. See Unit 3, exercise 3 for an idea on how to collect words starting with a particular consonant cluster.

8 jump, next, glimpsed
Consonant clusters at the end of words

A A26 There are many more combinations of consonant sounds possible at the end of English words than at the beginning (see Unit 7). There can be up to four consonant sounds in a final consonant cluster:

Words with...	2 final consonants	3 final consonants	4 final consonants
	honest /st/ jump /mp/ wrapped /pt/	helped /lpt/ next /kst/ crisps /sps/	prompts /mpts/ glimpsed /mpst/ texts /ksts/

B A27 Some final clusters with three or four consonants can be difficult to pronounce even for native English speakers, so in some words these are commonly simplified. For example, the middle consonant of the clusters /kts/, /mps/, /mpt/, /nts/, /ndz/ and /skt/ is hardly heard or sometimes even left out (see also Unit 29A):

products → produc~~t~~s /prɒdʌks/
camped → cam~~p~~ed /kæmt/
hands → han~~d~~s /hænz/
jumps → jum~~p~~s /dʒʌm^{p}s/
clients → clien~~t~~s /klaɪən^{t}s/
asked → as~~k~~ed /ɑːst/

Notice also:

twelfth → twel~~f~~th /twelθ/
fifths → fi~~f~~ths /fɪθs/ or fif~~th~~s /fɪfs/

C Leaving *final* consonants out of consonant clusters at the end of words can cause misunderstanding, and you should avoid this. For example, say:

product (not: produc~~t~~) jump (not: jum~~p~~) hand (not: han~~d~~)

In particular, avoid leaving out /z/ or /s/ in plurals and third person singular verb forms, and /t/ or /d/ in *-ed* verbs and adjectives:

jobs (not: job~~s~~)
laughed (not: laugh~~ed~~)
sleeps (not: sleep~~s~~)
curved (not: curv~~ed~~)

D Don't be tempted to add vowels to consonant clusters in order to make them easier to say, as this can also cause misunderstanding. You should –

- avoid adding an extra vowel (usually /ɪ/ or /ə/) between consonants:
  watched (not: watch^{ɪ}d) health (not: heal^{ə}th) dogs (not: dog^{ə}s)
- avoid adding an extra vowel (usually /ə/ or /uː/) at the end of the word:
  last (not: last^{ə}) announce (not: announce^{ə}) attempts (not: attempts^{uː})
- avoid adding an extra vowel at the end of an adjective, as this can sound like a comparative form:
  fast (not: fast^{ə} because it sounds like 'faster')
  damp (not: damp^{ə} because it sounds like 'damper')

You can find more practice of consonant clusters at the end of words in Section E2.

Exercises

8.1 How many final consonant *sounds* – 1, 2, 3 or 4 – do the words in the box have when they are spoken slowly and carefully? (Note that the number of consonant *sounds* may be different from the number of consonant *letters*.) Write the words in the appropriate row.

~~accents~~ against aspects ~~attempts~~ axe catch contexts diamonds ears earth grasped laughed ledge next risked sculpts stamps tempts touched

1 final consonant sound	
2 final consonant sounds	
3 final consonant sounds	*accents* /nts/
4 final consonant sounds	*attempts* /mpts/

Now check your answers, listen and say the words.

8.2 (A29) Listen to some of the words from exercise 8.1 (in **bold**) used in conversation. Some final clusters are simplified. Underline the words which are simplified and show which sound is left out or reduced.

EXAMPLES It was a long jump, but he <u>**risked**</u> it. ~~k~~ (the /k/ sound is left out)
He **helped** us a lot. (no simplification)

1 It's my turn **next.**
2 It's a recording of regional **accents.**
3 Don't forget to buy some **stamps.**
4 I've always been **against** it.
5 The question has a number of **aspects.**
6 She loved **diamonds.**
7 It was taken out of **context.**
8 They **grasped** it easily.

8.3 (A30) Listen and underline the word you hear.

EXAMPLE I *accept* / <u>*accepted*</u> the award gratefully.

1 I couldn't go on without more *paint* / *pain*.
2 The company has some innovative *designers* / *designs*.
3 I couldn't go *faster* / *fast* in my old car.
4 The factory makes *trays* / *trains*.
5 We wore heavy boots with thick, *ridged* / *rigid* soles.
6 They're one of Brazil's main *exports* / *exporters*.

8.4 (A31) Anna failed her test to become a newsreader for her local English language radio station. Look at the transcript of the news item that she read. Then listen to the news being read clearly and correct the words that Anna pronounced wrongly.

The police ~~thin~~ *think* the rose on the south coat will be pack when the seven Felton Pop Festival beginners neck weekend. Lass year more than 10,000 pop fan pack into the feel where the festival was hell. There is simpler accommodation on a nearby farm, but most people will camper in small tense.

Now check your answers in the Key. Then read aloud the (correct) news item.

Follow up: What is the maximum number of final consonant sounds that can occur in your first language?

9 abstract, next Friday
Consonant clusters within and across words

A

(A32) Consonant clusters also occur within words. For example:

Clusters with...	2 consonant sounds	3 consonant sounds	4 consonant sounds
	escape	complete	abstract
	approach	control	expression
	dislike	expert	upstream
	address	translate	exquisite (/kskw/)
	important	hundred	excruciating

⚠ **Note:** Some clusters found within words can also be found at the beginning of words (dislike – slow), at the end of words (important – lamp), or both (escape – Scotland/ask); but others can't (abstract, invisible).

B

(A33) When a word ending with a consonant or consonants is followed by a word beginning with a consonant or consonants, a new consonant cluster across words is formed. These can be particularly difficult to pronounce when they come within a speech unit without a pause (see Section E4 *Glossary* for a definition of *speech unit*):

// it's an elm tree//
// there's a children's playground//

When consonant clusters are divided by a pause, they are often easier to pronounce:

// if Tom can't take you to the film// try Mike//
// there'll be three suitcases// two of Joan's// plus my own//

C

(A34) Important for listening

All the consonant clusters within the speech units in this conversation are underlined. Listen and follow the notes. Some clusters are simplified with sounds left out or changed to make them easier to pronounce. (Units 26–31 give detailed information on all these features of fluent speech.)

A: // next Friday// I'll meet you around four//
B: // by the bus station//
A: // no// the art gallery// then we can collect Steve at five//

- next Friday: pronounced /ksfr/
- meet you: /t/ and /j/ are pronounced /tʃ/
- around four: /d/ is left out
- bus station: One lengthened /s/ is said
- art gallery: /t/ is pronounced like /k/
- then we: /n/ is pronounced like /m/
- can collect: /n/ is pronounced like /ŋ/
- collect Steve: /t/ is left out
- at five: /t/ is left out

D

(A35) Words that commonly go together in phrases and compounds (examples of these are given in Units 16–18) are generally said within speech units. Consonants at the word boundaries are usually run together in a cluster. For example:

Clusters with...	2 consonant sounds	3 consonant sounds	4 consonant sounds
	civil servant	vacuum cleaner	television screen
	cough medicine	flash flood	winning streak
	electric fence	asking price	false friends
	full marks	present simple	lunch break
	language lab	passive smoking	film credits

Exercises

9.1 Underline all the consonant clusters *within* the words in this text (i.e. not at the beginning or end of words). Note that some words have two consonant clusters.

When I started playing badminton, I was sixty and I hadn't done any strenuous exercise for almost twenty years. But after just a few months I'd won the over-fifties national championship and an international competition. My husband thinks I'm crazy and that I'll injure myself. But I've found a number of advantages in taking up a sport. I feel much healthier, and it's important to be active at my age. And meeting new people has improved my social life. So I'll carry on playing until I get too old.

Now check your answers in the Key. Then read the text aloud, focusing on the pronunciation of words with underlined consonant clusters.

9.2 (A36) Listen and repeat phrase 1 in column A with a slight pause between the two speech units. Then listen and repeat phrase 1 in column B, making sure you run the words together *without* a pause. Then do the same for phrases 2–10 (notice that the underlined clusters are the same in columns A and B). Some underlined consonant clusters in column B are simplified. Try to make the same simplifications when you repeat them (see Key for details of simplifications).

	A	B
1	// Jack was in the audience// trying not to laugh//	// she's a freelance translator//
2	// the ring looked very elegant// sparkling in the sunlight//	// the president spoke next//
3	// here's some milk// drink it now//	// she wore a silk dress//
4	// I hear you won the contract// great news//	// it looked green to me//
5	// if you're going to the coast// fly there//	// it's on the first floor//
6	// if you find any of my old books// throw them away//	// he speaks three languages//
7	// it's got two bedrooms// slightly small//	// lift your arms slowly//
8	// it's very old// Bridget says//	// there was a cold breeze//
9	// there was a footprint// small like a child's//	// what's that unpleasant smell//
10	// it was sad in some parts// humorous in others//	// it's huge//

9.3 Match a word from box A with a word from box B to make compound nouns. Say the compounds aloud, making sure you run the words in the compound together.

A

~~blood~~ direct general golf lamp
first passive rock lost speech
time tourist

B

club property music ~~poisoning~~
class shade smoking speech
strike therapist trap travel

EXAMPLE *blood poisoning* (/d/ in 'blood' is pronounced like /b/)

(A37) Listen, check your answers and repeat the compounds, making the same simplifications of consonant clusters where these occur (see Key for details of simplifications).

Follow up: Find two-word compound nouns used in a topic that interests you or in your area of study. Which of them have consonant clusters across the two words? Record yourself saying them, and listen to the recording.

10 ˌcontroˈversial and controVERsial Word stress and prominence

A (A38) In this book we use two terms that are related but different: *stress* and *prominence*. Most dictionaries which give the pronunciation of words also indicate which syllable(s) have *stress*. For example, *CALD* shows that 'party' and 'remember' have stress on only one syllable:

party /ˈpɑː.ti/ **remember** /rɪˈmem.bəʳ/

and that 'controversial' and 'kindergarten' have stress on two syllables:

controversial /ˌkɒn.trəˈvɜː.ʃəl/ **kindergarten** /ˈkɪn.dəˌɡɑː.tən/

ˈ shows main stress and ˌ shows secondary stress.

When a word is used in conversation and emphasised (see Unit 33), one of the stressed syllables is made *prominent*. In a one-stress word this is the stressed syllable, and in a two-stress word it is usually the syllable with main stress. Prominent syllables are shown in this book in capital letters:

I'm going to a PARty. I can't reMEMber.
It was controVERsial. She goes to KINdergarten.

B (A39) Prominence can move to the secondary stressed syllable in a word like 'controversial' when it is followed by a word with another prominent syllable, particularly when the first syllable of the following word is prominent:

She gave a CONtroversial ANswer.

This is sometimes called *stress shift*. Stress shift can only happen in words where a secondary stress comes *before* main stress. Here are some more examples:

ˌunderˈstand I UNderstand EVerything.
ˌdisapˈpointing It was a DISappointing OUTcome.

Other words which often have stress shift include:

- ˌaltoˈgether, ˌindeˈpendent, ˌindiˈstinct, ˌmediˈocre, ˌsatisˈfactory, ˌuniˈversity, ˌweekˈend, ˌworthˈwhile.
- some place names which have main stress on the last syllable, such as: ˌBerˈlin, ˌKowˈloon, ˌMontreˈal.
- *-teen* numbers – ˌthirˈteen, ˌnineˈteen; and two-part numbers – ˌforty-ˈfive, ˌseventy-ˈeight.

For others, see Units 11C, 12A and 15C.

Note: Some other words with secondary stress rarely have stress shift. For example: aˌpproxiˈmation, ˌcorreˈspondence, ˌindeˈcision, proˌnunciˈation.

C (A40) For particular emphasis or contrast, syllables other than those with main or secondary stress can be made prominent (see also Unit 47C):

ˈhopeful A: I agree with you that it's HOPEless.
B: No, I said it was hopeFUL.

reˈported A: Apparently, Kim's been dePORTed.
B: No, he's been REported.

Exercises

10.1 Are these one-stress words (write 1) or two-stress words (2)? Circle the main stressed syllables and underline the secondary stressed syllables. Use your dictionary if necessary.

EXAMPLES experiment (1) thermostatic (2)

1 occasional ( )
2 supplement ( )
3 temperamental ( )
4 cosmopolitan ( )
5 pedestrian ( )
6 incoherent ( )
7 electronic ( )
8 spectacular ( )
9 documentary ( )

A41 Now listen, check your answers and repeat the words.

10.2 Underline the syllable you think is most likely to have prominence in the words in **bold**. In which two of these words is stress shift *not* possible?

EXAMPLES We used to live near the **Berlin** Wall. She's got a job in **Berlin**.

1 I'm working on my **pronunciation.**
2 It was just a **routine** job.
3 The film was made for **propaganda** purposes.
4 The region has a **Mediterranean** climate.
5 Next month she'll be **sixteen.**
6 There was a **satisfactory** outcome.
7 The country was declared **independent.**
8 I love living next to the **Mediterranean.**
9 It cost **sixteen** euros.
10 The book was just political **propaganda.**
11 The operation was quite **routine.**
12 They appointed an **independent** judge.
13 The result was **satisfactory.**
14 I'm doing a **pronunciation** course.

A42 Now listen and check your answers. Then say the sentences aloud.

10.3 Listen and underline the syllable that has main stress in these words.
A43

handbag	concise	disarming	footbridge
lifelike	paintbox	subjective	tablecloth

Now use the words to complete these conversations. Then underline the syllable in the word that you think is likely to be prominent.

EXAMPLE A: So we have to take the old footpath?
B: No, we take the old footbridge .

1 A: So you thought the work was precise?
B: No, I said it was ....
2 A: You've lost your handbook, have you?
B: No, I've lost my ....
3 A: Yes, I thought the performance was lifeless, too.
B: No, I said I thought it was ....
4 A: I didn't think his findings were very objective.
B: No, they were very ....
5 A: Does the tabletop need washing?
B: No, the ....
6 A: I've brought you the paintbrush you asked for.
B: No, I wanted my ....
7 A: Did you say the country's rearming?
B: No, it's ....

A44 Now listen, check your answers and repeat the corrections .

Follow up: Do you know of any differences in stress in words in British English and in another variety of English you are familiar with?

11 'comfort and 'comfortable Suffixes and word stress (1)

A (A45) Some words are made up of a *root* and a *suffix*:

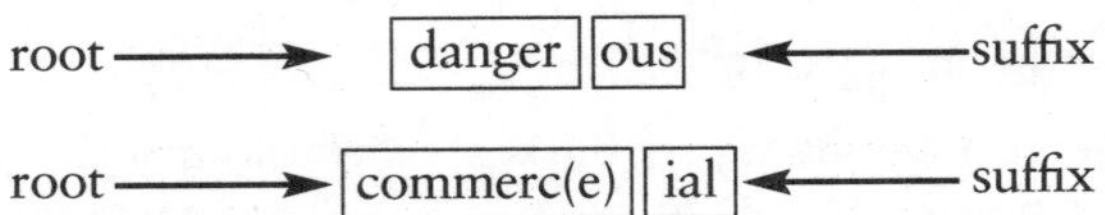

In some words with suffixes, the stress stays on the same syllable as in the root. Compare:

'danger and: 'dangerous

In other words, the suffix changes the stressed syllable. Compare:

'commerce and: com'mercial

B (A46) Suffixes which don't usually change the stress pattern in the root word include *-able*, *-age*, *-al* (but see Unit 12 for *-ial*), *-er*, *-ful*, *-less*, *-ness*, *-ous* and *-fy*. For example:

'comfort – 'comfortable
'amplify – 'amplifier
'foolish – 'foolishness
per'cent – per'centage
re'gret – re'gretful
di'saster – di'sastrous
e'lectric – e'lectrical
re'gard – re'gardless
'beauty – 'beautify

Exceptions with *-able* and *-al* include:

ad'mire – 'admirable
'medicine – me'dicinal
pre'fer – 'preferable
'agriculture – agri'cultural

Note that before the suffixes *-ious*, *-ulous*, *-orous* and *-eous* main stress usually comes in the syllable before the suffix:

'industry – in'dustrious
'miracle – mi'raculous
ad'vantage – advan'tageous
'mystery – my'sterious
'carnivore – car'nivorous
'outrage – out'rageous

C (A47) Some suffixes themselves usually have the main stress. These include *-ee*, *-eer*, *-ese* and *-ette*. For example:

ˌabsen'tee ˌrefu'gee ˌengi'neer ˌmountai'neer
ˌJapan'ese ˌNepal'ese ˌcigar'ette di'skette

Exceptions include: 'omelette, 'etiquette, em'ployee (although less commonly we use ˌemploy'ee).

⚠ **Note:** Some people say 'cigarette.

Words with these suffixes can often have *stress shift* (see Unit 10):

She's japanESE. but: She's a JAPanese JOURnalist.
He's a refuGEE. but: We saw photos of REFugee CHILdren.

You can find more practice of words with suffixes in Section E3.

Exercises

11.1 Complete the sentences with pairs of words from B opposite. You should also mark the stress.

EXAMPLE The herb is used for ....me'dicinal.... purposes, although it isn't usually thought of as a ....'medicine.... .

1 The journey was a ....; in fact, the whole vacation was ....
2 The decision was an .... – quite .... I was appalled.
3 .... of his mistakes, the president continues to be held in high ....
4 Workers in the steel .... are generally skilled and ....
5 The Democrats' lead is now eight .... points, and has risen three .... in the last week.
6 Her .... disappearance was never explained, and her whereabouts remain a .... until today.
7 The region is mainly .... land and most people here still work in ....

A48 Now listen and check your answers. Then say the sentences aloud, paying attention to the stress in the words you have written.

11.2 A49 This speaker is talking about the difficulty of getting cars repaired. Focus on the words ending with the suffixes *-able* and *-al* (in **bold**). Listen and tick (✓) the words which follow the rule given in B – that is, they have the same stress pattern as their root.

You hear about the poor quality of car repairs so often nowadays. You just can't find **dependable** (✓) mechanics, and the problem seems to be **universal** (✗). For example, the other day I was having problems starting my car, so I took it to a **reputable** ( ) garage. At least I'd heard it was quite **reliable** ( ). The people there seemed quite **professional** ( ), and they said it looked like just a minor **mechanical** ( ) problem. They said it would cost about €100, which seemed quite **acceptable** ( ). But when I picked it up, they'd badly scratched the paintwork. They apologised, and said it was **accidental** ( ) and offered to re-spray it, but whether they'll do a good job is **debatable** ( ).

11.3 Here are some extracts from a radio news programme. Underline the syllable in each word in **bold** that you think is likely to be made prominent. Remember, some of the words in bold are likely to have *stress shift*.

EXAMPLE An aircraft that crashed three years ago in the Andes has been found by **mountain<u>eers</u>**.

1 A report on the problem of **absentee** landlords is to be published today.
2 Five thousand **volunteer** helpers are to be recruited for the next Olympic Games.
3 Mandarin and **Cantonese** are the most widely spoken languages in China.
4 The government is considering a ban on **roulette**.
5 There has been an outbreak of cholera among **Sudanese** villagers.

A50 Now listen and check your answers. Then read the extracts aloud.

Follow up: How many other country adjectives ending in *-ese* can you think of? How would you say them: (i) on their own; (ii) in the context 'the .... people' (e.g. the Japanese people)?

12 ac'celerate and ac,cele'ration
Suffixes and word stress (2)

A (A51) In words with the following suffixes, main stress is usually on the syllable immediately before the suffix: *-ial*, *-ic*, *-ion*, *-ive*, and *-ity*. For example:

'editor – edi'torial
ac'celerate – ac,cele'ration
'generous – ,gene'rosity
'atmosphere – ,atmos'pheric
'instinct – in'stinctive
di'verse – di'versity

Note: In words ending *-ative*, stress is usually on the same syllable as in the root word. For example:
in'vestigate – in'vestigative 'speculate – 'speculative

Many words with these suffixes can have *stress shift* (see Unit 10). For example:

He faces proseCUtion. but: He's a PROSecution WITness.

When a word ends with one of the consonants *t* or *s* and the suffix *-ion*, this is how they are pronounced:

-tion is pronounced /tʃən/ after the letter *s*: suggestion, digestion
/ʃən/ after other letters: education, adoption

-sion is pronounced /ʃən/ after a consonant: extension, comprehension
/ʒən/ after a vowel: decision, persuasion

-ssion is pronounced /ʃən/: admission, expression

B (A52) In nouns and adjectives ending with the suffixes *-ant*, *-ent*, *-ance*, or *-ence*, stress placement depends on the spelling of the syllable before the suffix (the *pre-suffix syllable*).

- If the pre-suffix syllable ends with a single vowel letter (V) or a single vowel letter plus a single consonant letter (VC), stress usually goes on the syllable before the pre-suffix syllable if there is one:
  'ignorant (VC) 'variant (V) 'fraudulent (VC)
  con'tinuance (V) 'reference (VC) 'ambience (V)
- If the pre-suffix syllable has any other spelling, then stress is usually on the pre-suffix syllable itself:
  ap'pearance (VVC) ,corre'spondent (VCC) con'vergence (VCC)
- If the pre-suffix syllable ends with the letter *i* and the root word ends with the letter *y* in a *stressed* syllable, the stress is usually on the pre-suffix syllable:
  com'ply – com'pliance re'ly – re'liant

Some of these words ending with the suffixes *-ant*, *-ent*, *-ance* or *-ence* have a different stress placement from the root:

ig'nore – 'ignorant re'fer – 'reference

while others have the same stress placement:

con'tinue – con'tinuance ap'pear – ap'pearance

C (A53) Notice that the suffix *-ment* doesn't usually change the stress pattern in the root:

a'gree – a'greement 'govern – 'government

although a common exception is: 'advertise – ad'vertisement

You can find more practice of words with suffixes in Section E3.

Exercises

12.1 (A54) You will hear some short definitions. After each definition press 'pause', choose from the box and write the word that it relates to. When you press 'play' again you will hear the correct answer. Repeat it and then continue in the same way.

cooperative	~~allergic~~	photographic	editorial	familiarity
prosecution	hostility	impulsive	speculation	

Example Having an allergy. ....allergic........

1 .... 5 ....
2 .... 6 ....
3 .... 7 ....
4 .... 8 ....

One of the words in the box above is an exception to the rule given at the beginning of A opposite. Which is it?

12.2 Write the words from the box in the correct column according to the pronunciation of *-tion*, *-sion*, or *-ssion*.

~~accommodation~~	celebration	combustion	comprehension	
congestion	depression	digestion	erosion	exhaustion
explosion	expression	invasion	revision	suspension

/tʃən/ (e.g. suggestion)	/ʃən/ (e.g. education)	/ʒən/ (e.g. decision)
	accommodation	

(A55) Now listen and check your answers. Then say the words aloud.

12.3 Underline the syllable which you think has the main stress in the following words.

<u>res</u>ident	performance	defiant	convergence	reference
excellence	correspondent	assistant	maintenance	applicant
coincidence	informant	acceptance	insistence	significance

(A56) Now listen and check your answers. Then say the words aloud.
One of these words is an exception to the rules in B opposite. Which is it?

12.4 Decide whether the words in exercise 12.3 have the same stress pattern as their root word (write S) or a different stress pattern (write D).

Examples resident (D) ('resident – re'side)
performance (S) (per'formance – per'form)

(A57) Now listen to the root words and check your answers.

Follow up: Next time you read a book or an article, note down words ending in *-ion*. Mark the stress on them, then check in a dictionary to see if you were right. You can also add words ending in *-tion*, *-sion* and *-ssion* to the appropriate column in the table in exercise 12.2.

13 ex'treme and ex'tremity
Suffixes and word stress (3)

A

Some words *don't* change their stress pattern when a suffix is added to the root word, but *do* change the pronunciation of the vowel in the main stressed syllable. Compare:

ex'treme – ex'tremity   de'rive – de'rivative
/iː/   /e/   /aɪ/   /ɪ/

The following table shows a number of possible vowel changes. The main stressed syllable and the pronunciation of the vowel in this syllable are shown:

⇒ /ɪ/	⇒ /æ/	⇒ /e/
/aɪ/ 'bible – 'biblical /ɪ/	/eɪ/ 'nation – 'national /æ/	/iː/ com'pete – com'petitive /e/
/aɪ/ type – 'typical /ɪ/	/eɪ/ de'fame – de'famatory /æ/	/iː/ inter'vene – inter'vention /e/
/aɪ/ wise – 'wisdom /ɪ/	/eɪ/ sane – 'sanity /æ/	/iː/ ob'scene – ob'scenity /e/
⇒ /ɒ/	/eə/ com'pare – com'parative /æ/	⇒ /ʌ/
/ɔː/ ex'plore – ex'ploratory /ɒ/	/eə/ de'clare – de'clarative /æ/	/uː/ as'sume – as'sumption /ʌ/
/əʊ/ know – 'knowledge /ɒ/	/ɑː/ 'drama – 'dramatise /æ/	/uː/ pre'sume – pre'sumption /ʌ/

B

In some words, as well as a change in the pronunciation of the vowel in the stressed syllable, there is also a change in the pronunciation of the *consonant(s)* that follow it.

/aɪt/ ig'nite – ig'nition /ɪʃ/
/aɪn/ sign – 'signature /ɪgn/
/uːs/ pro'duce – pro'duction, pro'ductive /ʌk/
/uːs/ intro'duce – intro'duction, intro'ductory /ʌk/

C

In other words like this, there is a change in the pronunciation of the vowel in the stressed syllable and also the *spelling* of either this vowel and/or the consonant(s) that follow it:

/aɪd/ col'lide – col'lision /ɪʒ/
/aɪd/ di'vide – di'vision /ɪʒ/
/aɪd/ pro'vide – pro'vision /ɪʒ/
/aɪb/ de'scribe – de'scription, de'scriptive /ɪp/
/aɪb/ pre'scribe – pre'scription, pre'scriptive /ɪp/
/aɪb/ sub'scribe – sub'scription /ɪp/
/iːv/ de'ceive – de'ception, de'ceptive /ep/
/iː/ re'peat – re'petitive /e/
/ɑː/ ex'ample – ex'emplary /e/
/eɪ/ re'tain – re'tention /e/
/eɪ/ ex'plain – ex'planatory /æ/
/aɪ/ ap'ply – ap'plicable /ɪ/

D

Words that *do* change their stress pattern when a suffix is added to the root also commonly change their pronunciation in one or more syllable:

pro'nounce – pronunci'ation   pre'fer – 'preferable
/ə/ /aʊ/   /ə/ /ʌ/   /ɪ/ /ɜː/   /e/ /ə/

There are many words like this, and a great variety of pronunciation changes. For these words it is best to check pronunciation in a dictionary such as *CALD* or *CEPD* (see Section E5 *Further reading*).

Exercises

13.1 Which of these words have main stress on the same syllable as their root word? Write S (Same) or D (Different).

EXAMPLES familiarise (S) (fa'miliarise – fa'miliar) cancellation (D) (cancel'lation – 'cancel)

intervention ( )	security ( )	advantageous ( )	Canadian ( )	consumption ( )
maturity ( )	stupidity ( )	application ( )	sanity ( )	normality ( )
delivery ( )	precision ( )	preference ( )	sincerity ( )	diversion ( )

A62 Now listen and check your answers.

13.2 Look again at the words in exercise 13.1 with main stress on the same syllable as their root. Underline the ones which have a *different* vowel sound in the main stressed syllable from that in the main stressed syllable in their root. (Some of these are given in A and B opposite.)

EXAMPLE <u>intervention</u> (inter'vention /e/ – inter'vene /iː/)

Now listen again to the words in exercise 13.1 and check your answers.

13.3 Complete each pair of sentences using pairs of words from the box.

collide–collision	compete–competitive	divide–division	example–exemplary
nation–national	~~subscribe–subscription~~		

EXAMPLE a It costs £10 a year to ......subscribe...... to the sports centre.
b I've taken out an annual ......subscription...... to the magazine.

1 a We'll .... the money between us.
b Brighton football club was promoted to the first ....
2 a It's difficult to stay .... in business.
b He was much faster and I couldn't .... with him.
3 a Rod broke his leg in the ....
b They say the comet is going to .... with Saturn.
4 a She set a good .... to her younger sister.
b Their behaviour was ....
5 a The first of May is a .... holiday.
b Practically the whole .... watched the eclipse.

A63 Now listen and check your answers. Then read the sentences aloud.

13.4 Write the words from the box in the correct column according to the vowel sound in the main stressed syllable of their *root word*. There are three words in each column.

~~commercial~~	applicant	speciality	financial	symbolic
~~evolution~~	accidental	historic	decision	demonstration
influential	~~modernity~~	calculation	magnetic	medicinal

Vowel sound in main stressed syllable of root	/ɒ/ (as in stop)	/ɪ/ (as in sit)	/aɪ/ (as in drive)	/æ/ (as in black)	/e/ (as in pen)
	commercial evolution modernity				

Their roots all have /ɒ/ in their main stressed syllable: commerce, evolve, modern

14 dis'organised and ˌrecon'sider
Prefixes and word stress (1)

A

Some words are made up of a *prefix* and a *root*:

prefix ⟶ [dis][like] ⟵ root

Common prefixes include: *de-*, *dis-*, *il-*, *re-*, *un-*. Sometimes the root can be used as an independent word (e.g. like), but other roots cannot (e.g. renounce and denounce, but not 'nounce').

B

A64 In some words the prefix is unstressed and is only made prominent (see Unit 10) for particular contrast. Compare:

A: Do you enjoy driving?
B: No, I really disLIKE it.

A: I thought you LIKED driving?
B: No, I really DISlike it.

In *CALD*, words like this are usually shown as having only one (main) stressed syllable:

dislike /dɪ'slaɪk/

Other words like *dislike* include:

de'grade	di'scolour	il'legal	re'claim	un'easy
de'flect	di'scourage	il'legible	re'fresh	un'pack
de'fraud	di'sintegrate	il'literate	re'place	un'wise

Other words with these prefixes have secondary stress on the prefix:

ˌdecom'pose ˌrecon'sider ˌunaf'fected

(See Unit 15C for stress shift in words like these.)

C

A65 In words with *de-* and *re-* prefixes, the prefix is usually pronounced /dɪ-/ and /rɪ-/ if it is unstressed and /diː-/ and /riː-/ if it has secondary stress. Compare:

de'grade /dɪ-/ but: ˌdecom'pose /diː-/
re'claim /rɪ-/ but: ˌrecon'sider /riː-/

A few words with *de-* and *re-* prefixes are usually pronounced with an unstressed /-ɪ-/ in the prefix when they are used as a verb and a stressed /-iː-/ in the prefix when they are used as a noun. Compare:

Interest is likely to decrease. (/dɪ'kriːs/)
but: There has been a decrease (/'diːkriːs/) in interest.

D

A66 Some words beginning *re-* have the same spelling but a different stress and meaning depending on whether *re-* means 'again' or not. Compare:

recover	/ˌriː'kʌvə/ (= cover again)	/rɪ'kʌvə/ (= get well)
recount	/ˌriː'kaʊnt/ (= count again)	/rɪ'kaʊnt/ (= describe)
reform	/ˌriː'fɔːm/ (= form again)	/rɪ'fɔːm/ (= improve)
remark	/ˌriː'mɑːk/ (= mark again)	/rɪ'mɑːk/ (=comment)
resort	/ˌriː'sɔːt/ (= sort again)	/rɪ'zɔːt/ (= turn to)
resign	/ˌriː'saɪn/ (= sign again)	/rɪ'zaɪn/ (= give up a job)

⚠ **Note:** When *re-* means 'again', the words are sometimes spelt with a hyphen, e.g. re-cover, re-count.

Exercises

14.1 Complete the sentences with words from the box in **B** opposite. Underline the syllable that you think will have the main stress in these words.

EXAMPLE They're going to ....replace.... most of the workers with machines.

1 It's .... to forecast the weather too far ahead.
2 I haven't had time to .... since I got back from holiday.
3 We have to .... her from working too hard.
4 Parking on a double yellow line is ....

A67 Now listen and check your answers. Then say the sentences aloud.

14.2 Write the same words from exercise 14.1 (including the example) in the spaces in these conversations. Again, underline the syllables that you think will have the main stress in these words.

EXAMPLE A: Would it be a wise investment? B: No, I think it would be very ....unwise.... .

1 A: Did you say you've misplaced your keys? B: No, I said I have to .... them.
2 A: I suppose it's legal to bring alcohol into the country? B: No, it's completely ....
3 A: Did it take long to pack your case? B: Ages, but it won't take long to .... it.
4 A: Did your teacher encourage you to do the maths course? B: No, she tried to .... me from doing it.

A68 Now listen, check your answers and say the B parts aloud.

14.3 Write the verbs from the box in the correct column according to the usual pronunciation of the *de-* or *re-* prefix. Some are done for you.

~~debug~~	~~deflate~~	deform	delineate	demote	deregulate	descend
destabilise	devalue	~~reapply~~	~~reflect~~	recharge	reconsider	refresh
relapse	replace	resit	restructure	review		

/diː-/	/dɪ-/	/riː-/	/rɪ-/
debug	deflate	reapply	reflect

A69 Now listen and check your answers. Then say the words aloud.

14.4 Choose words from **D** opposite to complete the pairs of sentences. Use the same word in each pair. Think about the pronunciation of the words you have written and say the sentences aloud.

EXAMPLE a The band hasn't played together for years, but they've said they'll ....reform.... for the charity concert. (/ˌriːˈfɔːm/ = form again)
b The government are going to ....reform.... health care. (/rɪˈfɔːm/ = improve)

1 a She'd been seriously ill and it took her a long time to ....
b The chair was badly stained, so we had to .... it.
2 a He hasn't agreed yet to .... for the club for the next baseball season.
b If working conditions don't improve soon, she's threatening to ....
3 a When the phone rang, I forgot how many books I'd already put in the box, so I had to .... them.
b He liked to .... his wartime experiences to anyone who'd listen.

A70 Now listen and check.

15 ˈsubway and ˈsuperˌpower
Prefixes and word stress (2)

A (A71) In some words with prefixes, the prefix itself is stressed. In *CALD*, most of these words are shown as having main stress on the prefix and, in some cases, secondary stress later in the word:

subway – /ˈsʌbweɪ/ superpower – /ˈsuːpəˌpaʊə[r]/

Most words like this are nouns and include:

ˈco-driver	ˈcounteratˌtack	ˈhyperspace	ˈinterface
ˈco-writer	ˈcounterˌclaim	ˈhypertext	ˈinterchange
ˈco-star	ˈcounterpart	ˈhyperlink	ˈinterplay
ˈsubˌsection	ˈsuperˌmarket	ˈunderˌcurrent	
ˈsubtext	ˈsuperˌstructure	ˈundergrowth	
ˈsubsoil	ˈsuperˌmodel	ˈunderwear	

In these words the syllable with main stress usually has prominence in discourse:

We took the SUBway. I'm just off to the SUpermarket.

B (A72) However, other words with these prefixes have main stress on a syllable after the prefix. Most words like this are adjectives and include:

ˌco-eduˈcation	ˌcounterinˈtelligence	ˌhyperˈactive	ˌinterˈchangeable
coˈoperate	ˌcounterproˈductive	ˌhyperˈsensitive	ˌintercontiˈnental
ˌco-eˈxist	ˌcounterˈmand	ˌhyperˈcritical	ˌinterˈactive
ˌsubˈconscious	ˌsuperˈnatural	ˌunderˈcover	
subˈstandard	ˌsuperaˈbundant	ˌunderˈline	
ˌsubˈtropical	ˌsuperimˈpose	ˌunderˈage	

In these words the syllable with main stress usually has prominence in conversation:

They have to learn to co-eXIST. The climate here is subTROPical.

but prominence may go on the syllable with secondary stress in some cases (see **C**).

C (A73) In many words with a prefix, there is secondary stress on the prefix, with main stress later in the word:

ˌimpreˈcise ˌdisaˈgree ˌhyperˈactive

When these words are used in conversation they can have *stress shift* (see Unit 10**B**), with the prefix made prominent rather than the main stressed syllable. Compare:

Her answer was impreCISE. but: She gave an IMprecise ANswer.
He's hyperACtive. but: I work with HYperactive CHILdren.
He disaGREED. but: He DISagreed STRONGly.

Here are some more words with prefixes which commonly have stress shift: ˌdecomˈpose, ˌdeˈcode; ˌdisoˈbedient, ˌdisreˈspectful; ˌimmaˈture, ˌimpoˈlite; ˌmisˈplace, ˌmisˈspelt; ˌreconˈsider, ˌreproˈduce; ˌunacˈceptable, ˌunsucˈcessful.

However, some other words with these prefixes rarely have stress shift, including: deˈfame, disˈhonest, imˈpractical, ˌmisˈjudge, reˈplace, unˈpopular.

Exercises

15.1 Here are the titles of some research papers given at a conference on education. Look at the words in **bold** (some are given in A opposite) and underline the syllable that you think will be prominent.

EXAMPLE Why do children become **hyperactive**?

Conference	Time	Room No.	Coffee Break @
1 Assessing the benefits of **co-education**	12.00	13	12.30
2 Activating the **subconscious** for reading development	12.00	11	12.30
3 Technology and tradition in the classroom: exploring the **interface**	12.30	14	13.15
4 Motivating **underachievers**: using **subtitles** in language learning	13.00	13	13.30
5 **Superstars** as role models for children: going on the **counteroffensive**	14.00	14	14.45
6 Children's interest in the **supernatural**: some worrying **undercurrents**	14.00	10	14.30
7 Teachers and pupils as **co-writers**: an experiment in the use of **hypertext**	15.00	15	15.30
8 Making science education **international**: a study of British teachers and their Kenyan **counterparts**	14.45	13	15.15

 Now listen and check your answers. Then read the titles aloud.

15.2 Match each word 1–7 with a word from the list a–g. Matched words must have the same number of syllables *and* follow the same stress pattern. Words 1–7 are from A and B opposite.

EXAMPLE 1–c (*co-exist* and *interlinked* both have three syllables with main stress on the last syllable – o o O)

1 ~~co-exist~~	**a** cohabit
2 counterproductive	**b** counterclockwise
3 interchangeable	**c** ~~interlinked~~
4 hyperspace	**d** hypersensitive
5 substandard	**e** subcommittee
6 superstructure	**f** superstore
7 undercover	**g** underdeveloped

 Now listen and check your answers. Then listen again and repeat the words.

15.3 Focus on the words in **bold** (some are given in C opposite), and underline the syllable you think is likely to have prominence. Which words have stress shift (that is, prominence on the prefix), and which do not?

EXAMPLE He was sacked for **unacceptable conduct.** (has stress shift)

1 She was wearing **impractical** shoes.
2 The government has promised to **review** hospital funding.
3 He tends to use rather **impolite** language.
4 There were too many **misplaced** passes in the football match.
5 The police have prosecuted a number of **dishonest** landlords.
6 The cream is very good for **dehydrated** skin.
7 He **undressed** quickly.

 Now listen and check your answers. Then listen again and repeat the sentences.

Follow up: What other words do you know beginning *sub-* or *super-*? Where do they have their main stress? (Use a dictionary to check.)

16 'newsˌpaper and ˌabsolute 'zero Stress in compound nouns

A

A compound noun is a fixed expression which is made up of more than one word and which has the function of a noun. Some are written as two words, some with a hyphen, and some as one word:

'crash ˌbarrier ˌdouble-'glazing 'babyˌsitter

Notice that some compound nouns have main stress on the *first* part and others have main stress on the *second* part.

B

A77 The following types of compound noun usually have main stress on the *first* part:

- noun + noun
  'arms race 'fire exˌtinguisher 'night-time 'pillar-box
  'lipstick 'newsˌpaper 'airport 'poverty ˌtrap
  Exceptions: inforˌmation tech'nology, ˌtown 'hall, ˌfamily 'doctor

Notice, however, that if the first part gives the material that the second part is made out of, main stress usually goes on the second part. Compare:
ˌcotton 'wool but: a 'cotton ˌplant
Exceptions are most compounds ending with *-cake*, *-bread* and *-juice*:
'cheesecake, 'gingerbread, 'orange ˌjuice

- noun + *-ing* form
  'bird-ˌwatching 'house-ˌhunting 'fly-ˌfishing
  Exceptions: peˌdestrian 'crossing, ˌball 'bearing, ˌthanks'giving
- *-ing* form + noun
  'dressing ˌgown 'sitting ˌroom 'freezing ˌpoint
  Exceptions: ˌmanaging di'rector, deˌfining 'moment, ˌcasting 'vote
- verb + noun
  'search ˌparty con'trol ˌtower 'think ˌtank

Note: Other phrases may have the same forms, but are not compounds. In these, main stress usually goes on the *second* word. Compare:
'driving ˌlicence (a compound) but: ˌdriving 'rain (a normal adjective + noun)

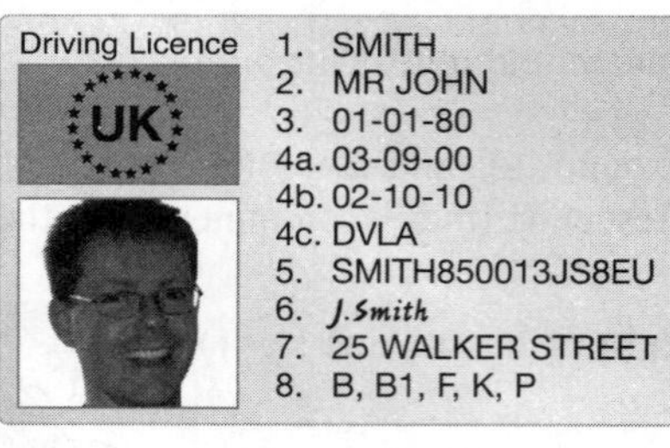

Driving Licence
UK
1. SMITH
2. MR JOHN
3. 01-01-80
4a. 03-09-00
4b. 02-10-10
4c. DVLA
5. SMITH850013JS8EU
6. J.Smith
7. 25 WALKER STREET
8. B, B1, F, K, P

C

A78 Most adjective + noun compound nouns have main stress on the *second* part and secondary stress on the first part:

ˌsocial se'curity ˌhot po'tato ˌabsolute 'zero
Exceptions: 'blind spot, 'dental ˌfloss, 'easy ˌchair, 'broadband, 'greenhouse

Note that this includes:

- adjective + *-ing* form
  ˌcentral 'heating ˌglobal 'warming ˌpassive 'smoking
- past participle + noun
  ˌsplit in'finitive inˌverted 'commas ˌlost 'property

Exercises

16.1 Do these compounds have main stress on their first part or their second part? Underline the syllable with the main stress. (Hint: Think about whether they are noun + noun compounds or adjective + noun compounds.)

EXAMPLES <u>saf</u>ety valve (noun + noun)
guilty <u>par</u>ty (adjective + noun)

1 chemical formula	5 coffee shop	9 sofa bed
2 bank account	6 best man	10 magnetic field
3 American football	7 mobile phone	11 tea strainer
4 artificial intelligence	8 flight attendant	12 space station

Now listen and check your answers. Then say the words aloud.

16.2 Use the compounds in the box to answer the questions. Think carefully about where main stress is placed and say your answers aloud. (Some of the words are given in **B** and **C** opposite.)

boiling point	civil war	claim form	defining moment	dental floss
distance learning	greenhouse	hot potato	house-hunting	ice rink
lipstick	loudspeaker	orange juice	pay phone	rubber band
search party	shop assistant	towel	town hall	~~voicemail~~

What is…
1 a system that records phone messages for you? 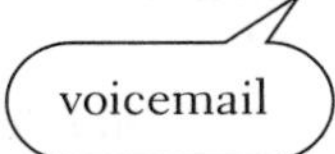

2 a sheet of thick paper for drying your hands?
3 battles between different groups of people living in the same country?
4 a building made of glass used for growing plants?
5 a level area of ice for people to skate on?
6 a way of studying where you mainly study at home?
7 a piece of equipment that sound comes out of?
8 a problem that no-one wants to deal with?
9 a legal document that you use to try to get compensation from an organisation?
10 the activity of looking for a house to live in?
11 a building where the local government usually meets?
12 a public telephone that you have to put money in to use?
13 a point at which a situation clearly starts to change?
14 a drink made from crushed oranges?
15 a coloured substance that women put on their lips?
16 the temperature at which liquid becomes a gas?
17 a group of people who look for someone who is missing?
18 someone who serves customers in a shop?
19 thread used for cleaning between the teeth?
20 a ring of rubber for holding things together?

Now listen and check your answers. Which five compounds are exceptions to the rules in **B** and **C** opposite?

Follow up: List ten compound nouns commonly used in a subject that interests you (e.g. an academic subject, or a hobby). Make sure you know where the main stress falls in each. Add to the list when you find new compound nouns in the subject.

17 ˈhair-ˌraising and ˌhard-ˈworking
Stress in compound adjectives and in abbreviations

A A compound adjective is a fixed expression which is made up of more than one word and which has the function of an adjective. Most compound adjectives are written with a hyphen, but a few are written as one word:

skin-deep   long-term   threadbare

B (A81) The following types of compound adjective usually have main stress on the *first* part:

- compound adjectives usually written as one word
  ˈairtight   ˈcarefree   ˈpraiseˌworthy
  Exceptions: ˌnationˈwide, ˌhandˈmade
- noun + *-ing* form
  ˈhair-ˌraising   ˈfee-ˌpaying   ˈtime-conˌsuming
- noun + past participle
  ˈpoverty-ˌstricken   ˈpear-shaped   ˈhealth-reˌlated
  Exceptions: ˌeagle-ˈeyed, ˌhome-ˈgrown

C (A82) The following types of compound adjective usually have main stress on the *second* part:

- noun + adjective
  ˌfat-ˈfree   ˌsky-ˈhigh   ˌsnow-ˈwhite (and other colour compounds)
  Exception: ˈcamera-shy
- adjective + noun
  ˌlong-ˈterm   ˌfull-ˈlength   ˌhigh-ˈprofile
- adverb or adjective + past participle
  ˌfully-ˈgrown   ˌlong-ˈsighted   ˌwell-ˈdressed
- adverb or adjective + *-ing* form
  ˌeasy-ˈgoing   ˌhard-ˈworking   ˌwell-ˈmeaning
  Exceptions: ˈbackward-ˌlooking, ˈforward-ˌlooking
- *self-* as the first part
  ˌself-ˈconfident   ˌself-inˈflicted   ˌself-ˈgoverning

Most compound adjectives with main stress on the second part (including the exceptions in 17B) can have *stress shift* (see Unit 10B). Compare:

The tiger was fully-GROWN.   but: It was a FULly-grown TIger.
The prices were sky-HIGH.   but: They were SKY-high PRIces.

D (A83) Two-, three- and four-letter abbreviations said as individual letters often have main stress on the last letter and secondary stress on the first:

the ˌEˈU   the ˌUˈK   the ˌBBˈC   ˌDNˈA   the ˌYMCˈA

Abbreviations like this usually have stress shift. Compare:

He works for the BBC.   but: He works for BBC RAdio.
She's from the UK.   but: She's a UK CITizen.

Exercises

17.1 Do these compound adjectives have main stress in their first part or their second part? Underline the syllable with main stress.

EXAMPLES sky-high colour-coded

1 homesick
2 far-fetched
3 spine-chilling
4 mind-blowing
5 armour-plated
6 cinemagoing
7 gift-wrapped
8 well-meaning
9 empty-handed
10 fireproof
11 self-financing
12 machine-readable

A84 Now listen and check your answers. Then say the compounds aloud. Which one is an exception to the rules given in **B** and **C** opposite?

17.2 Read the profile of Sarah Fox. Focus on the compound adjectives in **bold** (some are given in **B** and **C** opposite) and circle the syllable you think will have main stress. Remember some have stress shift.

High-flying surgeon introduces ground-breaking changes...

Sarah Fox is **easy-going** and is rarely **bad-tempered**. She's very **public-spirited** and does a lot of **time-consuming** work for charity. She's quite **good-looking**. She has **close-cropped** hair and wears glasses because she's **short-sighted**. She's a **high-flying** surgeon, **world-famous** in her field, and is extremely **hard-working**. She's recently introduced some **ground-breaking** changes into her hospital. She's always **well-dressed** at work. At home, though, she prefers to wear **loose-fitting** shirts, often in **eye-catching** colours. Surprisingly, she's a rather introverted person, and sometimes gets a bit **tongue-tied** in public. And she's rather **camera-shy**, too. Because of a **long-term** problem with her health, her diet has to be **fat-free**. At the moment she's taking a **well-earned** holiday in Majorca.

A85 Now listen and check your answers. Finally, read the description aloud.

17.3 Do you know the meaning of the abbreviations in column A? If not, check in a dictionary or the Key.
A86 Then listen to the abbreviations and repeat them. Notice that the main stress is always on the last letter. Finally, choose an appropriate abbreviation from each pair to complete the sentence in column B.

	A	B
1	CEO / DVD	She's the company's ....*CEO*.... .
2	AOB / PC	My laptop was advertised in a magazine called .... *World.*
3	OHP / NHS	She works as a nurse for the ....
4	ATM / RP	There aren't many people here who speak ....
5	AGM / RSI	The ....'s cancelled.
6	TLC / VAT	She just needs a lot of rest and a bit of ....
7	UFO / WHO	We've followed all the .... guidelines.
8	EU / RSVP	They're meeting at the .... summit in Brussels.
9	CV / ETA	If there are no delays, what's your ....?
10	CD / IT	The software's on a ....-ROM.
11	CND / DIY	He spends most weekends doing ....
12	GMT / HGV	The eclipse is at 9 o'clock ....

A87 Now listen and check your answers. Finally, say the sentences aloud. The Key gives details of stress shift.

Follow up: Skim through an English newspaper (either a paper copy or online), and find 10 compound adjectives. Do you know where the main stress is in each of them? (Use a dictionary to check.)

18 ,closed-circuit 'television and 'sell-by date
Stress in longer compound nouns

A

Some compounds are made up of *three* parts. They may have two words or three words, and sometimes the first and second words are hyphenated:

	desktop publishing	central nervous system	left-luggage office
part:	1 2 3	1 2 3	1 2 3

B

(A88) Many three-part compounds have secondary stress on the first part and main stress on the *third* part:

,first-degree 'burns ,three-point 'turn ,cheque-book 'journalism

Some of these use an established two-part compound with stress on the first part. In the new three-part compound, however, main stress is on the third part:

two-part:	'ballroom	'desktop
three-part:	,ballroom 'dancing	,desktop 'publishing

Other examples: ,cheque-book 'journalism, ,hairpin 'bend, ,rush hour 'traffic

In other three-part compounds the first two parts (often joined with a hyphen) function as an adjective to describe the third part:

,state-owned 'industry (the industry is state-owned)
,closed-circuit 'television (the television is closed-circuit)
Other examples: ,ball-point 'pen, ,button-down 'collar, ,first-degree 'burns, ,drop-down 'menu, ,semi-detached 'house, ,wide-angle 'lens

Note: Compounds beginning with a number usually have this pattern, too:
,ten-pin 'bowling ,one-man 'band
Other examples: ,one-parent 'family, ,two-horse 'race

C

(A89) Other three-part compounds have secondary stress on the first part and main stress on the *second* part:

,school 'leaving age ,left-'luggage office ,parent-'teacher association

Some of these use an established two-part compound with main stress on the second part. In the new three-part compound the stress remains on the second part:

two-part:	,washing-'up	,central 'heating
three-part:	,washing-'up liquid	,central 'heating system

Other examples: ,hard-'luck story, ,C'D player, ,wild-'goose chase

In others, a first part with secondary stress is added to an established two-part compound with stress on the first part. Compare:

'carriageway and: ,dual 'carriageway
Other examples: ,armoured person'nel carrier, ,safety de'posit box, ,travelling 'salesman, ,white 'blood cells

D

(A90) Some three-part compounds have main stress on the *first* part. Most of these also have secondary stress on the third part:

'no-man's land 'real estate ,agent 'pick-up ,truck

Other examples: 'fallout ,shelter, 'greenhouse ef,fect, 'sell-by ,date, 'housewarming ,party, 'payback ,period, 'windscreen ,wipers, 'sister-in-law ('brother-in-law, etc.)

Exercises

18.1 A91 You will hear 15 three-part compound nouns. Press 'pause' after each one and write it in the correct column, according to whether the first, second or third part has the main stress.

main stress on the first part	main stress on the second part	main stress on the third part
pinball machine	left-luggage office	first-time buyer

Now check your answers in the Key and then say the compounds aloud.

18.2 Choose a compound noun from each pair to complete the sentence. The compound should have main stress on the first, second or third part, as indicated. (Some of these are given in **B**, **C** and **D** opposite.)

EXAMPLE Don't forget to buy some ......washing-up liquid...... . (*stress on second part*)
(peanut butter / washing-up liquid)

1 She teaches in a .... (*third*)
(grant-maintained school / teacher-training college)
2 He lives in a/an .... (*second*)
(old-people's home / semi-detached house)
3 He spent some time working as a/an .... (*third*)
(travelling salesman / air traffic controller)
4 As I was driving I had a problem with my .... (*first*)
(rear-view mirror / windscreen wipers)
5 You'll recognise him easily. He's the one with the .... (*first*)
(baseball cap / shoulder-length hair)

A92 Now listen and check your answers. Then say the sentences aloud.

18.3 What do these pictures show? Choose words from the box to make three-part compound nouns. With one exception, they all have main stress on the third part. Which is the exception?

angled bottle ~~bus~~ bullet clover ~~decker~~ ~~double~~ four hot
leaf piece proof right suit three triangle vest water

1 ......double-decker bus......

2 ....

3 ....

4 ....

5 ....

6 ....

Now listen and check your answers. Then say the compounds aloud.

Follow up: Look around your house and list all the things you can see that are three-word compounds. These may be parts of your house or objects inside it. Do you know where the main stress is placed in each?

19 'dream of and 'live for One-stress phrasal verbs

A (B2) Some two-word phrasal verbs have main stress on the verb and no stress on the particle. These are *one-stress phrasal verbs*:

'dream of	I wouldn't DREAM of asking you to do it.
'hear from	We never HEARD from them again.

Note: The particle in most one-stress phrasal verbs is a preposition.

Other two-word phrasal verbs have main stress on the particle and secondary stress on the verb. These are *two-stress phrasal verbs* (see Unit 20):

ˌdoze 'off	The sun came out and I DOZED OFF.
ˌlet 'out	Please LET me OUT.

Note: The particle in most two-stress phrasal verbs is an adverb.

B (B3) In conversation, it is unusual for the particle in one-stress phrasal verbs to be prominent (see Unit 10). However, we can make the particle prominent if we want to highlight it for emphasis or contrast:

'smell of	The room SMELT of roses. It certainly smells odd, but I'm not sure what it smells OF.
'hear of 'hear from	A: I'm surprised you've never HEARD of him. B: I didn't say I hadn't HEARD OF him, I said I hadn't HEARD FROM him.

C (B4) A number of the particles in one-stress phrasal verbs have a weak and a strong form (see Unit 21), for example: *at*, *for*, *from*, *of* and *to*. We usually use the weak form of these particles in conversation, but the strong form is used when the particle comes at the end of a clause:

'live for	He LIVES for /fə/ his work. She felt she had nothing to LIVE for /fɔː/.
'think of	I was just THINKing of /əv/ you. What on earth were you THINKing of /ɒv/?

D (B5) A few phrasal verbs can be either one-stress or two-stress phrasal verbs, but with different meanings. For example:

'live on	He had to LIVE on less than $10 a day. (= the amount of money he had to buy things)
ˌlive 'on	The tradition LIVES ON in many parts of the country. (= continues)
'come to	How much does all that COME to? (= what's the total cost)
ˌcome 'to	She hasn't COME TO yet after the accident. (= regained consciousness)

Exercises

19.1 Do you think each part in **bold** includes a one-stress (write 1) or two-stress (write 2) phrasal verb?

EXAMPLE The birds came quite close, but when I sneezed I **frightened them away.** ...2...

1 She said she'd be early, but I wouldn't **bank on it.** ....
2 He gave us a lot of information that I couldn't **take in.** ....
3 I couldn't do question six, so I **left it out.** ....
4 Dan said he'd phone today, but I haven't **heard from him.** ....
5 If you're passing, why don't you **stop by**? ....
6 You look well. Living by the sea must **agree with you.** ....
7 There isn't anyone but you that I can **confide in.** ....
8 Having my own boat is something I've always **dreamed about.** ....

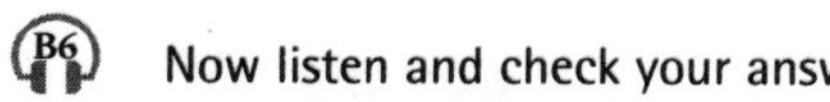
B6 Now listen and check your answers.

19.2 Read each A part and say each B part aloud, thinking about how the phrasal verb will be pronounced. All the phrasal verbs in the B parts are one-stress phrasal verbs, but sometimes the particle is made prominent for special emphasis or contrast.

1 A: I suppose your parents are quite well off?
B: What are you driving at?
2 A: Why didn't you show your mother your new shoes?
B: I thought she'd disapprove of them.
3 A: So you think the damage results from climate change?
B: I said I think it will result in climate change.
4 A: Apparently, they are forecasting a really cold winter.
B: Yes, I read about it.
5 A: My pen friend's planning to visit.
B: Where does she come from?
6 A: All you've got to do is aim and fire.
B: But I don't know what to aim at.
7 A: There are so many mosquitoes around the tent!
B: Yes, it's teeming with them.

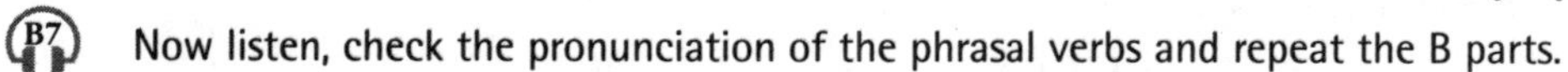
B7 Now listen, check the pronunciation of the phrasal verbs and repeat the B parts.

19.3 Do you think each part in **bold** includes a one-stress or two-stress phrasal verb? Think about how each phrasal verb will be pronounced in these dialogues.

1 A: We must get together again soon.
B: Yes, when you're next in town, why don't you **come by**?
2 A: This cabbage doesn't look very good.
B: Well, at this time of year fresh vegetables are difficult to **come by.**
3 A: What happened to your hand?
B: I was stroking Susan's cat when it just **turned on me.**
4 A: Mr Simpson can be very charming, can't he?
B: Yes, he certainly knows how to **turn it on.**

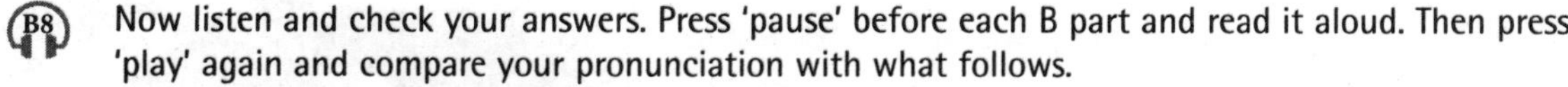
B8 Now listen and check your answers. Press 'pause' before each B part and read it aloud. Then press 'play' again and compare your pronunciation with what follows.

Follow up: When you learn a new phrasal verb, it is helpful to note whether it is a one-stress phrasal verb (if it has a preposition) or a two-stress phrasal verb (if it has an adverb).

20 ˌhang a'round and ˌlook 'up to Two-stress phrasal verbs

A

B9 When two-stress phrasal verbs (see Unit 19A) are used in conversation, both the verb and the particle are usually made prominent:

ˌhang a'round	It was freezing cold, so I didn't want to HANG aROUND.
ˌget a'long	My brother and I don't really GET aLONG together.
ˌcall 'back	I'm busy at the moment. Can I CALL you BACK?
ˌwrite 'down	I'll never remember the number. Can you WRITE it DOWN for me?

Notice that a pronoun between the verb and the particle is not usually prominent.

However, the particle is often non-prominent –

- when there is a noun (the object) after the phrasal verb but still in the same clause:
  Shall I WRITE down the NUMber for you?
- when we want to put special emphasis on the verb:
  A: I can't remember Trudi's address.
  B: Why didn't you WRITE it DOWN?
  A: I WROTE it down. (or: I DID write it down.)
- when there is a prominent noun (the object) between the verb and the particle. Compare:
  Can you CALL the DOCtor back? He called about your test results.
  but: I didn't understand the message about these pills.
  I'm going to CALL the doctor BACK. ← 'the doctor' is not prominent because it is information already understood (see Unit 33)

B

B10 Three-word phrasal verbs also have two stresses, with secondary stress on the first word (the verb) and main stress on the second word (the first particle):

ˌlook 'up to	I'd always LOOKED UP to her.
ˌgrow 'out of	The dress was small and she soon GREW OUT of it.
ˌgo 'through with	When the time came to leave I couldn't GO THROUGH with it.
ˌput 'up with	I was finding it hard to PUT UP with him.

Unlike two-word phrasal verbs with two stresses (see **A**), three-word phrasal verbs often have prominence on the first and second words even when there is a noun (the object) after the phrasal verb but still in the same clause. Compare:

ˌcut 'back on	I've CUT BACK on it.
	I've CUT BACK on SMOKing.
	I've CUT back on SMOKing.

(both of these are correct)

C

B11 Many compound nouns (see Unit 16) come from two-stress phrasal verbs. These nouns usually have stress on the first part. Compare:

'mix-up	I got the times MIXED UP.
	There was a MIX-up over times.
'warm-up	It's important to WARM UP before exercise.
	He hurt his ankle during the WARM-up.
'washout	The tennis match was WASHED OUT.
	It was a WASHout.

Exercises

20.1 B12 Listen and underline the prominent syllable(s) in each part in **bold**. All the phrasal verbs are two-stress phrasal verbs but sometimes the particle is non-prominent.

Can you call me back?

EXAMPLE I'm busy now. Can you call me back?

1 Have you **handed your homework in** yet?
2 The fire's on. Don't forget to **turn it off** before you go out.
3 At the stream I **rolled my trousers up** and paddled across.
4 We don't have much money, but I'm sure we'll **get by**.
5 My father and I didn't really **get along**.
6 My handwriting is terrible, as my teachers are always **pointing out**.
7 The painting suddenly **fell off the wall**.
8 If any letters come for me, can you **send them on**?

20.2 B13 You will hear seven questions. After each question, press 'pause' and say one of the responses in the box. (Think carefully about prominence in the phrasal verb.) When you press 'play' again you will hear the correct answer. (Note that all the responses include three-word phrasal verbs.)

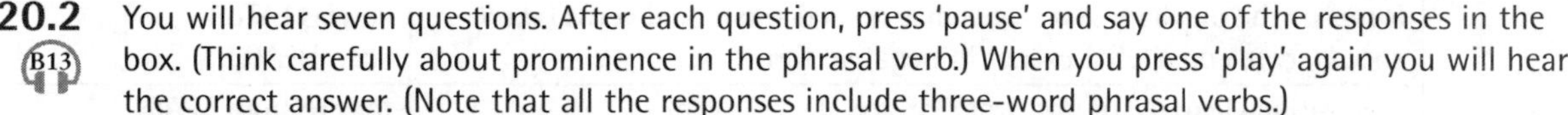

If I can come up with the money.
No, but I don't know how I'm going to get out of it.
~~We'll come on to it next semester.~~
Well, first, we should do away with private schools.
No, she just walked off with it.
Yes, I think he's hoping to put in for a promotion.
I've only just sent away for them.

EXAMPLE *You hear* Are we going to study ecology soon?
You reply We'll **COME ON to** it next semester.

20.3 Complete each (a) part of these pairs of sentences using one of the phrasal verbs in the box. (You may need to change the form of the verb.) Then form a compound noun from each phrasal verb to complete each corresponding (b) part.

back up	check in	follow up	~~hand over~~	get together

EXAMPLE **a** When he demanded my wallet I ....handed.... it ....over.... .
b United Nations troops supervised the ....handover.... .

1 **a** I only had a small bag, but I still had to .... it ....
b When you get to the airport go straight to the ....

2 **a** The whole family usually .... on our mother's birthday.
b All the neighbours had a .... to celebrate the New Year.

3 **a** The files are important, so make sure you .... them ....
b Before I shut down my computer I always make a ....

4 **a** Her suggestion was interesting, so I decided to .... it ....
b The first meeting on the subject was two years ago, and this one is a ....

B14 Now listen and check your answers. Then say the sentences aloud, making sure you put prominence in the correct place in the words you have written.

Follow up: When you read about a topic that interests you, keep a note of compound nouns from phrasal verbs and their related phrasal verbs. Make sure you know where the main stress goes.

21 some, the, from, etc. Weak forms of function words

A B15 Some words are not usually made prominent (see Unit 10) in conversation. These include the following groups of function words. (For exceptions, see Unit 22.)

the personal pronouns *I, me, we, us, you, he, him, she, her, it, they, them*	she SAW me.
the possessive determiners *my, your, his, her, its, our, their*	He's my BROTHer.
each other, one another	They were HITting each other.
the articles *a, an, the*	It's an OWL.
the determiners *some* and *any*	Do you WANT some?
the indefinite pronouns *some-/anybody, some-/anyone, some-/anything* when they are used as the object of a sentence	I didn't SEE anyone.
there used to introduce a sentence	There's some CAKE left.
forms of the auxiliary verbs *be, have, do* and the modal verbs (*shall, should, can, could,* etc.) except in negative forms	He was LATE. I can HEAR it.
prepositions (e.g. *as, at, for, from, of, to*)	They're from SPAIN.
the conjunctions *and, but, or, as, than, that*	He's OLDer than me.

B B16 Some of these function words have a *weak* form and a *strong* form. The weak form is the usual pronunciation, but the strong form is used when the word is –

- prominent (see Unit 22)
- said on its own
- at the end of the sentence

	Example with weak form	Example with strong form
The following have weak forms with /ə/: *the, a, an, and, but, that, than, your, them, us, at, for, from, of, to, as, there, can, could, shall, should, would, must, do, does, am, are, was, were, some*	I can (/kən/) SWIM. This is for (/fə/) YOU.	I CAN (/kæn/) come after ALL. who's it FOR (/fɔː/)?
she, he, we, you are pronounced with reduced vowels in their weak forms: /ʃi/, /hi/, /wi/, /ju/ (or /jə/)	Are you (/ju/ or /jə/) TIRED?	A: who DID it? B: YOU (/juː/)!
his, her, he, him, her, has, had are often pronounced without /h/ in their weak forms (except at the beginning of a sentence)	was he (/hi/ or /i/) THERE?	HE (/hiː/) was THERE, but SHE (/ʃiː/) wasn't.

B17

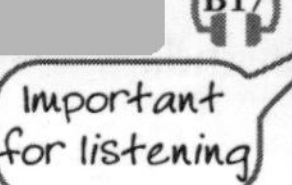

It can be difficult to hear the weak forms of function words in fast speech, particularly when a number of them come together, because they are often said quickly. Compare:

slow speech:	When are you taking him to see her?	There are some over there.
fast speech:	When /əju/ taking /ɪmtə/ see /ə/?	/ðərəsəm/ over there.

It is not always necessary to produce weak forms in your own speech in order to be understood, but they help to make your English sound more fluent and natural.

Exercises

21.1 Listen and repeat these sentences. Prominent syllables are in capital letters. Focus in particular on copying the non-prominent forms of the function words, in green.

B18

1 Do they LIKE each other?
2 I SAW somebody at the WINdow.
3 There was a LETter from his BROther.
4 There should be some MORE in the BOX.
5 We were GOing to see her PArents.
6 She doesn't LOOK as OLD as me.
7 WHEN do you get the reSULTS of your TESTS?
8 I was at HOME from EIGHT o'CLOCK.

21.2 Do you think the words in **bold** will have their weak (write W) or strong form (S) in these dialogues?

EXAMPLE a A: That ice-cream looks nice. B: Do you want **some**? S
b A: I'm really thirsty. B: There's **some** orange juice in the kitchen. W

1 **a** A: Do you think I should apologise? B: Yes, I'm sure that **would** help.
b A: Did you get 100% on the test? B: No, I spelt '**would**' wrong.

2 **a** A: I was in Slovenia last weekend. B: What **were** you doing there?
b A: Why weren't you and Amy at the party? B: But we **were**.

3 **a** A: What have you got there? B: It's a present **from** Alex.
b A: Is this a card for Simon's birthday? B: No, it's **from** Simon.

4 **a** A: Why did you mark it wrong? B: You wrote '**your**' instead of 'you'.
b A: We are off to Scotland again in the summer. B: Are you going with **your** sister?

5 **a** A: Can I borrow your screwdriver? B: What do you want it **for**?
b A: Did the phone ring? B: Yes, it was **for** David.

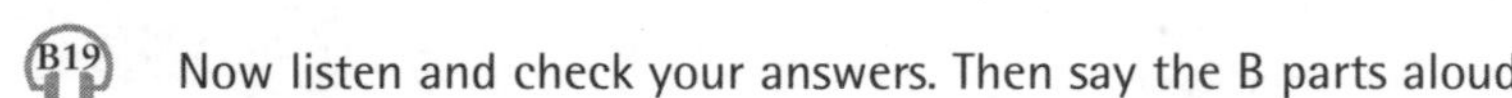

B19 Now listen and check your answers. Then say the B parts aloud.

21.3 Listen. Write the number of words you hear in each space.

EXAMPLE ....2.... leaving now ....3.... staying?
Are you leaving now or are you staying?

1 .... waiting .... brother.
2 I knew .... going .... late again.
3 .... take .... swimming pool?
4 I thought .... station already, ... wrong.
5 .... go to the zoo, ... before?
6 .... more books here .... have.
7 He asked .... money .... lent ....
8 She told .... better off going by bus.

Now check your answers in the Key. Then listen again and repeat the sentences.

Follow up: Find a recording of speech at normal speed with a transcript (see Unit 4 for suggestions). Take an extract and try to write down what the speakers are saying. Then check what you have written against the transcript. Note in particular the pronunciation of function words.

22 Well, YOU do it then! Prominent function words

The function words listed in Unit 21A are not usually prominent. However, there are a number of exceptions.

A B21 Function words are usually made prominent when a contrast is expressed or implied:

A: I'll leave it on the table, shall I? B: No, put it UNder the table.
A: That looks pretty easy. B: Well, YOU do it then! (because I can't)

B B22 *It* is rarely prominent except at the end of a number of fixed phrases with *this* and *that*:

You know I was buying a new car? Well, THIS is IT. (= this is the one)
A: People are only interested in money these days. B: THIS is IT. (= I agree)
THIS is IT, then. (= it's time to do something I don't want to – leave, part, etc.)
I just signed my name, and THAT was IT. (= nothing more had to be done)
A: Here's your pocket money. B: Is THAT IT? (= is that all there is?)
A: Just swim across. B: THAT'S just IT. (= that's the problem) I can't swim.

C B23 *Some* is often prominent (and pronounced /sʌm/) when –

- it means 'some people'
  SOME consider him to be the best golfer in the world.
- it means a large number or amount
  I didn't see her again for SOME YEARS.
- it means a particular person or thing, without saying exactly which
  There must be SOME time we're all free for a meeting.

Any is often prominent (and pronounced /'eni/) when –

- it means 'it's not important which'
  ANY of the camera shops in town will sell them.
- it is used for emphasis after a negative verb
  Haven't you done ANY of your homework yet?

Somebody, anybody, etc. are often prominent when they are the subject of a sentence:

A: Apparently, there were no witnesses. B: But SOMEbody must have seen it.

D B24 *The* is prominent (and pronounced /ðiː/) when we say that something is the best, most important, etc. of its kind:

You should go to the Maldives. It's THE place to see coral.

E B25 The auxiliary verbs *be*, *have* and *do* and the modal verbs are often prominent –

• in negative forms	I CAN'T wait.
• for special emphasis	I SHOULD have left earlier.
• in contradictions	A: You HAVEn't ironed your shirt. B: I HAVE ironed it.
• in time contrasts	It WAS in the cupboard, but it ISn't there now.

Do, did and *does* are often made prominent for emphasis with the present and past simple:

I DO like this cheese. We DID warn you.

F B26 In a piece of new information or a question made up only of function words, the last function word is often made prominent:

There was nothing I could DO.
A: I've just finished a really good book. B: What was it aBOUT?

Exercises

22.1 B27 Think about the words in **bold** in these dialogues and underline them if they are likely to be prominent. Then listen and check your answers.

1 A: **Do** you know of **any** good restaurants in Brockhurst?
B: Well, I haven't been for **some** years, but there used to be **some** very good ones. *The Oyster* was **the** place to eat seafood.
A: Mmm. I **do** like seafood.
B: But I'm sure **any** of **the** restaurants there will be good.

2 A: Try turning the tap off.
B: I **have** tried turning it, but it's stuck.
A: **Did you** ask **anyone** for help?
B: No. Look, why don't **you** try?
A: Okay. Hmmm. There must be **some** way of doing it.
B: I **did** tell you it was stuck.
A: There. It just needed **some** strength! **Anyone** could **have** done it.

Now listen again. Press 'pause' before each B part and read it aloud. Then press 'play' again and compare your pronunciation with what follows. Then do the same for the A parts.

22.2 B28 Play the recording. Press 'pause' before each B part and read it aloud. Then press 'play' again and compare your pronunciation with what follows. Did you put prominence in the same places?

1 A: There you are. All finished. B: Is that it?
2 A: You can't sit there, it's Kate's place. B: Oh, is it?
3 A: Are we there yet? B: Yes, this is it.
4 A: Have you finished? B: Yes, that's it.
5 A: Which coat is yours? B: That's it.
6 A: Your train's arriving. B: This is it, then.
7 A: Do you like my painting? B: What is it?
8 A: Come on, get up now. B: I can't. That's just it.

22.3 B29 You will hear seven sentences. After each sentence, press 'pause' and say one of the responses in the box. (Make sure you make the last word prominent.) When you press 'play' again you will hear the correct answer.

Who could it have been?	Where was he from?
There was nothing we could have done.	~~I wish I had.~~
How many is it for?	But isn't there anything I can do?
Yes, but I don't know who she was.	

EXAMPLE *You hear* I thought you were going to sell your old car.
You say I wish I HAD.

Follow up: Try to use the phrase 'THIS is IT' (= I agree) in the next conversation you have in English. Make sure you pronounce it correctly.

23 calcu/ʊ/late and calcu/ə/late
Vowels in unstressed syllables in content words

A

Vowels in *stressed* syllables of a content word are usually pronounced in the same way whether they are made prominent or not (see also Unit 10):

A: Is she a DOCtor?	/dɒktə/
B: NO, her SISter's a doctor.	/dɒktə/

The vowel in a one-syllable content word doesn't change its pronunciation, although the vowel in a one-syllable function word can (see Unit 21):

content word:	It's a big CAT. /bɪg/		It's really BIG. /bɪg/
function word:	It's for YOU. /fə/	but:	WHAT'S it FOR? /fɔː/

What's it for?

B

B31

Important for listening

However, the vowels in *unstressed* syllables of a content word can vary a lot. In slow, careful speech the vowel may have its full form, but in normal speech these vowels are often reduced to /ə/ (or sometimes /ɪ/). For example, 'calendar' can be said /kælɪndə/ or /kæləndə/; the second vowel varies from /ɪ/ to /ə/. Here are some more words which have variable vowels in unstressed syllables.

/æ/ to /ə/	/ʊ/ to /ə/	/əʊ/ to /ə/	/ɒ/ to /ə/	
accelerate	calculate	omit	comparison	
accept	documentary	proclaim	complain	
cassette	regular	microcosm	concise	
/ɔː/ to /ə/	**/aɪ/ to /ə/ or /ɪ/**	**/ɪ/ to /ə/**	Notice also the common ending *-ity*: /ɪti/ to /əti/	
forbid	director	begin	ability	scarcity
forever	dilemma	hopeless	density	security
corridor	financial	effective		

It is not essential to reduce these vowels in your own speech in order to be understood, although reduced vowels usually sound more natural and fluent.

C

Important for listening

In some words, when an unstressed syllable *ending* in a vowel is followed by another unstressed syllable *beginning* with a vowel, the two syllables may merge into one. This only happens in normal speech; in slow, careful speech both syllables are said:

slow speech:	casual	/kæʒ.ju.el/ = three syllables
normal speech:	casual	/kæʒ.jəl/ = two syllables

Other words like this include:

virtual, actual, adverbial, colonial, studious, obedient, ingredient, gradient

Exercises

23.1 Listen and compare the pronunciation of these words, first said slowly and carefully, and then used in normal speech. In which words does the pronunciation of the highlighted vowel sound change (write C), and in which is there no change (write NC)? (Some of these words are given in **B** opposite.)

EXAMPLES diagram — I didn't understand the diagram. NC
accept — I just couldn't accept their decision. C (accept /æ/ – accept /ə/)

1 musician — She's a musician in an orchestra.
2 director — He's a company director.
3 December — Her birthday's in December.
4 minute (= tiny) — The painting was minute.
5 ambulance — The ambulance came immediately.
6 cricket — I play cricket every weekend.
7 hotel — We stayed in a smart hotel.
8 vocabulary — I'm terrible at learning vocabulary.
9 Mongolia — She's from Mongolia.
10 corridor — Her office is across the corridor.
11 consent — He gave his consent.
12 airport — We live near the airport.

Now listen again and repeat, first the words alone and then the sentences with the words in context.

23.2 You will hear short definitions. After each definition, press 'pause', choose an answer from the box and say it aloud. (Use slow, careful speech.) When you press 'play' again you will hear the correct answer.

adverbial	celebrity	colonial	curiosity	furious	gravity
~~infinity~~	ingredient	majority	studious	virtual	

EXAMPLE *You hear* Time that has no end.
You say infinity /ɪn'fɪnɪti/

23.3 Use the words from exercise 23.2 to complete these sentences.

EXAMPLE The graph goes from zero to ......infinity...... (/ɪn'fɪnəti/)

1 I was late again and my boss was .... with me.
2 He was a .... boy who was happiest when he was reading.
3 Since he appeared on TV he's become a bit of a ....
4 The country used to be an important .... power.
5 The .... of people didn't bother to vote in the election.
6 I want you to underline the .... in each sentence.
7 Honey's the main .... in the sauce.
8 Just out of ...., how old are your sisters?
9 It seemed to defy the laws of ....
10 Because of the snow, we were .... prisoners in our own home.

Now say the sentences aloud (with the words you have written pronounced as in normal speech). Then listen and check your answers.

Follow up: Think about how you pronounce the words listed in **B** opposite. Which of the vowels indicated for the unstressed syllable do you normally use?

24 listen, bottle, politician, etc. Syllabic consonants

A

Most syllables contain a vowel sound. However, sometimes a syllable consists only of a consonant. In dictionaries, these are usually shown either with a ˌ symbol under the consonant or a ᵊ symbol before the consonant. Consonants like this are called *syllabic consonants.*

article /ˈɑː.tɪ.kl̩/ **listen** /ˈlɪs.ᵊn/

It is always possible to pronounce a syllabic consonant as an ordinary syllable with a vowel (/ə/) and a consonant (or consonants), although the syllabic consonant is usually more natural and fluent:

article = /ɑːtɪkəl/ or: /ɑːtɪkl/ listen = /lɪsən/ or: /lɪsn/

B

/l/ syllabic consonants are usually found in unstressed syllables after the following consonants:

/t/	bottle, little, hospital, pistol	/s/	hassle, parcel, whistle, colossal
/d/	saddle, muddle, handle, pedal	/z/	puzzle, drizzle, dazzle, hazel
/p/	couple, people, example, principal	/k/	knuckle, article, classical, comical
/b/	able, trouble, global, jumble	/n/	communal, channel, tunnel, panel

Most of these consonants are spelt *-le*, but a few are spelt *-al*, *-el* and *-ol*.

/n/ syllabic consonants are usually found in unstressed syllables after the following consonants:

/t/	button, rotten, threaten, kitten	/f/	often, deafen, stiffen, soften
/d/	sadden, widen, garden, pardon	/v/	seven, given, eleven, proven
/p/	happen, deepen, open, sharpen	/θ/	marathon, python, strengthen, lengthen
/s/	listen, loosen, comparison, person	/ʃ/	fashion, action, politician, musician
/z/	cousin, horizon, poison, prison	/ʒ/	illusion, collision, occasion, precision

Most of these consonants are spelt *-en*, *-on*, *-ion* or *-ian*.

Words ending *-sm* have an /m/ syllabic consonant. For example:

Buddhism, capitalism, criticism, journalism, mannerism, socialism, chasm, enthusiasm

Note: Contracted forms such as *didn't, haven't, shouldn't, wouldn't,* etc. have a syllabic 'nt':
haven't = /hævnt/ or /hævənt/

C

Some words have two syllabic consonants together, including: *conditional, diagonal, general, literal, national, veteran.* But notice that these can be pronounced in a number of ways. For example:

diagonal = /daɪægənəl/ or /daɪægənl/ or /daɪægnəl/ or /daɪægnl/

D

When *-ing* is added to a verb ending with a syllabic consonant (e.g. *handling, troubling, happening, gardening*) the consonant + *-ing* is usually said as one syllable. The syllabic consonant is the first consonant of the last syllable:

handle /hændᵊl/ – handling /hændlɪŋ/
happen /hæpᵊn/ – happening /hæpnɪŋ/

Notice that it is also possible to say the syllabic consonant with a vowel (/ə/): /hændəlɪŋ/, /hæpənɪŋ/

Exercises

24.1 Complete each sentence with words from the same group.

musician ambition classical	~~button~~ ~~middle~~ ~~happen~~	wobble pedal bicycle	candle knuckle hospital
mansion cousin garden	article prison politician	collision eleven people	little bottle poison

EXAMPLE What will ....happen.......... if I press this ....button.......... in the ....middle..........?

1 My .... lives in a .... with a huge ....
2 He took out a .... full of .... and poured it into her tea.
3 .... were injured in the ....
4 When she got on the .... and began to .... she started to ....
5 Since she started playing the violin, her .... has been to be a ....
6 I burnt my .... on a .... and had to go to ....
7 He wrote an .... about a famous .... who was sent to ....

B40 Now listen and check your answers. Then say the sentences aloud, focusing on saying the words you have written with syllabic consonants.

24.2 B41 Listen to the recording. Press 'pause' before each B part and read it aloud. (Focus on using syllabic consonants.) Then press 'play' again and compare your pronunciation with what follows.

1 A: Stop whistling! B: I *wasn't* whistling.
2 A: I wish you'd stop criticising me. B: It *wasn't* a criticism.
3 A: Why did you unfasten it? B: I *didn't* unfasten it.
4 A: It was drizzling all day. B: It *wasn't* drizzling.
5 A: Stop listening to our conversation. B: I *wasn't* listening.
6 A: It was broken when you gave it to me. B: It *wasn't* broken.
7 A: Don't threaten me! B: I *wasn't* threatening you.
8 A: You've jumbled them up. B: I *didn't* jumble them up.

24.3 Can you find two ... ?

... styles of painting — Cubism and Impressionism
... religions
... political systems
... things to avoid when appointing someone to a job
... good qualities for someone to have in a job
... feelings you might have about a situation

ageism	Buddhism
capitalism	communism
~~Cubism~~	enthusiasm
favouritism	Hinduism
~~Impressionism~~	optimism
pessimism	professionalism

B42 Say your answers aloud. Then listen and check your answers.

Follow up: Can you say 'The Channel Tunnel' with syllabic consonants? Do you know where it is?

25 déjà vu, angst, tsunami
Foreign words in English

Many English words have their origins in other languages. Some of these words are no longer thought of as 'foreign'; for example, *bungalow* (Hindi origin), *caravan* (Persian origin), *tomato* (Spanish origin). Others, however, are still associated with the language they are borrowed from, either because they are recent borrowings or because they keep the appearance of a foreign word. This unit looks at the pronunciation of words in this second group.

Some of these words are said with a pronunciation that makes them sound like English words; others may also be said in a way that is close to their pronunciation in the original language (marked * below).

A (B43) French words used in English

I'm not really au fait with the rules of cricket. /ˌəʊ'feɪ/ (= familiar with)
The negotiations have reached an impasse, with neither side wanting to back down. /'æmpɑːs/ or /'æ̃mpɑːs/* (= a situation where progress is impossible)

The symbol ˜ is put over a vowel when it is pronounced with a nasal sound.

Other examples: faux pas /ˌfəʊ'pɑː/, joie de vivre /ˌʒwɑːdə'viːvrə/, déjà vu /ˌdeɪʒɑː'vuː/, fait accompli /ˌfeɪtə'kɒmpliː/ or /ˌfetəkɔ̃ːm'pliː/*.

You can find the meaning of these and other foreign words in this unit in the Key.

A number of French words in English are pronounced with a /ɑ̃ː/ sound:

They show a lot of avant-garde films at the cinema. /ˌævɑ̃ːŋ'gɑːd/ (= original and modern)

Other examples: carte blanche /ˌkɑːt'blɑ̃ːntʃ/, entre nous /ˌɒntrə'nuː/ or /ˌɑ̃ːntrə'nuː/*, en route /ˌɒn'ruːt/ or /ˌɑ̃ːn'ruːt/*, nuance /'njuːɑːnts/ or /'njuːɑ̃ːns/*.

B (B44) German words used in English

He went through a long period of angst during his teens. /æŋkst/ (= worry and unhappiness about personal problems)

Other examples: doppelgänger /'dɒpəlˌgæŋəʳ/, realpolitik /reɪ'ɑːlpɒlɪˌtiːk/, wanderlust /'wɒndəlʌst/ or /'vɑːndəlʊst/*.

C (B45) Spanish words used in English

She's an aficionado of Spanish literature. /əˌfɪʃiən'ɑːdəʊ/ or /æˌfɪθjə'nɑːdəʊ/*
(= very interested and enthusiastic about the subject)

Other examples: incommunicado /ˌɪnkəˌmjuːnɪ'kɑːdəʊ/, mañana /mæn'jɑːnə/, El Nino (or El Niño) /el'niːnjəʊ/.

D (B46) Italian words used in English

He complained that he couldn't go anywhere without being followed by the paparazzi. /ˌpæpər'ætsi/ (= photographers who follow famous people to get pictures for newspapers)

Other examples: cognoscente /ˌkɒnjəʊ'ʃenti/, prima donna /ˌpriːmə'dɒnə/.

E (B47) Japanese words used in English

The tsunami killed over a million people. /tsu'nɑːmi/ or /su'nɑːmi/ (= a huge wave)

Other examples: bonsai /'bɒnsaɪ/, kimono /kɪ'məʊnəʊ/, origami /ˌɒrɪ'gɑːmi/.

F (B48) Chinese words used in English

He does an hour of t'ai chi every morning. /ˌtaɪ'tʃiː/ (= a form of exercise originally from China)

Other examples: feng shui /ˌfeŋ'ʃuːi/ or /ˌfʌŋ'ʃweɪ/*, lychee /ˌlaɪ'tʃiː/, typhoon /taɪ'fuːn/.

Exercises

25.1 B49 Listen and repeat these foreign words used in English. What language do you think each word comes from: French, Chinese, Italian, German, Japanese or Spanish? If you are not sure, use the examples on the page opposite and try to notice similar spellings or sounds.

denouement	diva	ersatz	haiku	macho	ninja
nouvelle cuisine	ginseng	schadenfreude	sotto voce	kumquat	pronto

Check your answers in the Key, where you can also find the meaning of the words.

25.2 B50 Listen and repeat the French words in column A. Then try to match them with the brief definition in column B. Use the example sentences below the table to help you.

	A	B
1	bête noire	a describing something you must have or do to appear fashionable
2	cause célèbre	b a false name used by a writer
3	de rigueur	c an embarrassing small disagreement
4	clientele	d a person or thing that particularly annoys you or that you dislike
5	contretemps	e being able to do or say the right thing in any situation
6	en suite	f the customers or clients of a business
7	nom de plume	g a controversial event that attracts a lot of public attention
8	savoir-faire	h describing a connected bathroom and bedroom

1 My particular bête noire is people who use mobile phones when they are driving.
2 The trial of the two teenagers became an international cause célèbre.
3 Where I work, smart suits are de rigueur for the women.
4 The restaurant has a clientele that includes film stars and famous sportspeople.
5 There was a contretemps between the neighbours over the fence dividing their gardens.
6 All the rooms in the hotel are en suite.
7 She writes under the nom de plume of Cathy Kay.
8 I really envy him for his savoir-faire.

Check your answers in the Key, then read the sentences aloud, paying particular attention to the pronunciation of the foreign words.

25.3 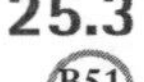 Here are some Russian words used in English. First, try reading them aloud. Then listen and compare your pronunciation with the recording. You can find the meaning of the words in the Key.

glasnost intelligentsia politburo samovar troika

Follow up: Do you know any (other) words from your first language that are used in English? How does the pronunciation of the words in the first language and in English differ? Check the English pronunciation in a dictionary.

26 one_evening, stop_now, go_away, etc. Linking sounds

Important for listening

In fluent speech, words within a speech unit (see Section E4 *Glossary*) are usually said without a break. The sound at the end of one word is linked to the sound at the beginning of the next so that there is a smooth connection between them.

A B52 A consonant sound at the end of a word is linked smoothly to a vowel sound at the beginning of the next:

one_evening a serious_accident the exact_opposite

B B53 When a word ending with a consonant sound is followed by a word beginning with another consonant sound there is no break between them, although the first consonant sound may change its pronunciation a little to make it easier to move to the next consonant sound:

a warm_breeze I've_seen it starting_tomorrow

Notice also that when a word ending with one of the consonants /p/, /b/, /t/, /d/, /k/, /g/, is followed by a word beginning with a different one of these (or /m/ or /n/), no air is released at the end of the first consonant and there is a smooth change to the second:

stop_now heard_tell make_bread

C B54 When a word ending with a consonant sound is followed by a word beginning with the same consonant sound, one lengthened consonant sound is made:

some_milk glorious_sunshine it's half_full

D B55 A vowel sound at the end of a word is linked to a vowel sound at the beginning of the next by an inserted /w/ or /j/ ('y') sound:

who_is it? /w/ go_away /w/ can you see_it? /j/ it's completely_empty /j/

The choice of either /w/ or /j/ depends on the vowel sound that ends the first word. If the vowel is produced with the highest part of the tongue close to the *front* of the mouth (/iː/, /eɪ/, /aɪ/, /ɔɪ/) then the linking sound will be /j/. If the vowel is produced with the highest part of the tongue close to the *back* of the mouth (/uː/, /aʊ/, /əʊ/) then the linking sound will be /w/.

E B56 Words ending with the letters *-r* or *-re* have a final vowel sound: e.g. car /kɑː/, more /mɔː/, fir /fɜː/, other /ˈʌðə/, fear /fɪə/, hair /heə/, pure /pjʊə/. When a word like this is followed by a word beginning with a vowel, a /r/ sound is inserted:

car_engine /r/ my other_uncle /r/ pure_oxygen /r/

In some dictionaries this /r/ before a vowel is shown with the symbol ʳ.
For example: /kɑːʳ/ (car) /ˈʌðəʳ/ (other) /pjʊəʳ/ (pure)

⚠ **Note:** In many other accents of English (e.g. Scottish, Irish and most North American accents) words ending in *-r* or *-re* always have a final /r/ sound: car /kɑːr/, more /mɔːr/, etc.

Less commonly, a /r/ sound is inserted when the word ends in one of the vowels /ɑː/, /ɔː/, /ɜː/, /ə/, /ɪə/, /eə/ or /ʊə/ but is not spelt with the letters *-r* or *-re*:

China_and Japan /r/ the area_is flooded /r/

However, some native speakers of British English think this is incorrect pronunciation.

When sounds merge or a sound changes at the end of a word, it may sound like another word, but usually any misunderstanding is resolved by context. For example, 'talk Danish' might sound like 'taught Danish', but these are unlikely to be confused in context.

Exercises

26.1 First match A's questions with B's answers in this conversation. Then look at the B parts and decide whether the links marked are /w/ links (write /w/) or /j/ links (write /j/).

	A	B
1	A: Where are you going?	.... B: By‿air.
2	A: When?	.... B: Yes, I grew‿up there.
3	A: Why?	.... B: Yes, a new‿umbrella.
4	A: Who is he?	.... B: He‿asked me for one.
5	A: Have you got cousins there, too?	.... B: Tomorrow‿afternoon.
6	A: How will you get there?	.... B: I'll stay‿a week.
7	A: How long will it take?	...1... B: To‿Austria. /w/
8	A: Have you been there before?	.... B: No, they‿all live in France.
9	A: How long will you be there?	.... B: It's too‿expensive.
10	A: Why don't you stay longer?	.... B: To see‿Adam.
11	A: Will you take Adam a present?	.... B: A few‿hours.
12	A: Why an umbrella?	.... B: My‿uncle.

Now listen and check your answers. Press 'pause' before each B part and read it aloud. Then press 'play' again and compare your pronunciation with what follows.

26.2 Mark all the possible /r/ links in these sentences containing idiomatic phrases. Say the sentences aloud and then listen and check your answers. (Check any idioms you don't know in a dictionary or in the Key.)

EXAMPLE I bought it on the spur‿of the moment.

1 He's got a finger in every pie.
2 It's in the nature of things.
3 She's without a care in the world.
4 It's as clear as mud.
5 It's the law of the jungle.
6 Let's focus on the matter in hand.
7 Is that your idea of a joke?
8 He's a creature of habit.
9 Pride comes before a fall.
10 Get your act together!

26.3 Listen and underline which of the words you hear in each sentence. As the pairs of words could be pronounced in a similar way in the sentences, you will need to use the context to help you choose.

EXAMPLE <u>held</u> / helped let / <u>led</u>
(She held my hand as she led me up the hill.)

1 lock / lot back / bat
2 play / played park / part
3 hit / hid trick / trip
4 like / light planned / plan
5 right / ride road / robe

Now check your answers in the Key. Then listen again and repeat the sentences.

> **Follow up:** My old English teacher, Mr Brookes, didn't like us to use /r/ links except after words spelt with *-r* or *-re*. Which of the links you have marked in exercise 26.2 would Mr Brookes have disapproved of? Do you think Mr Brookes was right in his view of the use of /r/ links?

27 I'*ll* get it, These'*re* mine
Contracted forms

A

(B60) A number of function words (see Unit 21) have *contracted* forms, written with an apostrophe:

contracted form	function word	pronunciation
'd	had, would	/d/ after vowels: I'd already seen it. /əd/ after consonants: It'd be wonderful.
's	is, has	/s/ after /p,t,k,f,θ/: It's interesting. /z/ after other sounds: She's left.
'll	will	/l/: I'll get it.
've	have	/v/ after vowels: You've got a letter. /əv/ after consonants: I could've gone.
're	are	/ər/ before a vowel: We're all right. /ə/ before a consonant: We're winning.
n't	not	/nt/: I haven't got any.

We don't use these contracted forms (except *n't*) at the end of a sentence:

I'm sure he will. (not: … ~~he'll~~.)

Note: *am* is contracted in *I'm* and *us* is contracted in *let's*.

B

(B61) In speech, we often use these contracted forms after –

• *wh-* words	Who'll be there?	Why's he doing that?
• nouns	The Smiths've gone away.	Now'd be a good time.
• *this, that, these, those*	These're mine.	This'll be fine.
• *there*	There're some over here.	There'll be rain later.

Note: *did* is sometimes contracted to *'d* after *wh-* words:
Why'd you do that? (= Why did you do that?)

Note: These contracted forms are less common in writing.

C

(B62) Important for listening

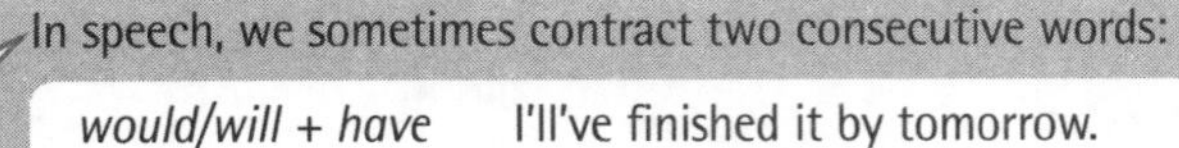

In speech, we sometimes contract two consecutive words:

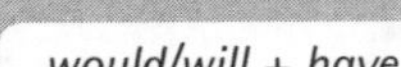

would/will + have	I'll've finished it by tomorrow. He'd've loved to have been there.
not + have	She couldn't've known about it. I wouldn't've minded doing it.

Note: These contracted forms are very uncommon in writing.

D

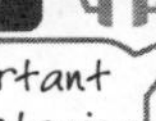

(B63) Important for listening

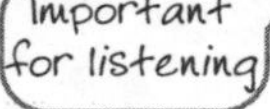

In informal speech, the contractions *'d* (*had*) and *'ve* (*have*) are sometimes left out in the verbs *had better* and *have got to* (see also Unit 28):

You ('d) better apologise to her.
You ('ve) gotta (= got to) be joking.

Exercises

27.1 First listen and repeat just the A parts, focusing on the contracted forms. Then match the A parts with the B parts.

	A	B
1	A: He's leaving now.	.... B: Let's ask the farmer.
2	A: We're arriving at ten.	...1... B: I thought he'd gone already.
3	A: I haven't got any money on me.	.... B: Yes, I think it's ridiculous.
4	A: Do you think it'd be okay to camp here?	.... B: It'll be good to see you.
5	A: You should've taken the job.	.... B: Well, let's eat now.
6	A: I suppose you've heard Kathy's idea?	.... B: Don't worry. I've got my credit card.
7	A: I'm starving.	.... B: You're right. I should.

Now listen and check your answers. Press 'pause' before each B part and read it aloud. Then press 'play' again and compare your pronunciation with what follows.

27.2 Underline words which could be contracted in these sentences. Then read the sentences aloud with contracted forms.

EXAMPLE Those are too big, but these will fit.

1 My feet will get wet because my shoes have got holes in.
2 There is no butter, but this will do instead.
3 I am sure Ann would help if she could.
4 How did they know we would be there?
5 Adam has phoned to say he is not ready to go yet, but he will call again when he is.
6 There have been four parcels delivered for you while you have been away.
7 What will you do if Tom has already gone?

Now listen and check your answers.

27.3 Listen. Write what you hear in each space. Use contracted forms, but also think about what the non-contracted forms would be.

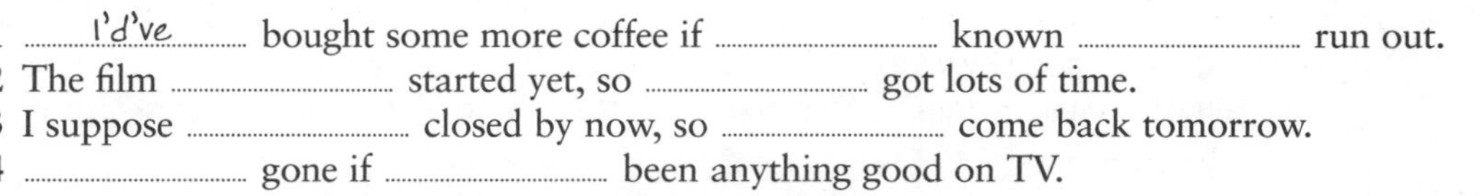

1 .....I'd've..... bought some more coffee if .... known .... run out.
2 The film .... started yet, so .... got lots of time.
3 I suppose .... closed by now, so .... come back tomorrow.
4 .... gone if .... been anything good on TV.

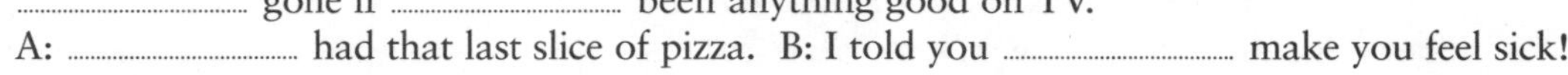

5 A: .... had that last slice of pizza. B: I told you .... make you feel sick!

Follow up: The lyrics to pop songs often contain contracted forms. Find lyrics to songs you know (you could search, for example, on http://www.azlyrics.com or http://risa.co.uk/sla). Which song contains the most contracted forms? Can you say (or sing!) them all fluently?

28 I'm not sure, Not sure, 'm not sure
Ellipsis and 'near ellipsis'

A

B68 Important for listening

In spoken English we often leave out words when they are obvious from the context:

A: What's the matter? B: Got a headache. (= I've got a headache.)

This process is called *ellipsis.* Often, however, the words are not omitted completely, but a very short sound from the omitted words is left behind:

've got a headache. (/vgɒt.../)

We will refer to this as *near ellipsis.*

Being aware of ellipsis and near ellipsis can help you to understand spoken English, and using it can make you sound more natural and fluent.

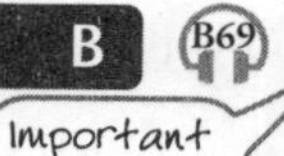

B

Important for listening

Ellipsis and near ellipsis are common at the beginning of an utterance. Here are some typical patterns. Examples give the complete (but often contracted) form, the form with ellipsis, and the form with near ellipsis:

- leaving out personal subject + *be/have*
  A: What time will we get there?
  B: I'm not sure. / Not sure. / 'm not sure.
  A: Where's Jack?
  B: He's gone home. / Gone home. / 's gone home.
- leaving out *it* before *is/has*
  A: What's the curry like?
  B: It's really hot. / Really hot. / 'ts really hot.
  A: What's wrong with your camera?
  B: It's broken. / Broken. / 'ts broken.
- leaving out *be*
  Is that Ken? / That Ken? / 's that Ken?
  Are we there yet? / We there yet? / 're (/ə/) we there yet?
- leaving out an auxiliary verb or *be* + subject
  Do you want another drink? / Want another drink? / d'y (/dʒ/) want another drink?
  Have you seen my keys? / Seen my keys? / v'y (/vj/) seen my keys?
  Are you leaving already? / Leaving already? / r'y (/əj/) leaving already or: 'y (/j/) leaving already?

What's the curry like?
'ts really hot.

The verbs *be* and *have* are often left out between the question word and subject in *wh-* questions:
What are you doing? / What you doing? / What're you doing?
What have you got there? / What you got there? / What've you got there?

Note: When *does* follows a *wh-* word, it can be pronounced /s/ or /z/, but isn't left out completely:
What does he do? / What's he do...? (not: ~~What he do?~~)
When does it start? / When's it start? (not: ~~When it start?~~)

Exercises

28.1 (B71) In the conversation below, the complete forms of the sections in **bold** are given. Listen and decide when the speakers actually use ellipsis (write E) or near ellipsis (write NE).

A: **What are you** making? ....NE....
B: **It's a cake** for Richard's birthday. ....E....
A: **It's amazing,** isn't it? ....
B: **Do you think** he'll like it? ....
A: **I'm sure** he will, although **he's a bit** fussy about food, isn't he? .... / ....
B: **Have you seen** this? ....
A: Wow! **Is that** a real flower? ....
B: No, **it's made** from sugar. ....
A: **When does it** have to be ready? ....
B: **It's his** birthday tomorrow. **Do you know** where he is now? .... / ....
A: **I've no** idea. ....

28.2 (B72) Listen to these conversations. Press 'pause' before each B part and read it aloud. (Use near ellipsis of the word(s) in **bold**.) Then press 'play' again and compare your pronunciation with what follows.

1 A: Have you heard from Paul recently? B: **I've** just phoned him.
2 A: My shoes feel tight. B: **Have** you got the right ones?
3 A: I retired last year. B: What **are** you doing now?
4 A: We're having a barbeque tonight. B: **It's** a good job it's not raining.
5 A: Marco's got a new job. B: What **does** he do?
6 A: Do you like my new hat? B: **Is** that a hat?
7 A: Pat looks really ill. B: **She's** got a terrible cold.
8 A: What time is it? B: **It's** half past.
9 A: We got that painting in Spain. B: **Do** you remember exactly where we bought it?
10 A: Have you taken my money? B: What **are** you talking about?
11 A: Do you think we can cut across that field? B: **I'm** pretty sure we can.
12 A: What's that thing? B: **It's** called a dibber.
13 A: I can't find my gloves. B: **Are** these yours?
14 A: We're having a brown-bag lunch. B: What **does** that mean?
15 A: We should be in Milton in about ten minutes. B: **Do** you know where to go when we get there?

Follow up: Ellipsis and near ellipsis happen in informal speech in most languages. Listen to conversations in your first language (or better still, listen to a recording) and find examples.

29 las~~t~~ night, I haven'~~t~~ seen her
Leaving out consonant sounds (1): /t/

Some consonant sounds tend to be left out in conversation. For example:

I was a~~l~~most lef~~t~~ behind. I practis~~ed~~ football with ~~h~~im.

Units 29 and 30 look at some of the most common consonant omissions. It is not necessary to leave these out in your own speech in order to be understood, but leaving them out can make your speech sound more fluent and natural, and being aware of these changes can help you understand fast speech.

A

B73

Important for listening

When a word with a final consonant cluster ending /t/ is followed by another word beginning with a consonant sound, /t/ is often left out (see also Unit 9):

Las~~t~~ night.	He stopp~~ed~~ breathing.	It kep~~t~~ still.
He was lef~~t~~ behind.	Just ac~~t~~ normal.	I collec~~t~~ coins.

Notice, however, that –

- we don't usually leave out /t/ before a vowel sound or /h/:
  First of May. You've bent it. She's left handed.
- when the final consonant cluster is /skt/ we often leave out /k/ before a vowel and /h/, and may leave out both /k/ and /t/ before a consonant. Compare:
  I as~~k~~ed Oliver. (.../ɑːstɒl/...) He ris~~k~~ed his life. (.../rɪstɪz/...)
  I as~~ked~~ Brian. (.../ɑːsbr/...) He ris~~ked~~ losing. (.../rɪsluː/...)

B

B74

Important for listening

In the informal speech of some speakers, a /t/ sound is commonly replaced by a *glottal stop* (ʔ), a sound made by stopping the flow of air by closing the vocal cords (see Section E4 *Glossary*). This change only happens at the end of a syllable and when the sound before /t/ is a vowel, /l/, /m/ or /n/.

In particular, it is used –

- within or at the end of a word when the next syllable or word begins with a consonant sound:
  football (.../ʊʔb/...) pointless (.../nʔl/...)
  Late at night. (.../əʔn/...) You're quite right. (.../aɪʔr/...)
- at the end of a sentence:
  Give me that. (.../ðæʔ/) It costs a lot. (.../lɒʔ/)

Note: Replacing /t/ with a glottal stop is found in Britain particularly in the accents of cities, but is also increasingly becoming part of the accents of educated young people. In some regional accents glottal stops replace /t/ even when the next syllable or word begins with a vowel sound, for example:

/bʌʔə/ (butter), /mɑːʔɪn/ (Martin), /nɒʔəʊnli/ (not only)

However, some people still consider this to be lazy speech.

C

B75

Important for listening

When a word ending with /t/ is followed by a word beginning with /j/ ('y'), the /t/ + /j/ is usually pronounced /tʃ/ (as in '<u>ch</u>eap'):

Has he left‿yet? (/tʃ/) Last‿year. (/tʃ/)

However, /t/ may also be replaced by a glottal stop, depending on the sound before /t/ (see **B**):

I can't let you do it. (.../letʃuː/... or .../leʔjuː/...)

/t/ may change its pronunciation before consonants in other ways to make it easier to move to the next sound (see also Unit 26**B**):

It's not me. (/t/ sounds like /p/) In the front garden. (/t/ sounds like /k/)

Exercises

29.1 Say these sentences aloud and cross out any letters representing /t/ at the end of words that you think are likely to be left out.

Example Nex~~t~~ Monday.

1 He wrote it.
2 A published article.
3 It's in first gear.
4 It was just him.
5 Take a left turn.
6 They kept quiet.
7 It looked good.
8 We reached Berlin.
9 We crossed over.
10 I'll contact Ann.
11 He finished first.
12 I slept badly.

Now listen, check your answers and repeat.

29.2 B77 Listen to these sentences and focus on the highlighted /t/ sounds. Write the number of the sentence in the table below according to what happens to the /t/ sound.

1 Almost there.
2 Have you passed your test?
3 I asked her to leave.
4 Just a bit.
5 We must be nearly there.
6 Tell us what you did.
7 Most Europeans agree.
8 I expect an answer soon.
9 She stopped playing.
10 Next year.
11 My left ankle hurts.
12 I'll have a soft drink.
13 Just use your common sense.
14 I've already dealt with it.
15 I washed all my clothes.
16 I can't wait.

A no change to /t/	B /t/ left out	C /t/ replaced with glottal stop	D /t/ + /j/ said /tʃ/
	1		2

Check your answers in the Key. Then say the sentences aloud as they are said on the recording.

29.3 All the possible /t/ sounds in this conversation are in green. Read the conversation and predict any likely omissions, replacements or changes to the /t/ sounds, using the four categories (A, B, C and D) in exercise 29.2.

A: What you got there?

B: It's Don Simpson's latest novel. Have you read it?

A: Bought it just the other day.

B: I don't think it's as good as his first.

A: Don't you? But then that was really tremendous.

B78 Now listen and check your predictions.

Follow up: If you have internet access, find recordings of people with regional English accents (see Unit 4 for suggested websites). Can you find speakers who very frequently replace /t/ with a glottal stop?

30 an ol~~d~~ car, a bottle o~~f~~ water
Leaving out consonant sounds (2): /d/, /h/, /l/, /v/

A Leaving out /d/ in consonant clusters

Important for listening

When a word with a final consonant cluster ending /d/ is followed by another word beginning with a consonant sound, /d/ is often left out (see also Unit 9):

An ol~~d~~ car. I chang~~ed~~ clothes. Can you fin~~d~~ Mark?

Notice, however, that –

- we don't usually leave out /d/ before vowel sounds or /h/
  Hand it over. They served apple pie. She seemed happy.
- we don't usually leave out /d/ before the sounds /l/, /w/, /r/ and /s/
  Do you mind walking? (compare: Do you min~~d~~ giving me a lift?)

Note: When a word ending with /d/ is followed by a word beginning with /j/ ('y'), the /d/+/j/ is usually pronounced /dʒ/ (as in '<u>J</u>une'). This happens both in consonant clusters and when the word ends with the single consonant sound /d/:

Had you met before? /dʒ/ I'll lend you one. /dʒ/

B Leaving out /h/

Important for listening

We often leave out /h/ at the beginning of –

- the pronouns *he, her, his, him*
  I thought ~~h~~e was. Did you meet ~~h~~er? Ask ~~h~~im.
- the auxiliary verbs *have, has, had*
  The students ~~h~~ave all left. Karen ~~h~~ad already left.
- the question word *who*
  Can you describe the person ~~wh~~o did it?

However, /h/ is not left out if it is stressed or at the beginning of an utterance:

It's not mine, it's his. It's him! Has Ken arrived? Who did it?

C Leaving out /l/ after /ɔː/

Important for listening

Many speakers leave out /l/ after the vowel /ɔː/ in words such as:

a~~l~~most a~~l~~ready a~~l~~right a~~l~~so a~~l~~though a~~l~~ways

D Leaving out /d/ in *and* and /v/ in *of*

Important for listening

Before consonant sounds, *and* is usually pronounced /ən/ or /n/ and *of* is pronounced /ə/:

red an~~d~~ blue now an~~d~~ then a bottle o~~f~~ water a waste o~~f~~ time

Before vowel sounds, *and* is usually pronounced /ən/ or /n/ but *of* is pronounced /əv/:

pen an~~d~~ ink Adam an~~d~~ Eve a bag of apples a can of oil

Exercises

30.1 Say these sentences aloud and cross out any letters representing /d/ at the ends of words that you think are likely to be left out.

EXAMPLE Hol~~d~~ tight.

1 She's world champion.
2 We sailed slowly.
3 She changed clothes.
4 I'll send Lucy.
5 I was pleased with it.
6 She arrived there.
7 Can you hold it?
8 I understand that.
9 We climbed over.
10 It moved towards us.
11 They're second-hand.
12 He turned round.

 Now listen, check your answers and repeat.

30.2 The /h/ sounds at the beginnings of words are highlighted in these conversations. Cross them out if you think they are likely to be left out in fast speech.

EXAMPLE A: Is that ~~h~~im over there?
B: Who?
A: The man ~~wh~~o took your bag.

1 A: He wasn't at home.
B: No, I think he's on holiday.

2 A: It says here, the President's coming.
B: Where?
A: Here.
B: I really hope we'll get to see her.

3 A: How's Tom these days?
B: Haven't you heard about his heart attack?

4 A: Kate says she left her handbag here. Have you seen it?
B: This one? But Judy says it's hers.

 Now listen and check your answers. Then repeat each line of the conversations.

30.3 B85 Make sure you have studied both Units 29 and 30 before doing this exercise. You will hear a conversation in which two students are talking about their teachers. Listen as many times as you need. Focus on the words in **bold** and –

(i) cross out any letters representing sounds that are missed out;
(ii) write ʔ above any /t/ sounds replaced by a glottal stop;
(iii) note any other changes to sounds at the end of the highlighted words.

A: Have you **got**$^{?}$ much work on **jus~~t~~** now?

B: Dr Thomas **has** given us a very hard essay, but I **mustn't get** a low mark this time.

A: I had an **argument** with my tutor **last** week.

B: **What** happened?

A: Well, I **couldn't find** my coursework, so I **asked** for a couple of days extra. She **got** really annoyed with me **and** complained I was **always late** for lectures. Anyway, I told **her** I thought **her** course was a waste **of** time.

B: **Did** you? Well, **at least** Dr Thomas **doesn't** shout at us, **although** I'm **not** very **confident** that I'll pass **his** exam.

Now check your answers in the Key.

31 average, novelist, happening
Words that lose a syllable

A

B86 Important for listening

In some words, vowels tend to be left out in conversation. When this happens, the word loses an unstressed syllable:

av~~e~~rage   nov~~e~~list   happ~~e~~ning

Some dictionaries show that the vowel /ə/ can be left out using the symbol ᵊ:

/ævᵊrɪdʒ/   /nɒvᵊlɪst/   /hæpᵊnɪŋ/

It is not necessary to leave these vowels out in your own speech in order to be understood, but leaving them out can make your speech sound more fluent and natural, and being aware of these changes can help you understand rapid speech.

B

B87 Important for listening

Most vowels left out in this way come before /r/, /l/ or /n/.

Before /r/ –

consid~~e~~rable	direct~~o~~ry	batt~~e~~ry	diction~~a~~ry	conf~~e~~rence	fav~~ou~~rite
fav~~ou~~rable	hist~~o~~ry	discov~~e~~ry	imagin~~a~~ry	diff~~e~~rence	int~~e~~rest
mis~~e~~rable	pref~~e~~rable	myst~~e~~ry	second~~a~~ry	ref~~e~~rence	rest~~au~~rant

Before /l/ –			Before /n/ –		
accident~~a~~lly	caref~~u~~lly	fam~~i~~ly	educati~~o~~nal	deaf~~e~~ning	def~~i~~nite
especi~~a~~lly	dreadf~~u~~lly	marv~~e~~llous	nati~~o~~nal	fright~~e~~ning	pris~~o~~ner
parti~~a~~lly	thankf~~u~~lly	speci~~a~~list	pers~~o~~nal	gard~~e~~ning	traditi~~o~~nal

Note: Some other words with these endings rarely lose a syllable (e.g. *theory, cookery, formally*), and some words with these endings almost always lose a syllable (e.g. *historic~~a~~lly, politic~~a~~lly, technic~~a~~lly*).

C

B88 Important for listening

In a few words, left-out vowels come before sounds other than /r/, /l/ and /n/. For example:

gove~~rn~~ment   med~~i~~cine   veg~~e~~table

D

B89 Important for listening

In a few two-syllable words with stress on the second syllable, the first vowel is often left out in rapid speech so that the word is said with only one syllable:

I don't b~~e~~lieve you. /bliːv/   What's the c~~o~~rrect answer? /krekt/
It's the p~~o~~lice. /pliːs/   I s~~u~~ppose so. /spəʊz/

E

B90 Important for listening

A few words lose their first syllable completely in rapid speech:

~~A~~bout five o'clock.
I bought it ~~be~~cause it was cheap.
I've invited everyone ~~ex~~cept Jack.

When these words are written to represent speech (for example, in novels) this pronunciation is sometimes indicated:

'bout, 'cause, 'cept

Exercises

31.1 Complete these sentences using the pairs of words below. (Notice that you may need to change the order of the words.)

frightening – discovery	considerable – difference	thankfully – battery
~~restaurant~~ – ~~favourite~~	mystery – prisoner	deafening – accidentally
interest – traditional	carefully – directory	secondary – miserable

EXAMPLE *Carlo's* is my ....favourite.......... Italian ....restaurant.......... .

1 When she lived in Shanghai she developed an .... in .... Chinese medicine.
2 The two cars seem identical, but there is a .... in how much they cost.
3 I had a .... time in .... school.
4 When he opened the door he made a ....
5 The .... escaped and where he's gone is a complete ....
6 I checked .... in the ...., but couldn't find his number.
7 The torch didn't work, but .... I had a spare .... in the kitchen.
8 When I .... pressed the button there was a .... bang.

B91 Now listen and check your answers. Then read aloud the sentences making sure you pronounce the words you have written with the appropriate vowels left out.

31.2 B92 Listen to the words in the box said slowly and carefully and write the number of syllables you hear (some of these are on the opposite page):

memory 3	formally 3	loyally	suppose	anniversary	police
machinery	technically	delivery	medicine	geometrically	
perhaps	historically	nursery			

31.3 B93 Listen to the words from exercise 31.2 used in sentences. Again, write the number of syllables you hear. Is this the same number as in exercise 31.2 (write S) or a different number (write D)?

EXAMPLES I must be losing my **memory.** 2 D He was dressed **formally.** 3 S

1 He supported her **loyally.**
2 I **suppose** not.
3 It's our wedding **anniversary.**
4 The **police** arrived.
5 The **machinery** broke down.
6 It's **technically** very advanced.
7 There's a special **delivery** for you.
8 I'm taking cough **medicine.**
9 It was **geometrically** patterned.
10 **Perhaps** you're right.
11 The play is **historically** accurate.
12 She goes to a **nursery.**

Now check your answers in the Key. Then say the sentences aloud, leaving out syllables where appropriate.

31.4 Here are some extracts from books. Read aloud the quoted speech as it is written.

'Well, no one's making any calls, and no one's sending no faxes either, so I guess you'll just have to start thinking 'bout being poor. So there!!'

'... I jus' felt I had to warn you, 'cause it don't look too healthy, y'unnersan'?...'

"He tried once or twice," said the boy dismissively, "but he couldn't see well enough to teach anything 'cept what was in his head. ..."

Follow up: If someone said 'scuseme' to you, what might they want you to do?

32 // we stuck a picture// of an elephant// Breaking speech into units

A (C2) As we speak, we group words into units depending on meaning and emphasis. Listen and notice how this speaker divides up what he is saying:

// I can remember as children// we were rather naughty// once// we stuck a picture// of an elephant// on the back of Dad's coat// before he went out// of course he couldn't see it// so he didn't know why everyone was laughing at him// until he got to work// and took it off//

In this book we call these *speech units* and mark them with //.

B (C3) Although there are no rules about how we divide speech into units, some words are more likely to go together than others in order to help make sense of the message. For example:

// we stuck a picture// of an elephant// is more likely than:
// we stuck a// picture of an elephant// or: // we stuck a picture of// an elephant//

// until he got to work// and took it off// is more likely than:
// until he got to// work and took it off// or: // until he got to work and took// it off//

C (C4) Sometimes the division of speech into units can make a difference in meaning:

(i) // we were rather naughty// once// we stuck a picture// of an elephant//…
(ii) // we were rather naughty once// we stuck a picture// of an elephant//…

In (i), 'once' goes with 'we stuck a picture of an elephant' and shows that the speaker is giving an example of the many times they were naughty. In (ii), 'once' goes with 'we were naughty' and suggests that we were naughty only one time.

(iii) // before he went out// of course he couldn't see it//
(iv) // before he went out of course// he couldn't see it//

In (iii), 'of course' goes with 'he couldn't see it' and means that it is obvious that he couldn't see it. In (iv), 'of course' goes with 'before he went out' and means that it is obvious that we stuck it on his coat before he went out.

D (C5) When we want to emphasise words in order to draw particular attention to them, we can put them into very short speech units:

// we were rather naughty// or for emphasis: // we were rather// naughty//
// on the back of Dad's coat// or for emphasis: // on the back// of Dad's// coat//

E (C6) Within speech units, words are usually linked smoothly together, without pauses between them (see also Unit 26):

// I can remember‿as children//
/r/

// of course he couldn't see‿it//
/j/

// until he got‿to work//

Exercises

32.1 (C7) Listen to the recording as many times as you need, and mark the boundaries between speech units with // in these extracts. The first one has been done for you.

1 that's the main thing // and then if you've got any questions afterwards hopefully we'll still have time to go through a few of them is that okay

2 she'd left when she had a baby and then decided not to go back although the job had been kept open for her

3 Tom dear where's the advert for this calculator because I don't know the address and I don't know who I've got to make the cheque payable to

Now check your answers in the Key. Then read the extracts aloud. Put short breaks between speech units and link the words within speech units smoothly together without pauses.

32.2 Each of these extracts consists of three speech units. Put // in two of the four spaces to show where you expect the speech unit boundaries to be.

EXAMPLE
when you read it carefully // it doesn't say anything // that's very critical

1 when I woke up I didn't even realise what time it was
2 of course it's written in a language that hardly anyone can understand
3 I was working late because they want it done as quickly as possible
4 because he was ill I didn't expect him to come to work
5 if I get some time I'll be over on the weekend to see you both
6 luckily we haven't had any rain since the day we arrived
7 it should never have been built in my opinion this new office building

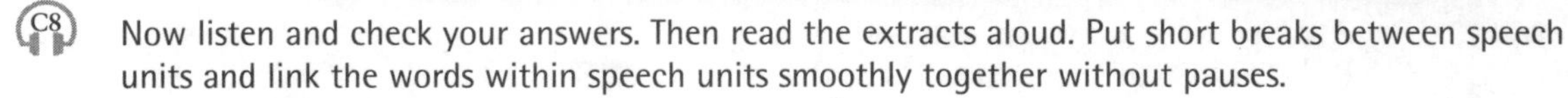

(C8) Now listen and check your answers. Then read the extracts aloud. Put short breaks between speech units and link the words within speech units smoothly together without pauses.

32.3 (C9) Give special emphasis to the words in **bold** by putting each one in a short speech unit. Read the extracts aloud and then compare your pronunciation with the recording.

1 I've never seen such an **incredibly exciting** football match.
2 She has always helped me and has **never refused** any request I've made.
3 After the day of climbing I was **completely exhausted.**
4 She looked much older – **grey** and **lined** – and she used a walking stick.

Follow up: Record a short extract (about 15 seconds) from a radio or TV programme. (See Unit 4 for suggestions.) Write out what was said and then try to mark speech unit boundaries in the text. Listen to the recording as many times as necessary.

33 // It's BLUE// DARK blue// Prominent words in speech units (1)

A (C10) Within a speech unit, some words are made *prominent* (see Unit 10) and others *non-prominent*. A prominent word is shown with its prominent syllable in capital letters:

A: Where's Kieron living now?
B: // He's got a HOUSE in LIVerpool//

> 'house' and 'Liverpool' are made prominent; the first syllable in 'Liverpool' has main stress and so is prominent

The prominent syllable in a word is usually the one shown in a dictionary as having main stress (see Unit 10).

Words are made prominent in order to emphasise them because they carry important or interesting information:

A: Why are you cleaning your shoes?
B: // I've got an INterview later today//

> the reason for needing clean shoes – the interview – is important here

A: When I was in New Zealand I went bungee jumping.
B: // It must have been TERrifying//

> B expresses his feelings about bungee jumping in 'terrifying'; note that just a one-word response – Terrifying! – would have a similar meaning

Non-prominent words are not so important (see also Unit 36). For example, they may –

- repeat information that has already been given:

A: What colour's your car?
B: // It's BLUE// DARK blue//

> 'blue' is non-prominent in the second speech unit because it repeats information given in the first

- or give information that is already understood:

A: Who are you waiting for?
B: // My BROTHer's supposed to be here by now//

> 'supposed to be here by now' is non-prominent because the question implies that someone should already be here; what's of interest is who the person is

B (C11) Some speech units have more than one prominent word in them. Each prominent word is emphasised because it carries important information. The last prominent word in a speech unit is where the main falling or rising tone in the speech unit starts (see also Unit 39):

A: How much further is the station?
B: // ONLy about a MILE //

A: Why did you buy such an old car?
B: // THAT'S all I can afFORD at the moment //

C (C12) Here is part of a conversation with speech units and prominent words marked. Listen and notice these in the recording:

A: // It's NICK'S BIRTHday coming up// ISn't it// WHAT are you doing for THAT//
B: // well I'd LIKE// to have a PARty// outSIDE// but we DON'T have a very big GARden// so that LIMits// HOW many people I can inVITE//
A: // MY garden's pretty big// WHY don't you use THAT//
B: // Are you SURE// that would be alRIGHT// that would be GREAT//
A: // NO problem at ALL//

Exercises

33.1 C13 These extracts are divided into speech units (see Unit 32), each containing one prominent word. Listen to the extracts as many times as you need and underline the prominent word in each speech unit.

1 // most of the time// we advertise jobs// in national newspapers// and on our website// occasionally however// we might approach someone// to see if they're interested// someone we might really want//

2 // when we ran out of money// we worked for a bit// and then got a train// somewhere else// and eventually we ended up// in a little village// in the Andes// way up high//

Now read the extracts aloud, making sure that you emphasise each prominent word and that you link words within speech units smoothly together without pauses.

33.2 C14 Listen to these extracts as many times as you need. Mark all the speech unit boundaries using // and underline the prominent word in each speech unit. (Each speech unit has only one prominent word.)

1 should the government pay // for health care or do you think it's the individual's responsibility to save money for when they need treatment my personal view is that we should pay for our own treatment

2 I'm impressed with your cooking Annie that was very nice I particularly liked how you did the rice I'd really like the recipe sometime if you could write it down for me

Now read the extracts aloud, making sure that you emphasise each prominent word and that you link words within speech units smoothly together without pauses.

33.3 Some of the speech units in these extracts have one prominent word and others have two. First, underline the words that you think are likely to be prominent.

1 // we've had wonderful weather// for the last two weeks// but Adam and Emma// have been up in Scotland// where they've had heavy rain// and even flooding// in the western parts of the country//

2 // I was thinking of buying// a second-hand car// from this garage// but because I don't know anything about cars// I paid for the AA// to inspect it// and they found all kinds of things wrong// so of course// I didn't buy it//

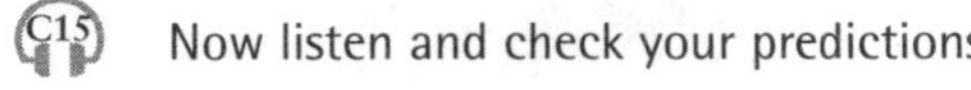

C15 Now listen and check your predictions.

There are many ways of saying these extracts, so if your predictions are different from those on the recording this doesn't necessarily mean they are wrong.

Follow up: If you made a recording for the activity at the end of Unit 32 and marked speech unit boundaries, listen to the recording again and try to underline all the prominent words.

34 // I've always been terrified of SPIders// Prominent words in speech units (2)

A C16 Within a speech unit, we can emphasise different words to convey different meanings. Compare the replies in these conversations:

A: How long have you been frightened of spiders?
B: // I've ALways been terrified of spiders// (saying how long)

A: Why don't you try keeping a spider as a pet?
B: // I've always been TERrified of spiders// (giving the reason)

A: Is there anything that really frightens you?
B: // I've always been terrified of SPIders// (saying what frightens him)

A: I've just finished reading *Homebush Boy*.
B: // THAT'S the book I wanted// (= I couldn't remember the title until you said it)

A: I'm going to read *The Riders* next.
B: // That's the book I wanted// (= it's a pity you got it first)

A: I couldn't get you *The Collector*, so I bought *The Magus* instead.
B: // That's the book I WANted// (= you were wrong; I *did* want *The Magus*)

B C17 We sometimes emphasise a word by making it prominent in order to –

- make a contrast with something previously said (see also Unit 46). Compare:
  A: Did you find your keys?
  B: Yes, // they were under the TAble//

  but: I left my keys on the table, but when I came back // they were UNder the table//
- correct something previously said (see also Unit 47). Compare:
  I noticed something white at the end of the garden, but when I got closer I couldn't believe it. // It was a white RABbit//

  but: A: When we were small we used to have this grey rabbit.
  B: // It was a WHITE rabbit//

A: How does your family know so much about medicine?
B: // My father's a DOCtor//

but: A: Your brother's a doctor, isn't he?
B: No, // my FAther's a doctor//

Exercises

34.1 Match each opening to the appropriate response. Prominent syllables in the responses have capital letters.

EXAMPLE a Have you never been to Spain before? → (ii) I WORKED in Spain.
b What did you do between school and university? → (i) I worked in SPAIN.

1 a That mobile looks familiar. (i) It's your PHONE.
b What's that ringing noise? (ii) It's YOUR phone.

2 a Do you like my glasses? (i) I thought they were NEW.
b I can't see very well through these glasses. (ii) I THOUGHT they were new.

3 a I see Terry's come bottom of the class again. (i) He's ALways last.
b Why's Gustav been dropped from the team? (ii) He's always LAST.

4 a She works at St Mary's, doesn't she? (i) She's an administrator at the HOSpital.
b She works in administration nearby, doesn't she? (ii) She's an adMINistrator at the hospital.

C18 Now listen and check your answers.

34.2 Underline the word in B's replies that you think is most likely to be prominent in each case.

EXAMPLE A: What do you think Jill will want for lunch? B: She's coming <u>after</u> lunch.

1 A: Jean's got three brothers. B: She's got three sisters.
2 A: Have a good time in Paris this week. B: I'm going next week.
3 A: I thought the office was in West Newtown. B: It's in East Newtown.
4 A: You're at fifty-seven, aren't you? B: We live at fifty-nine.
5 A: You said you'd be there at 8.00. B: I said I'd be there later.
6 A: Do you think leaving school at 16 was a mistake? B: It was a big mistake.
7 A: I'll see you in the office on Friday. B: But I work at home on Fridays.
8 A: We took the first on the left. B: You should have taken the first on the right.

C19 Now listen, check your answers and then say the B parts aloud. All of these are said in one speech unit with only one prominent word. Practise saying them without putting extra prominences in. (For example, say: // she's coming AFter lunch//, not: // she's COMing AFter lunch//.)

34.3 Each A part in this conversation is said as one speech unit with *two* prominent words. Underline the two words you think are most likely to be prominent in each A part.

A: <u>Why</u> don't you come and <u>see</u> us?
B: Where do you live?
A: In an old house by the river.
B: I'd probably come by train.
A: It's only a short walk from the station.
B: And if I came by bus?
A: It's five minutes from the bus stop.
B: It's in Mill Lane, isn't it? Where exactly?
A: The first house on the left.

Now listen, check your answers, and then say the A parts aloud. Make sure you emphasise the two prominent words in each speech unit and link all the words in the speech unit smoothly together without pauses.

Follow up: Suggest what might have been said immediately before each of these statements:
(i) // I've never SEEN him before// (ii) // I've never seen HIM before//

35 // I'll beLIEVE it when I SEE it// Fixed phrases and idioms in speech units

A  Fixed phrases and idioms are usually said together in one speech unit rather than being divided across speech units. For example:

// It's a race against time// to get help to the refugees before winter.
is more likely than:
// It's a race// against time// to get help to the refugees before winter.

It was so noisy in the room// I could barely hear myself think//.
is more likely than:
It was so noisy in the room// I could barely// hear myself think//.

Note: Longer idioms are more commonly divided into two or more speech units:
// I could count// on the fingers of one hand// the number of times I've seen her this year.

B (C22) Many fixed phrases and idioms are usually said with two prominent syllables, one of which is in the last word:

// what with ONE thing and aNOther// I forgot all about her birthday.
(= the reason I forgot is that I was very busy)

He's been around so long// he's just PART of the FURniture//.
(= so familiar that I no longer notice him)

A: Why don't you ask them for your money back?
B: Well// that's EAsier said than DONE//.
(= it's a good idea, but it's difficult)

They want me to go to Taiwan in January,// but that's OUT of the QUEStion//. (= cannot possibly happen)

Other examples include:

a RACE against TIME
it's just ONE of those THINGS
to CALL it a DAY
to SLIP [my] MIND
I COULDn't believe my EYES

C (C23) In some other fixed phrases and idioms, the last prominent syllable is not in the last word (see also Unit 36):

She says she's going to get a new job// but I'll beLIEVE it when I SEE it//.
(= I don't think it will happen)

Somehow// we'd GOT our WIRES crossed// and she turned up a week early.
(= we had understood things differently)

They'd like me to invest in the company now// but I want to SEE how the WIND'S blowing// first. (= see how the situation develops before making a decision)

// I've HAD my MONey's worth// out of this old car. I only paid £500 for it and I've been driving it for years. (= it was good value)

Other examples include:

THROW [your] WEIGHT around
[it]'s NOT to be SNEEZED at
PUT [your] FOOT down
a WHOLE new BALL game

Exercises

35.1 Ruth returns Maggie's phone call and leaves this message on her answering machine. Seven of the speech unit boundaries marked in Ruth's message (with //) are unlikely to occur because they split fixed phrases and idioms. Cross out the boundaries you think should not be marked.

> // hi Maggie// got your message// and your question about car repairs// sorry// but I haven't got~~//~~ a clue// the best person to contact is … //oh //it was on the tip// of my tongue// and my mind just// went blank// Peter Thomas// that was it// he's a mine// of information// about that sort of thing// anyway// I'll be over to see you// when I can// as soon as the doctor's given me// a clean bill// of health// the new medication// is doing me// a power of good// so I'm hoping to be up// and about// in the next week or so// speak to you soon//

Now listen and check your predictions.

35.2 Listen to these sentences with fixed phrases and idioms and underline the last prominent syllable in each. (Note: each sentence has just one speech unit.)

EXAMPLE Not in the <u>slight</u>est.

1 Don't jump to conclusions.
2 They're putting a brave face on it.
3 He's had a change of heart.
4 You can say that again.
5 You may well ask.
6 He took them in his stride.

Now listen again and repeat the sentences, putting prominence on the correct syllables. Make sure you say each sentence in one speech unit, running the words together smoothly without pauses.

35.3 Use the sentences with fixed phrases and idioms in exercise 35.2 (including the example) to complete this conversation.

A: How did Nick get on in his exams last week?
B: *He took them in his stride.*
A: Didn't get nervous?
B: (1) ……………………
A: I suppose he'll be off to university next year?
B: (2) ……………………
A: But I thought he wanted to be a doctor.
B: (3) ……………………
A: He'd be crazy not to go to university.
B: (4) ……………………
A: His parents must be really annoyed.
B: (5) ……………………
A: So what does he want to do now?
B: (6) ……………………

Now listen and check your answers. Finally, play the recording again. Press 'pause' before each B part and read it aloud. Then press 'play' again and compare your pronunciation with what follows.

Follow up: When you learn a new short fixed phrase or idiom, practise saying it as one speech unit. You may need to check with your teacher or a native speaker of English which syllables are made prominent.

36 she's got an ESSay *to write*
Non-prominence on final 'empty' content words

Some words at the end of a speech unit are non-prominent (see Unit 33) because they are 'empty' – that is, they don't carry new information.

A C27 Some words are empty because they refer to something or someone that has already been mentioned:

Gail talked to me about Oscar as if I knew him well, although I've never MET her brother. ('her brother' = Oscar)

He's always asking my advice on what flowers to plant, even though I don't know anything aBOUT gardening. ('gardening' = what flowers to plant)

or because they mean the same as something said before or implied in the previous context:

A: There's a meeting tonight at Carl's.
B: Hadn't I already TOLD you about that? ('that' refers to the meeting)

I thought Hiroshi lived in the north of Tokyo, but in fact he lives on the OTHer side of the city. ('the north of Tokyo' implies 'one [the north] side of the city')

A: Can you translate this for me?
B: But you KNOW I don't speak French. (asking for a translation implies that the speaker thinks I speak French)

B C28 Some words are empty because their meaning is obvious from what has been said before:

Who left the TAP running?
I must get my HAIR cut.
She says she can't come out. She's got an ESsay to write.
I'll see you in about an hour. First, I've got some SHOPping to do.

'running', 'cut', 'to write' and 'to do' are predictable meanings in these contexts

A: When does the eclipse start?
B: About an HOUR from now.

A: Where does Karen live?
B: A couple of MILES from here.

'now' and 'here' are the usual points of reference in contexts like this

I'm not going out in THIS weather.
Why don't we meet at YOUR house?

'weather' and 'house' are obvious: we could just say '... in THIS' and '... at YOURS'

or they may be empty because their meaning is obvious in the particular context in which they occur:

A: Look! There's a MOUSE in the corner of the room.
B: Careful! You're spilling your SOUP all over the table.

C C29 Some idiomatic phrases typically have 'empty' words at the end:

I found out that I didn't have to make a speech at the meeting after all. It was a REAL WEIGHT off my shoulders. (= I was pleased that I was no longer responsible)

It was with her fourth novel that she really MADE a NAME for herself. (= became famous)

A: How did you find out I was leaving?
B: Let's just say a LITTLE BIRD told me. (= I'm not going to tell you who told me)

Being a builder is a hard job, even at the BEST of times. (= even in the best conditions)

Exercises

36.1 Listen and underline the one prominent word in each of the speech units in green.

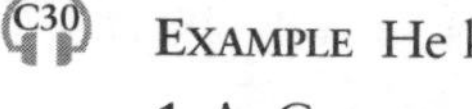

EXAMPLE He kept telling me to be careful with the bones// as if I'd never eaten fish before//.

1 A: Can you give me a lift?
B: // But you know I can't drive//.
2 A: Do you think England will beat Australia?
B: No idea.// I'm not interested in cricket//.
3 A: If I get the position I'm going to buy a new car.
B: // But you haven't even applied for the job yet//.
4 I could only see the end of the queue, but in fact // there were hundreds of people waiting//.

Now say the highlighted speech units aloud. Make sure you make only the underlined word prominent and link words within the speech units smoothly together without pauses.

36.2 Complete the sentences using words and phrases from the box.

to drink	from now	from there	going	place	~~rang~~
she's holding	in here	in my soup	you're reading		went off

EXAMPLE I was just going to bed when the doorbell ....rang........ .

1 We didn't have any water ....
2 Last night my car alarm ....
3 How's your work ....?
4 Waiter! There's a fly ....
5 Get to the bus station and our house is a couple of minutes walk ....
6 I wonder what's in that box ....
7 The bridge should be finished a year ....
8 Let's have the meeting at my ....
9 What's that book ....?
10 What's the smell ....?

Now listen and check your answers. Then say the sentences aloud, making sure you make the underlined words prominent and the words you have written non-prominent. (Note: there will be other prominent words in the sentences, too.)

36.3 Match A's statements and questions with B's responses to make short conversations.

	A		B
1	A: Still no word from Dan.	....	B: I'm sure he'll have a whale of a time.
2	A: Tim has raised some objections to your proposals.	....	B: You'll really have your work cut out for you.
3	A: I'm looking after my two nephews this weekend.	...1...	B: Oh, well, I suppose no news is good news.
4	A: He's working in Barcelona for the summer.	....	B: I bet that wiped the smile off her face.
5	A: These cakes are great. Can I have another one?	....	B: Sure, there's plenty more where that came from.
6	A: Paula didn't get the promotion she'd been expecting.	....	B: Trust him to throw a spanner in the works.

Now listen and check your answers. Then listen again and underline the *last* prominent word in the B parts. Finally, say the B parts aloud, making sure that all the words after the underlined word are non-prominent.

37 I can't STAND *the stuff*
Non-prominence on final vague expressions

Vague expressions are often used in conversation when we don't need to be exact or precise. Many of these expressions are found at the end of a speech unit (see Units 33 and 34). They are usually non-prominent, following a prominent word.

A C33 When we refer to something already mentioned, we can use *the stuff* (for uncountable nouns), *the place(s)* and *the thing(s)* (for countable nouns). Very often, some criticism is intended:

A: I've got some apple juice. Do you want some? B: No, I can't STAND the stuff.
Jack seems to spend all his time in his bedroom. Never LEAVES the place.
My car's always breaking down. I HATE the thing.

We can use these words with *sort of* to show that we have just given examples of a larger group of things. Often we use (*all*) *this/that/these/those* before *sort of*:

Before we could use the laboratory, we had to learn about safety and all THAT sort of stuff.
The book's about corruption in sport – taking bribes, placing illegal bets and all THIS sort of thing.
When we were in Rome we were taken to museums, art galleries and THOSE sorts of places.

We can use *and stuff*, *and things* and *and places* in a similar way to refer in a general way to things and places without giving any further detail:

I bought some CHEESE and stuff.
We went through Berlin, BONN and places.

The phrase *and that* is used to mean that other things were involved, without specifying more precisely what:

A: Where's Kate? B: She's gone upstairs to do her HAIR and that.

B C34 We use *or something/anything* (etc.) to make what we have just said more vague or indirect:

Didn't she use to be a VET or something?
He went off with KEN or somebody.
Isn't there any chocolate in the FRIDGE or anywhere?
Let me know if you want any HELP or anything.

In a similar way we can use *or something/anything* (etc.) *like that*:

A: Linda seems very lonely.
B: Doesn't she ever go out with FRIENDS or anything like that?

C C35 The phrases *or/and* + *whatever/whenever/wherever/whoever* are used to make a statement more informal or less direct:

We could meet about TEN or whenever.
When we move into the flat, we might change the carpets and LIGHTS and whatever.

D 

The phrase *or so* is used with expressions of number and time to make them less precise:

A: How long will it take? B: About a WEEK or so.
We'd been driving for an hour, but we'd only gone a MILE or so.

Note: Words like *thing, place, something, whenever*, etc. are not only used in vague expressions. For example:
This is the place I used to live. What's this thing for? We'll leave whenever you want.

Exercises

37.1 Complete the sentences using vague expressions from the box.

the place	~~the stuff~~	the things	or anything	or someone	or wherever

EXAMPLE Hannah asked me to get some goat's cheese, but I don't know where to buy ......the stuff...... .

1 She got the job without even an interview ....
2 You can buy them in a supermarket ....
3 I used to work at the airport, but now I never go near ....
4 I don't like mice or rats. I've always been terrified of ....
5 He's staying with his cousin ....

C37 Now listen and check your answers. Then say the sentences aloud, making sure you make the vague expressions non-prominent.

37.2 Read this conversation in which Belinda is talking about her holiday, and underline all the vague expressions you can find.

A: You've just got back from Italy, haven't you? The Amalfi coast <u>or somewhere</u>.
B: That's right. We stayed in Positano. Do you know it?
A: Yes, I went there twenty years ago or something. But I don't remember much about the place. A good holiday?
B: Well, we had some problems at first. They lost our luggage at the airport – it got put on the wrong plane or something like that. So the first night we didn't have a change of clothes or toothbrushes or whatever. It turned up the following day, though.
A: So how did you spend your time there?
B: We just relaxed, walked around, sat on the beach and that sort of thing. And we looked around the shops and places.
A: Did you buy a lot of stuff?
B: No, just a few presents and things.

C38 Now listen and circle the prominent word before each of these vague expressions.

EXAMPLE The Amalfi (coast) <u>or somewhere</u>.

Check your answers in the Key. Finally, read the conversation aloud making sure you make the circled words prominent, the underlined vague expressions non-prominent, and that you link them smoothly.

37.3 Here are more comments about holidays. Listen and write the vague expressions used in the spaces.

C39 EXAMPLE There's nowhere to leave the car: in a car park, at the hotel, along the street ......or anywhere...... .

1 All cars are banned from the town centre because of exhaust fumes ....
2 We'll probably go again for a month ....
3 When I got back to the hire car I couldn't start ....
4 I had to pay 450 euros ....
5 We're hoping to go back next year, in the spring ....
6 There were no museums or art galleries ....

Now read the sentences aloud, making sure you make the vague expressions non-prominent.

Follow up: What final vague expressions are used in other languages that you know? Are these also usually non-prominent?

38 Just help yourSELF; Throw it to ME
Prominence in reflexive and personal pronouns

A C40 When a reflexive pronoun follows a verb or preposition and refers to the subject, it is usually non-prominent (see Unit 33):

She locked herself OUT.
As he ran, he TIMED himself.
You should look AFTer yourself.
Make yourself at HOME.
Let me introDUCE myself.
He fell and HURT himself.

However, reflexive pronouns like this can be made prominent for contrast. Compare:

I stupidly left my wallet at home. I was really anNOYED with myself.

but: A: I bet you were angry with your sister.
B: In fact, I was MAINly annoyed with mySELF.

B C41 When we use reflexive pronouns for emphasis they are usually prominent. For example –

- after a noun or pronoun to emphasise it:
  I'm flying to Rome, but the AIRport itSELF is miles from the city.
  Many successful business people didn't go to college. I mySELF left school at 16.
- at the end of a clause to emphasise the subject:
  I'm arranging the office party, but I won't be there mySELF.
  They drew the posters themSELVES.
- to emphasise that someone did or will do something alone or without help:
  I made it mySELF.
  Did you paint it yourSELF?
  She went all by herSELF.
  We had the beach all to ourSELVES.

However, reflexive pronouns like this can be made non-prominent if we want to highlight a contrast somewhere else in the sentence. Compare:

I'm really thirsty. I could drink the whole BOTtle mySELF.

but: A: You look thirsty. Would you like a glass of this juice?
B: Actually, I could drink the whole BOTtle myself.

C C42 Personal pronouns (e.g. *they*, *me*, *we*, *you*) are usually non-prominent:

They WOULDn't let me IN. SHOULD we WAIT for you?

However, we can make them prominent in order to contrast one person or group of people with others:

Throw it to ME, not to HIM.
The only person who's applied so far is YOU. (An implied contrast between 'you' and 'others')

Note: The pronoun *it* is rarely stressed, except in some phrases with *this* and *that* (see Unit 22B).

Exercises

38.1 Listen and repeat these phrases.

C43

1 She was killing herself laughing.
2 We had to do all the cooking ourselves.
3 They blame themselves for it.
4 He didn't know what to do with himself.
5 Take care of yourself.
6 He made it all himself.
7 I'm going to get myself a bike.
8 They made fools of themselves.
9 I picked them myself.
10 Speak for yourself.
11 I just burned myself.
12 Take one for yourself, too.

Now underline only the reflexive pronouns you made prominent.

38.2 Is the reflexive pronoun in each sentence likely to be prominent or non-prominent? Underline reflexive pronouns you think will be prominent.

EXAMPLE He works for <u>himself</u>.

1 What did you do to yourself?
2 I fell asleep on the train and found myself in Cardiff.
3 The city centre itself is quite interesting.
4 She went for a walk by herself.
5 He's got himself a new car.
6 Have a good time. Enjoy yourselves.
7 Do they bake the bread themselves?
8 I'm keeping myself warm.
9 I grew all the vegetables myself.
10 She tried to defend herself.

Now listen, check your answers and repeat the sentences.

38.3 Listen and underline only the reflexive pronouns or personal pronouns in this conversation that are made prominent for contrast.

C45

A: I've made you a cake.

B: Is that <u>it</u>?

A: Yes, help yourself.

B: Er, you have some first.

A: But I didn't make it for me.

B: I can't eat it all myself. Marco would like it. Why not give some to him?

A: But I made it for you. You don't like it, do you?

B: Well, it's not the cake itself. It's the icing ...

A: And I was feeling so pleased with myself.

Now listen again. Press 'pause' before each B part and read it aloud. Then press 'play' again and compare your pronunciation with what follows.

Follow up: What does DIY stand for? Is the last word usually prominent or non-prominent?

39 I'm quite busy ↘ at the moment ↗ Falling and rising tones

A C46 In each speech unit (see Unit 32) there is one main movement of the voice, either up or down, starting on the last prominent word of the speech unit. Listen to this example:

// you'll arRIVE ↗// at CENtral STAtion ↘//
when you get OFF the TRAIN ↗//
turn LEFT along the PLATform ↘//
at the END of the platform ↗//
there's an EScalator ↘// go UP it ↗//
and you'll be in the MAIN SQUARE ↘//
there's a FOUNtain ↘// in the SQUARE ↗//
and I'll be WAITing for you THERE ↘//

These speech units have either a *falling tone* ↘ or a *rising tone* ↗.

B C47 A falling tone or a rising tone can extend over just one word (which may be only one syllable) or over a number of non-prominent syllables at the end of a speech unit:

// NO ↘//
// he WORKS in a SUpermarket ↘//
// I've ALways wanted to go there ↘//

// YES ↗//
// is that a CHOColate MILKshake ↗//
// do you LIKE living in Paris ↗//

C C48 Choosing a falling tone indicates that the information in the speech unit adds some 'news': it is information that the hearer is not expected to know already. Choosing a rising tone indicates that the information in the speech unit is 'not news': it is information that the speaker and hearer already share. Distinguishing 'news' from 'not news' in this way can help the hearer understand what is being said.

A: See you on Saturday.
B: // but I'll be in LONdon ↘// at the weekEND ↗//

LONdon: the fact that I'll be in London is 'news' to A

weekEND: the weekend is 'not news' – it is the time we are talking about (Saturday)

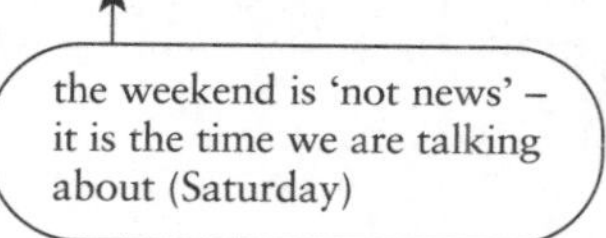

A: I'm trying to get fit, so I've decided to go on a diet.
B: // you CAN'T just eat LESS ↗// you'll HAVE to do more EXercise ↘//

LESS: 'eating less' has already been talked about (in 'go on a diet')

EXercise: B tells A that exercise is necessary, too

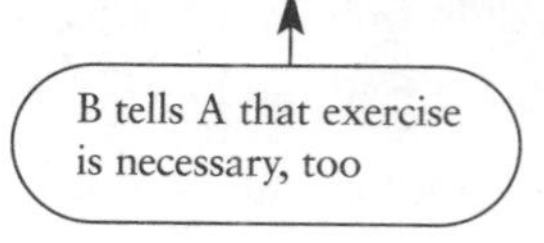

D C49 We can use a fall-rising tone instead of a rising tone to indicate that information is 'not news'. Compare these examples:

A: Can you come over now?
B: // I'm QUITE BUSy ↘// at the MOment ↗//
or: B: // I'm QUITE BUSy ↘// at the MOment ↘↗//

Note: It usually doesn't matter whether you use a rising or fall-rising tone. However, in some contexts one tone or the other is more likely. For more details, see Unit 43B.

Exercises

39.1 (C50) Listen to the sentences and underline the last prominent word (where the main movement of the voice begins). Then show whether the voice rises (put ↗ in the box) or falls (↘) from there. (Note that each sentence is one speech unit.)

EXAMPLE I'm quite <u>tired</u> again. ■

1 Was she really? ■
2 I suppose so. ■
3 I've always lived around here. ■
4 It's broken down again. ■
5 Shall I have a go? ■
6 You remember Pablo. ■
7 I gave it to my son. ■
8 Can we go now? ■
9 One moment, please. ■
10 There was dust all over the place. ■

Now say the phrases aloud in the same way.

39.2  Listen and decide whether the speech units in the B parts have a rising tone (put ↗ in the box) or a falling tone (↘).

EXAMPLE A: Where on earth did you find that?
B: // I came across it ■// in an antique shop ■//

1 A: What time shall we leave?
B: // We could go now ■// as you're ready ■//

2 A: What time did David get back?
B: // I heard him come in ■// at about three ■//

3 A: I'm not sure his plan would work very well.
B: // I thought his suggestion ■// was ridiculous ■//

4 A: The hall was packed, wasn't it?
B: // I hate it ■// when it's so crowded ■//

5 A: Do you want a drink?
B: // I wouldn't mind some orange juice ■// if you've got any ■//

6 A: When did they tell you it would get here?
B: // They said it would be delivered ■// by yesterday ■//

7 A: Have you heard *Trio Gitano* play before?
B: // I first saw them perform ■// a couple of years ago ■//

8 A: I could move that easily.
B: // Well why don't you try ■// if you think you're so strong ■//

Now listen again. Press 'pause' before each B part and read it aloud. Then press 'play' again and compare your pronunciation with what follows.

Follow up: Read again the explanation in C opposite. Use it to decide why falling and rising tones are used in the B parts in exercise 39.2.

40 They taste great, *these biscuits*
Tails

A C52 In informal spoken English, *tails* are sometimes used at the end of a sentence to emphasise or make clearer what we have just said. We often use them when we give an evaluation of something:

It's a really good PHOto, THAT one.

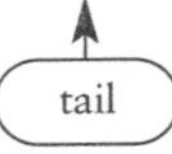

She's a JUDGE, my AUNT.

tail

Tails consist of a noun or a noun phrase. They usually have a rising tone because they are referring to or expanding on something that has been said before (see Unit 39).

B C53 Some tails consist of *this*, *that*, *these* or *those* or a phrase beginning with one of these words. These tails usually emphasise what we are saying:

They're all we've got LEFT, THOSE two.
They taste GREAT, these BIScuits.
It's BEAUtiful, THIS part of the COUNtry.
It says here that they're going to put up a new town hall. INteresting, THAT.

C C54 Other tails make clear who or what we are referring to:

He's a good COOK, NIgel. (= Nigel is a good cook)
She's really STRICT, the headTEAcher.
I can't STAND it, cigarETTE smoke. (= I can't stand cigarette smoke)
That's MY hat, the ONE you're WEAring.

D C55 Important for listening

Another type of tail, also with a rising tone, repeats the subject + verb in order to reinforce what we have just said. It is similar to a *tag* (see Unit 41), and is used mainly in very informal speech:

A: Maybe you could borrow the money from your brother?
B: No, he's incredibly MEAN, HE is.
subject + verb

A: Do you know those people over there?
B: Yeah, they LIVE near me, THEY do.
subject + verb

the subject in the tail is prominent and the verb non-prominent

E C56 Some other tails usually have a falling tone; for example, a tail added to a *wh-* question in order to clarify who or what the question refers to:

What time's it ON, this SHOW?
How OLD is she, your DAUGHter?

Exercises

40.1 Match the sentence beginnings and the tails.

1	It's so boring,	.... this cream.
2	I think it's gone off,	.... those two shirts.
3	I took them myself,	.... most of these photos.
4	That's my coat,	.... my sister.
5	They're a bit unfriendly,	.....1..... tennis.
6	It's really annoying,	.... that dripping tap.
7	They're quite similar,	.... the one with the fur collar.
8	She was the first one in our family to go to university,	.... our neighbours.

C57 Now listen and check your answers. Then say the full sentences aloud, making sure you use a falling tone before it and a rising tone on the tail.

EXAMPLE It's so boring ↘, tennis ↗.

40.2 Do you think the tails in these sentences are likely to have a rising tone (put ↗ in the box) or a falling tone (↘)?

EXAMPLE They're all over the kitchen, those beetles. ↗

1 Where's it being held, Friday's concert? ☐
2 What's it like, this cheese? ☐
3 It can be dangerous, skiing. ☐
4 It's made from Thai silk, Vicky's dress. ☐
5 When are they coming, Frank and Gill? ☐
6 How much did you pay for them, these tickets? ☐
7 It's not a great day for us to meet, Sunday. ☐

C58 Now listen and check your predictions. Then say the sentences aloud.

40.3 The speakers in this conversation actually used sentences with tails instead of the parts in green. Write down what you think they said and mark the likely intonation with arrows.

A: These things are fascinating.	They're fascinating ↘, these things ↗.
B: Careful, that knife's sharp.	....
A: Looks old, too.	
B: Most of those things've been in my family for over a hundred years.	....
A: That's amazing.	....
B: My grandfather brought them back from Nepal.	....
A: Nepal is somewhere I'd really like to go.	....
B: Me, too. But I'd have to go by plane, and I hate flying.	....

C59 Now listen and check your answers.

Follow up: Imagine you are being shown around a house that is for sale. Using sentences with tails, think of five criticisms and five compliments you might make. For example: 'It's very small, the garden'; 'It's nicely decorated, the sitting room.'

41 Great film, *wasn't it*? Question tags

A  C60 Question tags are short questions added to the end of a statement, usually to produce a response from a hearer. We use a falling tone for question tags when we expect the hearer to acknowledge that what we have just said is correct, for example, when we are giving our opinion:

> They didn't PLAY very well, DID they?
> GREAT FILM, WASn't it?

We use a rising tone when we invite the hearer to say whether what we have just said is correct or not, for example, when we are not certain that something is true:

> JapanESE, ISn't it?
> NOT on a DIet again, ARE you?

Notice that question tags are often used after statements where the subject or subject and verb have been left out.

B C61 Question tags usually have a falling tone when the statement is obviously correct:

> You're not WELL, ARE you?
> HOT, ISn't it?

We also use a falling tone when we want the hearer to admit that something they may not have accepted before is, in fact, correct:

> TOLD you I was RIGHT, DIDn't I?
> WRONG again, WEREN'T you?

Question tags can also follow exclamations, and these tags usually have a falling tone:

> what a riDICulous thing to SAY, WASn't it?

C C62 When both the statement and the question tag are positive, the question tag usually has a rising tone:

> Came by CAR, DID you?
> You've FINished, HAVE you?

This pattern is sometimes used to be critical or sarcastic. These sentences often begin with 'So…' or 'Oh, …':

> So you THINK you're CLEVer, DO you?

Question tags (usually *will you*, *can't you*, *won't you*, *would you*, or *shall we*) can be added to imperative sentences. These tags usually have a rising tone and are often used to soften a request or command:

> Let's get the EARlier train, SHALL we?
> TAKE care of THESE, WOULD you?

Exercises

41.1 Do you think the question tags in this conversation are likely to have a rising tone (put ↗ in the box) or a falling tone (↘)?

A: Wonderful view from up here, isn't it? ■
B: Great.
A: I said it would be worth the effort, didn't I? ■
B: Hmm.
A: You're not tired, are you? ■
B: Exhausted. Give me some water, will you? ■
A: Not very fit, are you? ■ Still, not much further.
B: But we're at the top, aren't we? ■
A: Just another kilometre to go. We can't turn round now, can we? ■
B: Of course we can. Let's go back now, shall we? ■ Please.

C63 Now listen and check your predictions.

41.2 C64 Listen and decide whether the question tags in B's responses have a rising tone (put ↗ in the box) or a falling tone (↘).

EXAMPLE A: Great race. B: She ran well, didn't she? ■

1 A: I can do that easily. B: Oh, you can, can you? ■
2 A: We'll have to wait ages for the bus. B: But they come every ten minutes, don't they? ■
3 A: What a boring lecture. B: Yes, dull, wasn't it? ■
4 A: Shame about the colour. B: What a hideous shade of purple, isn't it? ■
5 A: Where do you want these boxes? B: Put them over there, would you? ■
6 A: I think there's something wrong with the printer. B: You broke it, didn't you? ■
7 A: Can I get a discount on these tickets? B: You're a student, are you? ■

Now listen again. Press 'pause' before each B part and read it aloud. Then press 'play' again and compare your pronunciation with what follows.

41.3 Suggest an appropriate question tag to complete B's responses. Then read them aloud, using either a rising or falling tone on the tag as appropriate.

EXAMPLE A: Did you see the eclipse yesterday?
B: Fantastic, ...wasn't it......? ■

1 A: Don't forget your gloves.
B: They're yours, ...?
2 A: He could have been killed crossing the road like that.
B: What a stupid thing to do, ...?
3 A: Try to come early to get a good seat.
B: There'll be a lot of people, ...?
4 A: What a terrible noise.
B: You're not a rock music fan, ...?
5 A: Where shall I leave you?
B: Drop me in front of the station, ...?

C65 Now listen and check your answers.

Follow up: Many other languages have question tags, although in some a single question tag is used rather than the large number found in English. Think about the intonation of question tag(s) used in your first language. Does it follow a similar pattern to that described in this unit for English question tags?

42 What I don't understand is how it got there Cleft sentences

A

A cleft sentence is divided into two parts, allowing us to focus particular attention on information in one part of the sentence. Cleft sentences are common in speech. In these examples the focus is on 'my gold necklace':

What I lost was my gold necklace.

A *what-* cleft (sometimes called a *pseudo-cleft*) has *what + subject + verb* in the first clause followed by *be + the focus.*

It was my gold necklace that I lost.

An *it-* cleft has *it + be + the focus* in the first clause and is followed by a *relative* (*that* or *who*) *clause.*

B C66

What- clefts typically have a fall-rising tone at the end of the *what-* clause and a falling tone in the other part of the sentence. Remember that the tone begins on the last prominent syllable of the speech unit:

A: I can't get the chain back on my bike.
B: WHAT you need to DO is take the WHEEL off .

I hadn't seen Don since he went to Australia …
… and what surPRISED me about him was his ACcent .

I know there's a pool of water in the kitchen, but …
… what I DON'T understand is how it GOT there .

Notice that the order of information in the cleft sentence can often be reversed, but that the two parts keep the same tone:

I know there's a pool of water in the kitchen, but …
… how it GOT there is what I DON'T understand .

We can use *all* instead of *what* if we want to emphasise that only one thing is done:

A: Paul hasn't spoken to me since I scratched his car.
B: ALL you've got to SAY is that you're SORry .

C C67

It- clefts typically have a falling tone in the clause beginning with *it*. Tone choice in the relative clause depends on meaning in context (see Unit 39):

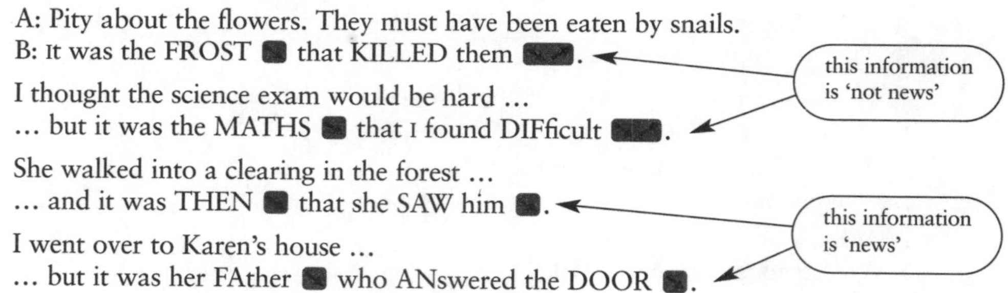

A: Pity about the flowers. They must have been eaten by snails.
B: IT was the FROST that KILLED them .

I thought the science exam would be hard …
… but it was the MATHS that I found DIFficult .

(this information is 'not news')

She walked into a clearing in the forest …
… and it was THEN that she SAW him .

I went over to Karen's house …
… but it was her FAther who ANswered the DOOR .

(this information is 'news')

Exercises

42.1 Listen to each A part. Press 'pause' before each B part and read it aloud using the intonation marked. Then press 'play' again and compare your pronunciation with what follows.

C68

1 A: Do you want some tea?
B: what I'd REALly like is a GLASS of WAter.

2 A: I see your neighbours keep goats.
B: what I obJECT to is the AWful SMELL.

3 A: What's for breakfast?
B: what I USually have is COFfee and TOAST.

4 A: What are you having for your birthday?
B: what I'm HOPing for is a NEW comPUter.

Now do the same with these. Before you answer, think about where the fall-rising and falling tones start.

5 A: My train to work was late yet again.
B: What you should do is write and complain.

6 A: All the plants in my garden are dying.
B: What we want is some rain.

7 A: What did you get from the butcher's?
B: All they had left were these sausages.

8 A: What's the view like from your bedroom window?
B: All I can see is a block of flats.

42.2 Give the answers in exercise 42.1 again. This time, however, reverse the order of the information. The first two answers are given with intonation marked.

1 A: Do you want some tea?
B: A GLASS of WAter is what I'd REALly like.

2 A: I see your neighbours keep goats.
B: The AWful SMELL is what I obJECT to.

42.3 Expand the notes to make *it*- cleft responses. Then draw a falling tone in the clause beginning with *it* and then either a falling or fall-rising tone, as appropriate, in the relative clause.

EXAMPLES

A: Your idea of having a street party was a really good one.
B: (my daughter – suggested it) *It was my daughter who suggested it.*

A: Why were you staring at that woman?
B: (her eyes – looked strange) *It was her eyes that looked strange.*

1 A: How is Dan getting on in Sydney?
B: (his brother – went to Australia)

2 A: You looked uncomfortable during the meeting.
B: (my back – aching)

3 A: I suppose the Liberals will raise taxes now they are in government.
B: (the Democrats – won the election)

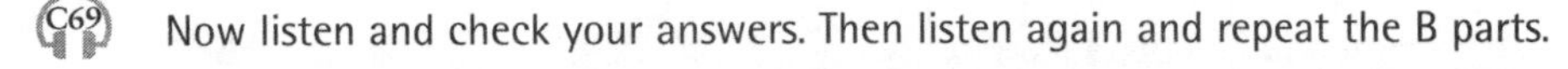

Now listen and check your answers. Then listen again and repeat the B parts.

Follow up: Make a conscious effort to use *what*- clefts and *it*- clefts in your speech, especially in informal contexts. Perhaps you could even plan ahead to use some in a particular conversation.

43 Finding out or making sure? Questions (1)

A

C70 When we ask a question, we might be trying to *find out* information that we don't already know. Alternatively, we might ask a question in order to *make sure* that information we think we know is, in fact, correct.

Finding out questions usually end with a falling tone:

WHAT part of SPAIN were you in ? HOW much ARE they ?

Note: Because *wh-* questions are often used to find out information, they often, although not always, end with a falling tone.

Making sure questions usually end with a rising or fall-rising tone (for the difference see **B**):

was BRIan there ? or: was BRIan there ?
DOESn't she WORK with you ? or: DOESn't she WORK with you ?

Note: Because *yes–no* questions are often used to make sure, they often, although not always, end with a rising or fall-rising tone.

However, *wh-* questions can have a rising or fall-rising tone when they are making sure, and *yes–no* question can have a falling tone when they are finding out:

WHEN'S your birthday ? ← a rising tone shows that I'm checking the date; it might be polite to suggest that I do know but have temporarily forgotten

Have you SEEN her recently ? ← I don't know whether you have or not

B

C71 In *making sure* questions we can usually use a fall-rising tone or a rising tone with little difference in meaning. However, a fall-rising tone often sounds more polite than a rising tone. In particular, a fall-rising tone is often preferred in questions asked for social reasons; that is, mainly to be polite and friendly rather than to check information (see also Unit 48C):

Do you WANT to take your COAT off ?
Are you SURE you can MANage that ?

C

C72 Other kinds of questions can also be used to produce a reply from a hearer. In these, too, we use a falling tone to find out and a rising (or fall-rising) tone to make sure. For example, sentences which ask for assistance with *would you mind*, *perhaps* or *I wonder* usually have a falling tone:

would you MIND holding THIS ? I WONder if you could HELP me ?

Note: *Wh-* and *yes–no* questions used to *offer* assistance often have a falling tone as this sounds more genuine, and therefore more polite, than a rising or fall-rising tone (see also Unit 48C):

can I HELP you ? WHAT can I DO for you ?

Statements which are intended to produce a reply often have a rising tone because they are usually asking for confirmation of something we think we already know:

You've FINished alREADy ? You HAVen't even STARted ?

Exercises

43.1 C73 Listen to each question and decide whether the speaker is *finding out* (with a falling tone) or *making sure* (with a rising tone). Underline your answer.

EXAMPLE Who are they playing next week? *finding out* ↘ / *making sure* ↗

1 Were the police involved? *finding out* ↘ / *making sure* ↗
2 Are you feeling okay now? *finding out* ↘ / *making sure* ↗
3 Don't we turn left here? *finding out* ↘ / *making sure* ↗
4 Why didn't you phone me earlier? *finding out* ↘ / *making sure* ↗
5 Have you discussed it with your parents yet? *finding out* ↘ / *making sure* ↗
6 How do you get the top off? *finding out* ↘ / *making sure* ↗
7 Did I see you in town on Saturday? *finding out* ↘ / *making sure* ↗
8 What happened after that? *finding out* ↘ / *making sure* ↗

Now check your answers in the Key. Then say the questions aloud with the same intonation.

43.2 Joe and Olivia are going on holiday in the morning, but Joe is excited and can't sleep. Do you think Joe's questions are likely to have a rising tone (put ↗ in the box) or a falling tone (↘)?

J: Are you awake? ☐ O: Mmm.
J: I wonder what time it is? ☐ O: Er, four o'clock.
J: When did you book the taxi for? ☐ O: Eight.
J: Which terminal does the plane leave from? ☐ O: Don't know.
J: You don't know? ☐ O: No.
J: Doesn't Philip work at the airport? ☐ O: No, Adam.
J: Are you sure? ☐ O: Yes.
J: What time is it again? ☐ O: Four.
J: Would you mind if I put the radio on? ☐ O: No.
J: When's the taxi coming? ☐ O: Zzzzz.

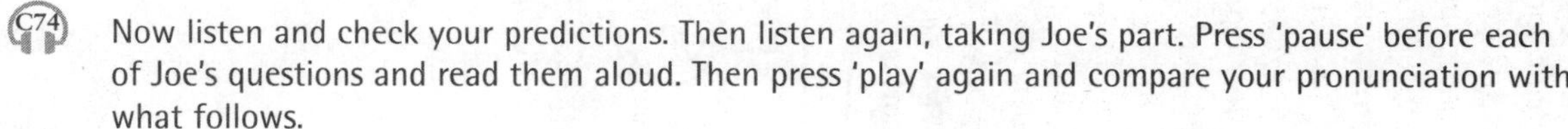

C74 Now listen and check your predictions. Then listen again, taking Joe's part. Press 'pause' before each of Joe's questions and read them aloud. Then press 'play' again and compare your pronunciation with what follows.

43.3 C75 Listen and decide whether each question is asked mainly for social reasons (with a fall-rising tone) or to make sure (with a rising tone). Underline ↘↗ or ↗.

EXAMPLE Is it okay to park here? ↘↗ / ↗

1 Can I get you another drink? ↘↗ / ↗
2 Have you been here before? ↘↗ / ↗
3 Wasn't Don at the meal? ↘↗ / ↗
4 Can you see it more clearly now? ↘↗ / ↗
5 Would you like me to fetch it for you? ↘↗ / ↗

Now check your answers in the Key. Then say the questions aloud with the same intonation.

Follow up: If you have internet access, go to the BBC Radio website (http://www.bbc.co.uk/radio) or another English language radio website (see Unit 4 for suggestions). Find a recording of an episode of a 'soap opera', that is, a series about the lives of a particular group of characters. Listen and write down the first ten *yes–no* and *wh-* questions that are spoken. Is the last tone in each a rise, a fall, or a fall-rise? Does the information in this unit help you to understand each choice?

44 Wasn't it terrible ? Are you crazy ? Questions (2)

A C76 Questions are often used to make a comment or exclamation rather than to find out or check information. An answer is not necessarily expected.

Negative *yes–no* questions are commonly used to show surprise, pleasure, etc., particularly when we encourage others to agree with us. These usually have a falling tone:

WASn't it TERrible ? DIDn't she sound riDICulous ?
HAVen't I been STUpid ? AREN'T they BEAUtiful ?

In informal English we can also use positive *yes–no* questions, particularly to express criticism. These often have a rising tone:

Are you CRAzy ? Have you gone MAD ?

Wh- questions are also used to make a comment, particularly ones with modal verbs. These usually have a falling tone:

HOW was I supposed to know ? WHAT'S it to do with YOU ?

B C77 Sometimes we ask a question and suggest a possible answer ourselves before the hearer replies. As the purpose of these possible answers is to make sure that what we think we know is correct, they usually have a fall-rising tone (see Unit 43):

Where are you off to? The SUpermarket ?
How are you getting there? With NICola ?
What are you going to wear? NOT that old JUMper again ?

C C78 We can use questions to give instructions or make suggestions. These usually have a falling tone, and often (but not always) include modal verbs:

will you PLEASE leave it aLONE ? COULD we have the BILL, please ?
WOULD you turn the LIGHT off ? COULDn't you just reFUSE ?
WHY don't you go by TRAIN ? HOW about putting it over THERE ?

Exercises

44.1 Do you think the questions in B's responses are more likely to have a rising tone (put ↗ in the box) or a falling tone (↘)?

EXAMPLE A: I thought Madrid played brilliantly. B: Weren't they amazing? ■

1 A: I've just got a job in Alaska. B: Are you serious? ■
2 A: I don't think any of these jackets will fit. B: How about this one? ■
3 A: You didn't tell your parents what you're going to do, did you? B: Certainly not. Do you think I'm stupid? ■
4 A: Great weather we're having. B: Isn't it fantastic? ■
5 A: So did you lend Barry your motorbike? B: Barry! Are you out of your mind? ■
6 A: Where do you want me to go? B: Can you stand over there? ■
7 A: What do you think of my new skirt? B: You can't go out dressed like that. Have you no shame? ■
8 A: Roz's exam results were good, weren't they? B: Didn't she do well? ■
9 A: The match is on TV tonight. B: Who cares? ■
10 A: David looks awful. B: Do you mind? ■ That's my brother you're talking about.

C79 Now listen and check your answers. Then listen again. Press 'pause' before each B part and read it aloud. Then press 'play' again and compare your pronunciation with what follows.

44.2 Choose an answer from the box to complete each conversation.

All of them	~~A cake~~	Any of it	This evening	Dr Ireland
Because your friends told you to		With her parents		Nothing serious

EXAMPLE A: What are you making? ......A cake......?
B: Yes, it's for Linda's birthday.

1 A: When are they supposed to be back? ....?
B: I think so.

2 A: Where's she living now? ....?
B: Yes, since last month.

3 A: How many of your cousins have you invited? ....?
B: Just a few.

4 A: Why did you do such a silly thing? ....?
B: I'm really sorry.

5 A: How much of the assignment have you written so far? ....?
B: A couple of pages.

6 A: What's wrong with your mother? ....?
B: No, she'll be fine soon.

7 A: Which doctor did you want to see? ....?
B: Yes, please, if he's free.

C80 Now listen and check your answers. Then listen again. Press 'pause' before each A part and read it aloud. Use a falling tone in the first question and a fall-rising tone in the possible answer. Then press 'play' again and compare your pronunciation with what follows.

EXAMPLE What are you making ■? A cake ■?

Follow up: Here are some more common short questions usually said with a falling tone. Do you know what they mean? *What for? How come? Why not? What's up? So what?*

45 'I paid €200,000 for it.' '*How much* ↗?' Repeat questions

We use some questions to get people to repeat all or part of what they have said. We may want to check that we heard it correctly, or perhaps we found it surprising. Because these questions are usually *making sure* (see Unit 43), they often have a rising tone.

A

C81 Some repeat questions consist of –

- a single *wh-* word (*who, what, where, when, why, how, which*)
  A: She used to work in Wollongong. B: WHERE ↗?
- a phrase beginning with a *wh-* word (e.g. *how many, what sort, what time*)
  A: I paid €200,000 for it. B: HOW much ↗?
- a longer question beginning with a *wh-* word (e.g. *When did you get there?*)
  A: It starts at midday. B: WHEN does it start ↗?

All these repeat questions have a rising tone starting on the *wh-* word.

When questions are used to *find out* (see Unit 43), they have a falling tone. In these *finding out* questions the falling tone starts after the *wh-* word. Compare:

A: I'll meet you at eight. B: WHAT time ↗? (*making sure*)
but: A: I'll meet you at the station. B: what TIME ↘? (*finding out*)

A: This parcel's for Mike. B: WHO'S it for ↗? (*making sure*)
but: A: This parcel's arrived. B: who's it FOR ↘? (*finding out*)

B

C82 In other questions used to check hearing or understanding, we repeat the whole of what was said:

A: Kathy's getting married again. B: she's getting MARried again ↗?

or we focus on part of what was said using a *wh-* word or phrase at the end:

A: We're staying with Zara. B: You're staying with WHO ↗?

A: There were at least 500 people in the room. B: There were HOW many ↗?

We can use *what* or *do* + *what* to focus on the verb or the part of the sentence beginning with the verb:

A: I bought Chris a rabbit. B: You WHAT ↗? or: You did WHAT ↗?

C

C83 A number of common phrases with rising tone are used to ask people to repeat. For example:

I'm SORRy ↗? SORRy ↗? PARdon ↗?
WHAT did you say ↗? SAY that aGAIN ↗? SAY it aGAIN ↗?
WHAT ↗? You WHAT ↗? (these two are less polite and some people avoid them)

⚠ **Note:** Some of these can also be used to *find out* (with falling tone):
A: Zak told me he was leaving. B: WHAT did you SAY ↘? (= What did you say to him?)

Exercises

45.1 Choose a question from the box to complete each conversation. (You won't need them all.)

How many?	What time was it?	She's doing what?	Why was he there?
How much?	Which one's yours?	How old is it?	When did you leave?
What were you looking for?	~~Who did you want to see?~~	What sort?	
You did what?	How far is it?	Where?	When do you need it?

EXAMPLE: A: I'd like to see Mrs Kirby, please. B: *Who did you want to see?*
A: Mrs Kirby.

1 A: It only cost me fifty pounds. B: ....
A: Fifty pounds.
2 A: I need it for Thursday. B: ....
A: Thursday.
3 A: It's a couple of centuries old. B: ....
A: About two hundred years.
4 A: I told him I thought he was stupid. B: ....
A: I said he was stupid.
5 A: It's only another five kilometres. B: ....
A: Five kilometres.
6 A: She's got seven sisters. B: ....
A: Seven.
7 A: I was looking for a spatula. B: ....
A: A spatula.
8 A: He's got a job in Port Moresby. B: ....
A: Port Moresby.
9 A: My bike's got the yellow saddle. B: ....
A: The one with the yellow saddle.
10 A: Margot's going abseiling next weekend. B: ....
A: Abseiling.

C84 Now listen and check your answers. Press 'pause' before each B part and read aloud what you have written with a rising tone. Then press 'play' again and compare your answer and your pronunciation with what follows.

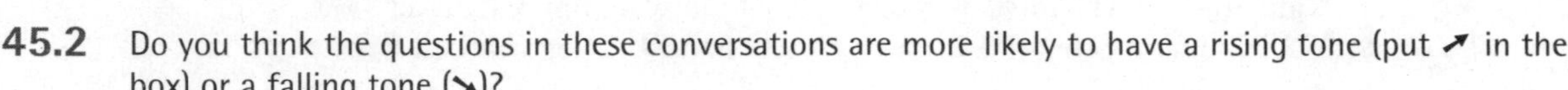

45.2 Do you think the questions in these conversations are more likely to have a rising tone (put ↗ in the box) or a falling tone (↘)?

EXAMPLE A: The play starts at 7.00. B: When have we got to be there? [↘] A: At 6.30.

1 A: She's quite upset, you know. B: What did you say? ■ A: She's quite upset.
2 A: There's a problem with the cooling system. B: How can you tell? ■
A: The engine's overheating.
3 A: I'd like an ice cream. Pistachio flavour. B: What sort do you want? ■ A: Pistachio.
4 A: He says he doesn't want to go because of the humidity. B: Why doesn't he want to go? ■
A: Because he doesn't like the humidity.
5 A: I think it's broken. B: What is? ■ A: The door bell.
6 A: There was a good attendance at the meeting. B: How many were there? ■ A: About 50.
7 A: I've bought this necklace for Jackie. B: Who did you buy it for? ■ A: Jackie.

C85 Now listen and check your answers.

Follow up: The questions with a rising tone in 45.2 could be said with a fall-rising tone with a similar meaning. Try saying those questions with a fall-rising tone.

46 Although I was tired, I couldn't get to sleep
Comparisons and contrasts

A

When we are contrasting two words or phrases, we emphasise the parts that we want to contrast by making them prominent:

A: You looked exhausted last night.
B: Yes, but even though I was TIRED,
I couldn't get to SLEEP.

A: Can I have some of this cake now?
B: The pudding's for toMORrow, not for toDAY.

Typically, the word or phrase that is 'news' – that is, information that the hearer is not expected to know – has a falling tone (e.g. that I couldn't get to sleep; that the cake is for tomorrow). This contrasts with information that the hearer and speaker already share, which has a rising or fall-rising tone (e.g. that I was tired; that A thinks the cake is for today). (See also Unit 39.)

Note: The contrasting phrase sometimes comes first and sometimes second.

B

Here are some common patterns of comparison and contrast –

- using a comparative form of an adjective:

  I think it's more important to have COMfortable clothes than STYlish ones.

  Notice that starting the falling or (fall-)rising tone on different words can affect meaning:

  watching FOOTball is much better than watching CRICKet.
  WATCHing football is much better than PLAYing football.

- using *either ... or*:

  You can either catch the EARlier train or the LATer one.
  I've either left my wallet at HOME or I've LOST it.

- using ..., *not* ... or ... *not* ..., ... :

  He's got bronCHItis, not just a COUGH.
  I'm not really ANgry with him, just a bit anNOYED.

- using other contrasting phrases (e.g. catch the bus *versus* walk home; reducing the cost of public transport *versus* increasing it):

  Rather than catch the BUS, maybe we could WALK home.
  We should be reDUcing the cost of public transport instead of inCREASing it.

Exercises

46.1 In B's responses one part is said with a falling tone and the other with a fall-rising tone. Write ↘ in the box for a falling tone or ↘ ↗ for a fall-rising tone where you think these tones are likely.

EXAMPLE A: How on earth do you sit down in those jeans?
B: They're really quite comfortable [ ], even though they're tight [ ].

1 A: You spoke to Bryan, didn't you?
B: I phoned him [ ], but there was no answer [ ].

2 A: It was interesting meeting the Education Minister yesterday, wasn't it?
B: I didn't get to speak to him [ ], though everyone else seemed to [ ].

3 A: I suppose your parents were in bed when you got home.
B: My Dad was asleep [ ], but my Mum was waiting up for me [ ].

4 A: Of course, you know Dartmoor well, don't you?
B: I used to live on Exmoor [ ], not Dartmoor [ ].

5 A: Ray's put on a lot of weight, hasn't he?
B: Although he's overweight [ ], he's actually quite fit [ ].

6 A: We're going late on Friday.
B: You'd be better off travelling on Saturday morning [ ], rather than Friday night [ ].

C88 Now listen and check your answers. Then listen again. Press 'pause' before each B part and read it aloud. Make sure you start the falling or fall-rising tone in the right place. Then press 'play' again and compare your pronunciation with what follows.

46.2 Choose a pair of phrases from the box to complete each conversation. (Notice that you may need to change the order.) The tone (falling or rising) is given for each of the two parts of the sentence.

short story – novel	on the phone – face-to-face	we can't afford it – we'd like to go
~~first one – second~~	new glasses – smaller fingers	Australia – Scotland
boat – helicopter		

EXAMPLE A: I really enjoyed her second film.
B: I actually liked her ......first one...... [ ] more than her ......second...... [ ].

1 A: We need to discuss this more. I'll give you a call.
B: But it's easier to talk .... [ ] than .... [ ].

2 A: I'll never be able to sew this. I need smaller fingers.
B: You either need .... [ ] or .... [ ].

3 A: Are you going to Malaysia again this holiday?
B: Much as .... [ ], ... [ ].

4 A: I hope Carla has a great time in Australia.
B: She's going to Perth in .... [ ], not Perth in .... [ ].

5 A: How are you getting on with your novel?
B: It's not a .... exactly [ ], more a .... [ ].

6 A: How was the boat journey to Capri?
B: Instead of going by .... [ ], we went by .... [ ].

C89 Now listen and check your answers. Then listen again. Press 'pause' before each B part and read it aloud. Make sure you use falling and rising tones as indicated. Then press 'play' again and compare your pronunciation with what follows.

Follow up: In some of B's replies in exercises 46.1 and 46.2 you could reverse the order of information, perhaps with some rewording of the sentence. Say the replies in this way, making sure that you keep the same tone on each piece of information.

47 'You were asleep in the class!' 'I ↑ WASn't asleep ↘.' Contradictions

A  C90 When we contradict something (perhaps to correct it or because we disagree with it) we emphasise the word that focuses on the difference between the other speaker's view and our own:

A: You were asleep in the class!
B: I ↑WASn't asleep ↘.

Usually this word (*wasn't* in this example) has falling tone and a step up in pitch.

The symbol ↑ is used to show a step up in pitch. In other words, the voice moves up to a noticeably higher level than it was at before.

B  C91
- To contradict a positive verb, we can use *not* or a contraction with *-n't* (*don't, can't, won't, shouldn't,* etc.). *Not* or the contraction is made prominent:

  A: It's your fault we're late.
  B: It's ↑ NOT my fault ↘.

  I thought Paul had the key, but he ↑ DIDn't have it ↘.

  A: You're not bringing your friends home. You'll be too noisy.
  B: But we ↑WON'T be noisy ↘.

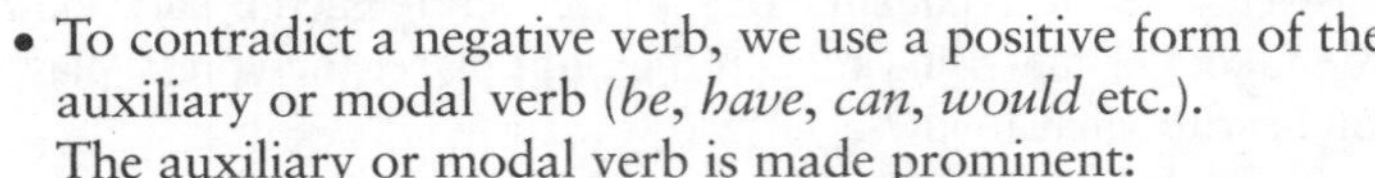

- To contradict a negative verb, we use a positive form of the auxiliary or modal verb (*be, have, can, would* etc.). The auxiliary or modal verb is made prominent:

  A: You can't remember your uncle Bob, can you?
  B: Yes, I ↑CAN remember him ↘.

  A: You don't seem to like my cooking.
  B: But I ↑DO like it ↘.

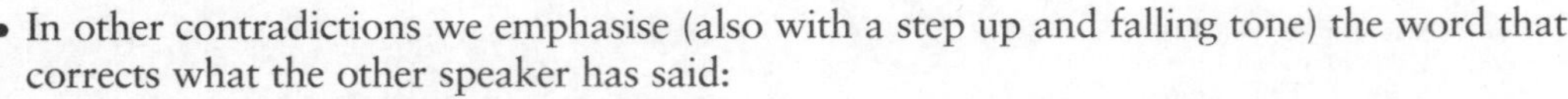

- In other contradictions we emphasise (also with a step up and falling tone) the word that corrects what the other speaker has said:

  A: Carmen must have overslept again.
  B: No, she's ↑ILL ↘. ← = she didn't oversleep, she's ill

  A: Did you take the wrong turning?
  B: Your in↑STRUCtions were wrong ↘. ← B contradicts A's suggestion that it was B who was at fault

Notice that there is sometimes a choice of words we can emphasise in order to contradict, although the meaning is similar. Compare:

A: I suppose she'd given up and gone home.
B: No, she ↑WAS waiting for me ↘.
B: No, she was ↑WAITing for me ↘. ← although a different word is emphasised, the meaning is similar

C C92 In comparisons and contrasts (see Unit 46) and in contradictions, we sometimes emphasise parts of words that are not normally emphasised. That is, we might make syllables prominent that are not shown as having primary or secondary stress in a dictionary (see also Unit 10):

A: So you think the troops are being reARMED?
B: No, I said they're being ↑DISarmed ↘. ← stress is normally on the second syllable in dis'armed, but here there is a contrast between re(armed) and dis(armed), so the first syllable is made prominent

Exercises

47.1 Catherine and her school friends are planning a holiday in Spain to celebrate the end of exams, but her father objects. Here is what she told her friends.

1 He says we're too young, but we're *not* too young.
2 He says I can't afford it, but I *can* afford it.
3 He thinks we'll stay out too late, but we *won't* stay out too late.
4 He says we'll make too much noise in the hotel, but we *won't* make too much noise.
5 He thinks I haven't got a passport, but I *have* got a passport.
6 He says I don't work hard enough at school, but I *do* work hard.
7 He says I've got school work to do, but I *haven't* got any school work to do.
8 He thinks we can't look after ourselves, but we *can* look after ourselves.

C93 Read each sentence aloud, stepping up on the word in italics and using a falling tone. Make sure that there are no prominent words after the word in italics. Then listen to the recording.

47.2 Underline the one word out of the two in **bold** that is more likely to be emphasised with a step up in pitch at the beginning of a falling tone.

EXAMPLE a A: The meeting's next Thursday, isn't it?	B: No, it's **next <u>Tuesday</u>**.
b A: The meeting's this Tuesday, isn't it?	B: No, it's **<u>next</u> Tuesday**.
1 a A: So I need to add three cupfuls of sugar?	B: No, three **spoonfuls** of **sugar**.
b A: So I need to add three spoonfuls of cream?	B: No, three **spoonfuls** of **sugar**.
2 a A: Your parents have lent you a car, then?	B: No, they've **bought** me a **car**.
b A: Your parents have bought you a bike, then?	B: No, they've **bought** me a **car**.
3 a A: Isn't it time for you to get up?	B: No, I'm not **going** to **school** today.
b A: Won't you be late for school?	B: No, I'm not **going** to **school** today.
4 a A: I want to use the laptop this afternoon.	B: But I **took** it to **work**.
b A: Alex just phoned. She wants you to bring the laptop into work.	B: But I **took** it to **work**.

C94 Now listen and check your answers. Then listen again. Press 'pause' before each B part and read it aloud. Make sure you step up in pitch in the right place. Then press 'play' again and compare your pronunciation with what follows.

47.3 Underline the syllable in each word in **bold** where you think the speaker will step up and start a falling tone.

EXAMPLE A: Here's the microscope you wanted. B: But I asked for a **micro<u>phone</u>**.

1 A: So you think it's a hardware problem? B: No, I said it's a **software** problem.
2 A: Yes, parties are always better outdoors. B: But we're holding it **indoors**.
3 A: I've deflated that airbed. B: But I asked you to **inflate** it.
4 A: I have rewound the hosepipe for you. B: But I wanted it **unwound**.
5 A: It is an unusual postcard, isn't it? B: No, I said an unusual **postcode**.
6 A: So you felt homesick while you were away? B: No, I was **seasick**.

C95 Now listen and check your answers. Then listen again. Press 'pause' before each B part and read it aloud. Make sure you step up in pitch in the right place. Then press 'play' again and compare your pronunciation with what follows.

Follow up: On a radio programme, a British opposition MP said: 'The government says it's going to happen, but this report shows it's not happen↑ING ↘'. Why do you think he said the last word in this way?

48 You couldn't carry it upSTAIRS for me ↘↗? Requests and reservation

A 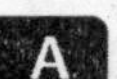 D2 When we want to get someone to do something for us, we often express this in a polite way by using a fall-rising tone:

> I need to get to the airport by six. Don't suppose you can give me a LIFT ↘↗?
> You couldn't carry it upSTAIRS for me ↘↗?
> I suppose I could come over on Saturday, but Sunday would be EAsier ↘↗.
> (= asking someone to change their plans)

Notice, however, that if we *offer* to do something for someone, it often sounds more sincere – that is, as a more genuine offer of help – if we use a falling rather that a rising or fall-rising tone (see also Unit 43C):

> Do you want a HAND ↘? can sound more genuine than:
> Do you want a HAND ↗? or: Do you want a HAND ↘↗?

B  D3 We commonly use a fall-rising tone when we want to indicate our *reservation* about something. For example, we may not completely agree with something, or we know that what we are saying is only partly correct, or we may not be sure that what we are saying will be accepted:

> A: Do you like her paintings?
> B: YES ↘. (= I do) but: B: YES ↘↗. (= I'm not sure, or I like *some* of them)
>
> A: Is it an interesting town?
> B: The OLD parts are ↘↗. (= other parts aren't)
>
> A: You lost again, I hear.
> B: I did my BEST ↘↗. (= you obviously expected more)

We also use a fall-rising tone when we talk about a cancelled arrangement:

> A: Are you going to the conference next week?
> B: Well, I was PLANning to go ↘↗, but I've got too much WORK ↘.

C  D4 In negative sentences, there is sometimes a difference in meaning when we use a falling tone and a fall-rising tone (see also Unit 43B). Compare:

> A: It's a pity Ann was ill and missed the party.
> B: She didn't miss the party because she was ILL ↘↗. (= it was for another reason)
>
> but: A: I wonder why Ann missed the party.
> B: She missed it because she was ILL ↘. (= this was the reason)
>
> A: I'll get some cheese while I'm out.
> B: I don't want ANy cheese ↘↗. (= I want a particular kind)
>
> but: A: How much cheese shall I get?
> B: I don't want ANy cheese ↘. (= none at all)

Exercises

48.1 Listen to these sentences and underline the syllable where the fall-rising tone starts.

D5

EXAMPLE I don't suppose you'd like to buy one?

1 You couldn't do me a favour?
2 Do you want to borrow my umbrella?
3 I'd rather meet at ten, if you can make it.
4 Couldn't you come another day?
5 Will you be able to write a reference for me?
6 Can I open the door for you?
7 Can you get something for me from town while you're there?

Now say the sentences aloud. Make sure you use a fall-rising tone, starting on the underlined syllable. Which two of the sentences would sound more polite or sincere with a falling tone?

48.2 Match A's statements with B's responses, which express reservation. Then underline the syllable in B's responses where you think the fall-rising tone will start.

1	A: Mr Brown's an excellent dentist.	....	B: His later ones were.
2	A: I've put on a lot of weight recently.	....	B: I wanted to come.
3	A: Dali's paintings were so strange.	....1....	B: He's very good with children.
4	A: You're very good at chess, aren't you?	....	B: It was certainly unexpected.
5	A: Great news about Martha's new job.	....	B: Well, I used to play well.
6	A: It's a pity you couldn't come skiing with us.	....	B: You still look fit, though.

D6

Now listen and check your answers. Press 'pause' before each B part and read it aloud. Then press 'play' again and compare your pronunciation with what follows.

48.3 Tick (✓) the more likely continuation in each case.

EXAMPLE I didn't decide not to buy the hat because it was too exPENsive ...
(i) I just didn't like the colour. ✓ (ii) I don't have much money at the moment.

1 I didn't buy the car because it was CHEAP ...
(i) I'd have been happy to pay a lot more for it. (ii) So I guessed it wouldn't be reliable.

2 She didn't fail the exam because she was LAzy ...
(i) I was always telling her to work harder. (ii) She was really ill on the day.

3 He won't play in ANy tournaments ...
(i) He says he's too old. (ii) He only plays where there's a lot of prize money.

4 I don't like ANyone borrowing my bike ...
(i) It's really valuable. (ii) I only lend it to my closest friends.

D7

Now listen and check your answers. Then say the sentences aloud, including the correct continuation.

Follow up: Think of a country (not your own) and write three positive things about it. Now imagine that you have been asked to move to that country, but you are reluctant to go. How might you only partly agree with positive comments about the country to express your reservation? For example, 'People are very friendly there.' 'Well, in the VILLages they are .' Use a fall-rising tone in your response. (If possible, you could do this activity with another student.)

49 *On the whole*, it went very well
Attitude words and phrases (1)

A (D8) A number of words and phrases are commonly used to indicate our attitude to what we are going to say, what we have just said, or what another speaker said. Words and phrases like this are often in a separate speech unit (see Unit 32), either at the beginning or at the end of a sentence, and when this happens many are typically said with a particular tone. For example:

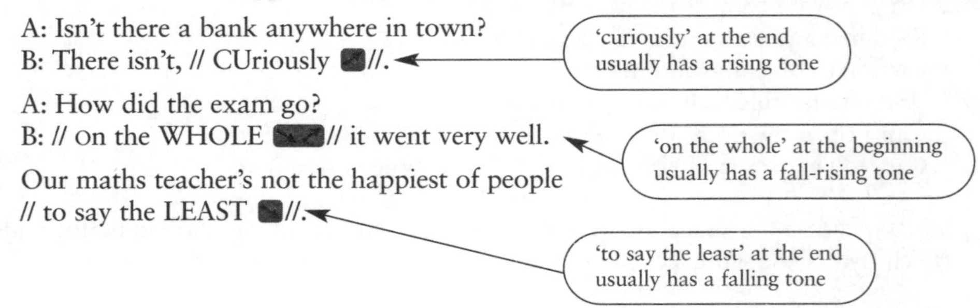

A: Isn't there a bank anywhere in town?
B: There isn't, // CUriously //.

'curiously' at the end usually has a rising tone

A: How did the exam go?
B: // On the WHOLE // it went very well.

'on the whole' at the beginning usually has a fall-rising tone

Our maths teacher's not the happiest of people // to say the LEAST //.

'to say the least' at the end usually has a falling tone

Units 49 and 50 look at intonation in these attitude words and phrases.

Note: Attitude words and phrases may be part of a longer speech unit and then intonation is less predictable. For example:

// PEOple on the whole were very KIND //

B (D9) Some attitude words and phrases are used to emphasise that what we are saying is true, and these typically have a falling tone both at the beginning and end of a sentence. Words and phrases like this include: *believe 'me*, *'surely*, *to put it 'mildly* and *to say the 'least* (note that the main stressed syllable is marked with '):

BeLIEVE ME, it's freezing out there.
She wasn't too pleased with me, to put it MILDly.

The phrase *mind you* is used at the beginning of a sentence, typically with a falling tone, to emphasise an added piece of information:

My granddad is always at the doctor's. MIND YOU, he smokes a huge amount.

C (D10) The phrase *The (only) thing is …* is used at the beginning of a sentence, typically with a rising or fall-rising tone to highlight a problem connected to what has just been said:

You know you lent me that money? Well, the THING IS, I need some more.

The phrases *The fact/point is …* indicate that what we are going to say is important, and *The question/problem is …* label what we are going to say as an important question or problem. These phrases also typically have a rising or fall-rising tone:

It might be a good car, but the FACT IS, it's too expensive.
I know you've applied for the job. The QUEStion IS, do you really want it?

D (D11) Some words are used to show what viewpoint we are speaking from; that is, identifying what features of something we are talking about. Typically, these phrases have either a rising or fall-rising tone:

PHYSically, he's in quite good shape.
I mean, LOGically, her answer was quite right.

Other examples are *economically*, *outwardly*, *politically*, *statistically*, *superficially*, *technically*.

Exercises

49.1 Listen to these conversations. Do the attitude words and phrases in **bold** have a falling tone (put ↘ in the box), rising tone (↗) or fall-rising tone (↘↗)?

D12

EXAMPLE A: **In my opinion** [↘↗], the government was wrong to go to war. What do you think?
B: I disagree, **actually** [↗].

1 A: These are new, **presumably** [ ].
B: I've had them a while. A few weeks, **in fact** [ ].

2 A: There was a terrible mess in the kitchen when I got home. Jack was to blame, **naturally** [ ].
B: And **of course** [ ] he said it wasn't his fault.
A: That's right.

3 A: **Apparently** [ ], Mike's getting married again.
B: I already knew, **as it happens** [ ].

4 A: **On reflection** [ ], I think Julia's right. The company needs to invest in people more.
B: She's got a point, **in fairness** [ ]. But she's also got to be ready to put her money where her mouth is, **so to speak** [ ].

49.2 Match A's questions and statements with B's responses to make five conversations.

1	A: Why don't you get a new job?	.... B: Yes. **Mind you**, it should at the price.
2	A: How did the workers feel about the decision?	.... B: It was unpopular, **to say the least.**
3	A: What did your mother say when you left?	.... B: You don't expect me to believe that, **surely?**
4	A: This wine tastes wonderful.	...1... B: **Believe me**, I would if I could.
5	A: My dog ate my homework.	.... B: She was disappointed, **to put it mildly.**

D13

Now listen and check your answers. Press 'pause' before each B part and read it aloud. (Make sure you use a falling tone on the words and phrases in **bold**.) Then press 'play' again and compare your pronunciation with what follows.

49.3 Repeat the words in the box after the recording. Use a fall-rising tone in each case.

D14

outwardly   politically   ~~statistically~~   superficially   technically

Now use the same words to complete the sentences, and then say the sentences aloud using a fall-rising tone on the words you have written.

EXAMPLE Average temperatures have risen a little over the last hundred years, although ......*statistically*...... [↘↗] the increase is insignificant.

1 He was quite hurt by her comments, although .... he showed no sign of being upset.
2 She plays the violin with a lot of feeling, although .... she's not that good.
3 The country is rebuilding after the war, but .... it's still unstable.
4 The job is quite interesting, although .... it looks repetitive.

D15

Now listen and check your answers.

Follow up: Write sentences using some of the phrases in **C** opposite. Read these aloud, making sure you use a rising or fall-rising tone in the phrase. For example, 'I was going to contact Ann. The only thing is [↘↗], I don't have her email address.'

50 She just forgot, *presumably*? Attitude words and phrases (2)

The words and phrases in this unit usually have a fall-rising tone at the beginning of a sentence (or after *and* or *but*) and a rising tone at the end of a sentence.

A D16 A number of one-word adverbs can be used to show your opinion of what you are talking about:

> I was hoping to go to Italy this week, but unFORtunately, I couldn't get a flight.
> A: Can you record DVDs on your computer? B: No, I can't, unFORtunately.

Other adverbs like this include: *amazingly*, *astonishingly*, *curiously*, *fortunately*, *funnily*, *interestingly*, *luckily*, *oddly*, *regrettably*, *remarkably*, *sadly*, *strangely*, *surprisingly*, *unbelievably*.

⚠ **Note:** Many of these adverbs are also used to describe adjectives, verbs or other adverbs, when they may have different intonation patterns:

> His cooking is surPRISingly GOOD.

Some of the adverbs listed above (in particular, *curiously*, *funnily*, *interestingly*, *luckily*, *oddly*, *strangely* and *surprisingly*) are used with *enough* in a phrase showing opinion:

> He went out without his wallet. LUCKily eNOUGH, he had some change in his jacket pocket.
> I use this bit of wire as a TV aerial, and it works, STRANGEly eNOUGH.

B D17 We can use *actually* at the beginning or end of a sentence to sound more polite, particularly if we are correcting what someone has said, giving a different opinion, or refusing a request or offer:

> A: I thought the concert was a bit dull. B: ACtually, I quite enjoyed it.
> A: Do you want a coffee? B: I've got one, ACtually.

C D18 The words *apparently*, *presumably* and *supposedly* show that we are not completely sure what we are saying is true, perhaps because someone else has told us (see also Unit 48):

> ApPARently, you can now fly from Bristol to Paris.
> She just forgot, preSUmably?

D D19 Some attitude words and phrases are used to show that what we are saying is only an approximate statement: that we are referring only to the main features of something, or that we know that there are exceptions. These include *'basically*, *by and 'large*, *as a 'rule*, *'generally*, *on the 'whole*, *es'sentially* and *in 'general* (note that the main stressed syllable is marked with '):

> A: What will you do after college? B: BAsically, I want to do some travelling.
> I only see my brother at Christmas, as a RULE.

Exercises

50.1 Choose one word or phrase from the box to complete each pair of sentences. Do you think each word or phrase is more likely to have a rising tone (write ↗) or a fall-rising tone (↘↗)?

frankly	strangely enough	~~interestingly~~	luckily	sadly

EXAMPLE a I heard from Dan's mother that he'd given up his course. He didn't tell me himself, ...interestingly ↗...... .

b We thought we'd find a difference in reading preferences between boys and girls but ......interestingly ↘↗......, they like the same books.

1 a Mona had a heart operation last week. .... , it wasn't successful.
  b I'll be leaving Australia at the end of the year, ...

2 a The kitchen ceiling completely collapsed. .... , I'd just gone out of the room.
  b The 5 o'clock train was delayed by snow. We'd caught the earlier one, ...

3 a Peter's lost his job and I don't care, ...
  b The business isn't doing well and .... , it's beginning to worry me.

4 a I hadn't seen Adam for years but then I bumped into him twice last week, ...
  b Sophia has got two sisters but .... , she never mentions the older one.

D20 Now listen and check your answers. Then say the sentences aloud using the same tones in the words and phrases you have written.

50.2 Are the words and phrases in **bold** more likely to have a rising tone (put ↗ in the box) or a fall-rising tone (↘↗)?

EXAMPLE A: They'll post the tickets to us, presumably [↗]?
B: Supposedly [↘↗], they've sent them already.

1 A: **Basically** [ ], you made the whole story up, didn't you?
  B: No, it was true, **essentially** [ ].

2 A: **Apparently** [ ], the car will be ready by tomorrow.
  B: Yes, the garage is quite efficient, **on the whole** [ ].

3 A: Theresa phoned this morning, **apparently** [ ].
  B: **Actually** [ ], it was her sister.

4 A: **Presumably** [ ], you've been to Canada recently?
  B: Not for many years, **actually** [ ].

D21 Now listen and check your answers. Then say each line aloud, using a rising or fall-rising tone on the words and phrases in bold as appropriate.

Follow up: Write three things that are *not* true about a relative or friend of yours. Now imagine that someone says these things about them. How might you correct them using *actually* either at the beginning or end of your correction? For example, 'Paul's 40 next year.' 'Actually [↘↗], he's 45.' (If possible, you could do this activity with another student.)

51 How embarrassing ! Exclamations

A

(D22) When we want to give our opinion on something that has been said or done, we can do this with particular emphasis, often to express enthusiasm, using an adjective. Typically, this has a rise-falling tone:

> A: Dan got the job! B: GREAT !
> A: It's incredible to think that it's over 100 years old. B: aMAzing !
> A: Sounds really good, doesn't it? B: fanTAStic !

However, when adjectives like this have a low falling tone, they can be used in a sarcastic way. A positive word is used, but in fact expresses lack of enthusiasm, disappointment, or criticism:

> A: The flight's been cancelled.
> B: GREAT .
>
> A: The computer's crashed again.
> B: WONderful .

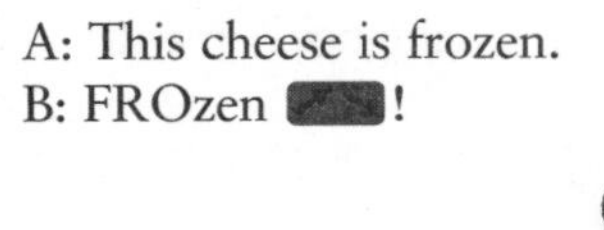

We can also use an adjective with a rise-falling tone to express surprise at what has been said:

> A: Jack's just bought a new car. It's pink.
> B: PINK !
>
> A: This cheese is frozen.
> B: FROzen !

B

(D23) Adjectives like this can also be used with a rise-falling tone as part of longer phrases, often emphasised with adverbs such as *absolutely*, *completely* and *totally*:

> A: They're stupid to close the school. B: ABsolutely riDICulous .
> A: Karl's given up his college course. B: he must be comPLEtely MAD .
> A: Were the instructions any good? B: they were TOtally incompreHENsible .

Some are also used in exclamations after *how*:

> HOW emBARrassing !
> HOW COOL ! (= very good; informal)

C

(D24) Nouns and phrases without adjectives may also be used to express surprise, anger, etc., typically with a rise-falling tone. Sometimes these repeat a part of what was previously said:

> you're JOking !
> NONsense !
> A: They've got diamonds in them. B: DIAmonds !

D

(D25) Notice that the word *really* can have different meanings, depending on the tone used with it. For example, with a rise-falling tone it often expresses surprise, but with a rising tone it often expresses doubt:

> A: It only cost me €10. B: REALly ! (= I'm surprised)
> B: REALly ? (= I'm not sure I believe you)

Exercises

51.1 Listen and decide whether B uses a rise-falling tone or a low falling tone in each response. Underline ↗↘ or ↘. In which responses is B being enthusiastic?

D26

EXAMPLE A: You had a good time, then. B: Superb! ↗↘ / ↘ *enthusiastic*

1 A: I can't find the tickets. B: Brilliant! ↗↘ / ↘
2 A: The house had a well in the kitchen. B: Extraordinary! ↗↘ / ↘
3 A: That's the third red bus I've seen today. B: Fascinating! ↗↘ / ↘
4 A: Dan's coming over at six. B: Great! ↗↘ / ↘
5 A: Kate's just phoned to say she'll be late. B: Marvellous! ↗↘ / ↘
6 A: She speaks 14 languages. B: Remarkable! ↗↘ / ↘
7 A: These beetles glow in the dark. B: Interesting! ↗↘ / ↘

Now listen again. Press 'pause' before each B part and read it aloud, using the tone you have underlined. Then press 'play' again and compare your pronunciation with what follows.

51.2 Choose the most likely adjective from the box to complete each conversation.

bizarre	convenient	~~dreadful~~	exhausting	horrified	stunning	useless

EXAMPLE A: How are you feeling? B: Absolutely ......*dreadful*......!

1 A: There's a coffee shop right next door. B: How .... !
2 A: Were you shocked by the news? B: Totally .... !
3 A: This heater isn't much good. B: Completely .... !
4 A: His paintings are weird, aren't they? B: Totally .... !
5 A: How did you find the heat in Malaysia? B: Completely .... !
6 A: The view from here is fantastic. B: Absolutely .... !

D27

Now listen and check your answers. Press 'pause' before each B part and read it aloud. Make sure you use a rise-falling tone on the words you have written.

51.3 You will hear five statements. After each statement, press 'pause' and say one of the responses in the box. Make sure you use a rise-falling tone. When you press 'play' again you will hear the correct answer. (Note: Other responses than those on the recording are also possible – see Key.)

D28

No way!	That's ridiculous!	A Porsche!	~~Tomorrow!~~	You're kidding!	You idiot!

EXAMPLE *You hear* The boss wants the report by tomorrow.
You respond ToMORrow ↗↘!

51.4 You will hear ten statements. Respond to each statement using the word 'Really'. Express surprise (with a rise-falling tone) or doubt (with a rising tone) as indicated.

D29

EXAMPLE *You hear* Marcus has left his job.
You respond REALly ↗↘! (surprise)

1 surprise	3 doubt	5 doubt	7 surprise	9 doubt
2 doubt	4 surprise	6 surprise	8 doubt	10 surprise

D30

Now listen to both the statements and responses on the recording.

Follow up: Write three ridiculous demands your teacher or boss might make of you. Reply with a short response, repeating part of their sentence and using a rise-falling tone to show your surprise. For example, 'I want you to write in green.' 'GREEN ↗↘!' (If possible, you could do this activity with another student.)

52 Mhm, Right, I see
Keeping conversation going

A

When we are taking part in a conversation, we often show the current speaker that we are following what they are saying, and that we want them to go on. A number of sounds, words and phrases are commonly used to do this, usually with a rising tone. These include *mm*, *uhuh*, *mhm*, *okay*, *right*, *yeah*, *I see*:

A: So how do I make a recording with this?
B: Well, you plug the microphone in this socket in the back [A: MHM] and you make sure that it's switched on and that the battery's working [A: RIGHT]. Then you press the play button and the pause button at the same time [A: oKAY] and then check that the recording level is okay [A: uHUH]. You can change it using this dial here [A: I SEE]. And then when you're ready you just …

B

When these are used with a falling tone, they often indicate that we think the speaker has finished or that we want to take a turn in the conversation ourselves (see also Unit 53):

B: … but make sure you don't move this switch.
A: RIGHT. What does it do?
B: It changes the voltage setting.
A: I SEE. And what would happen exactly?

C

Some words and phrases are added to positive sentences in order to check that something has been understood or accepted as true, usually with a rising tone. These include *alright*, *you know*, *okay*, *you see*, *right*:

I'll be over later, alRIGHT?
He was really odd, you KNOW?

They are often followed by the words and phrases in **A**, usually with a falling tone, indicating 'I have understood' or 'I agree':

A: I phoned Jerry straight away. He's a doctor, you SEE?
B: RIGHT.
A: So I thought he'd be able to help.

A: You're not to touch it, oKAY?
B: oKAY.

D

To show interest and to encourage the speaker to continue, we can also use short questions such as *Did you? Were they? Haven't we?*, typically with a fall-rising tone:

A: Saw Helen in town today.
B: DID you?
A: She said she's bought the flat [B: MHM] though she won't be able to move in until next year.
B: WON'T she?
A: No, some problem with the other people moving out. [B: RIGHT] Apparently they're going to …

We can also use *Really?* with a fall-rising tone for a similar purpose (see also Unit 51):

A: Did you hear there's been another earthquake in Iran?
B: REAlly?
A: Yeah, and another bad one, too.

Exercises

52.1  Listen and take B's part in this conversation. You will only hear the A parts. Use a falling tone in each case to show that you agree or have understood.

A: The coach leaves at six, alright?
B: Okay. ■

A: From outside the museum, you know?
B: Right.
A: You wanted two tickets, right?
B: Yeah.
A: That's $50, okay?
B: Mhm.
A: It costs more at the weekend, you know?
B: Mm.
A: 'Cause we have to pay the driver more, you see?
B: Uhuh.

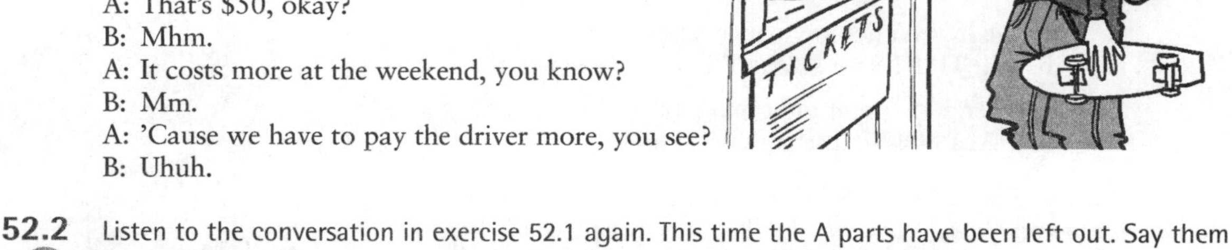

52.2 Listen to the conversation in exercise 52.1 again. This time the A parts have been left out. Say them aloud, using a rising tone on each final phrase to check that B understands.

EXAMPLE *You say* The coach leaves at six, alright ■?
You hear Okay.

52.3 Listen to this conversation. Two people are talking about a proposed new road through the countryside. Are the words and phrases in **bold** said with a falling tone (put ↘ in the box), rising tone (↗), or fall-rising tone (↘↗)?

A: So it'll go past those trees …
B: **Mhm** ■.
A: … across that footpath …
B: **Yeah** ■.
A: … and down across the top of that field.
B: **Right** ■, and who owns that?
A: All the fields around here are part of a big farm.
B: **Uhuh** ■.
A: Belongs to the farmer who lives in that white house.
B: **Right** ■.
A: Of course, he won't be happy about the plans.
B: **Won't he** ■?
A: No, I doubt that he'll want to sell any of his land.
B: **Okay** ■. So what'll happen then?
A: I suppose the council could force him to sell.
B: **Really** ■?
A: But that wouldn't be popular with the local community.
B: **I see** ■.

Now check your answers in the Key.

52.4 Listen to the conversation in exercise 52.3 again. This time the B parts have been left out. Say them aloud, using the same tones on the words in **bold**.

Follow up: English uses sounds such as *mm, uhuh,* and *mhm* to keep conversation going. Do you use the same or different sounds in your first language? Do you use the same pattern of rising, falling and fall-rising tones on these sounds that you have learned about in this unit?

53 On top of that... ; Anyway...
Adding information and changing topic

A D39 A number of words and phrases are used to introduce a piece of information that is related to what has just been said. Many of these are typically said in their own speech unit with a rising or fall-rising tone:

A: You can get a €100 fine for dropping litter in the city centre.
B: // on TOP of THAT //, the police can make you spend a whole day picking up rubbish.

A: I'll give you a ring later.
B: // BETter STILL //, why don't I come over and see you?

A: We haven't got any coffee left.
B: // in THAT case //, I'll just have water, thanks.

A: There's no point in keeping this jacket, it's full of holes.
B: // ALso //, the zip's broken.

Other words and phrases like this include: *at the same 'time, in the same 'way, 'similarly, by the same 'token, even 'better, worse 'still, 'otherwise, in other 'words* (or *in 'other words*). (Note that the main stressed syllable is marked with '.)

B  When we want to change the topic in a conversation or to start talking about a different aspect of the same topic, we often begin with a word or phrase with a falling tone in its own speech unit:

A: So where did you say they lived?
B: Cornwall.
A: Great, it's really nice there.
B: Yeah. // ANyway //, I must dash. See you later.

A: I really like the town square.
B: Lovely, isn't it? // RIGHT //, so what would you like to see next?

Other words and phrases like this include: *'anyhow, by the 'way, inci'dentally* (this suggests that what is going to be said is less important than what has come before), *'now (then), o'kay, well.*

Some people use *look* to introduce an aspect of the same topic that they particularly want the hearer(s) to pay attention to:

A: There's a meeting this Friday afternoon.
B: // LOOK //, I won't be able to get there, so can you tell me what happens?

However, other people only use it in this way to show that they are annoyed:

A: I don't want to go to the dentist.
B: // LOOK //, don't be so childish!

We can use *besides* to give another reason or argument for something:

A: Maybe we could look around the castle?
B: It's really expensive to get in. // BeSIDES //, it's only open in the morning.

Exercises

53.1 Listen and write what you hear in the space. Does this word or phrase have a falling tone (puts ↘ in the box), rising tone (↗), or fall-rising tone (↘↗)?

D41

EXAMPLE A: The new radio's very easy to carry around.
B: ....Even better........ [↘↗], it's got a built-in alarm clock.

1 A: Perhaps we could meet and have lunch?
B: .... [ ], we could just have a coffee.
2 A: Did your dad see you in the pub?
B: .... [ ], he caught me smoking.
3 A: When I gave them cabbage for dinner, they wouldn't eat it.
B: .... [ ], young children often don't like green vegetables.
4 A: I'll probably drive over early in the morning when it's cooler.
B: .... [ ], the roads won't be as busy then.
5 A: Mr Jenkins should be back in a few minutes.
B: .... [ ], I'll wait for him.

53.2 Underline the word or phrase in **bold** that is more natural in these conversations. Then underline the tone that is more likely with the word or phrase you have chosen.

EXAMPLE A: I'm sure I put your camera somewhere safe.
B: **In other words** / **Incidentally**, you've lost it, haven't you? [↘]/[↘↗]

1 A: So eventually, the holiday turned out really well.
B: Sounds great. **In the same way / By the way**, how's your mother feeling now? [↘]/[↘↗]
2 A: We could go to Paris by train rather than taking the car.
B: **Better still / Similarly**, we could travel first class. [↘]/[↘↗]
3 A: I wouldn't mind something to eat.
B: **Also / Well**, there's some leftover chicken in the fridge. [↘]/[↘↗]
4 A: It would be good to get together soon.
B: Yes, we really should. **Anyway / On top of that**, thanks for ringing. [↘]/[↘↗]
5 A: The factory needs improved safety conditions for its workers.
B: And **anyhow / by the same token**, workers need to follow safety guidelines. [↘]/[↘↗]

D42 Now listen and check your answers. Press 'pause' before each B part and read it aloud. Then press 'play' again and compare your answer and intonation with what follows.

53.3 Think of a suitable way to complete each B part and write it in the space. Then say the B part aloud, using an appropriate tone on the phrase in **bold**. (If you can, find a partner to take the A part.)

EXAMPLE A: I think it's really good that they're going to use the old town hall as a library.
B: But **at the same time** [↘↗], they've got to preserve the character of the place.

1 A: Bridget and Steve are coming next week.
B: **In that case** [ ], ...
2 A: I've got an assignment to do by Monday.
B: I won't see you over the weekend, then. **Incidentally** [ ], ...
3 A: Will you be coming to watch the concert?
B: No, it's too expensive. **Besides** [ ], ...
4 A: Have you thought any more about my offer to buy your car?
B: **Look** [ ], ...

D43 Now listen to some example answers.

Follow up: The phrase 'then again' usually has a rising or fall-rising tone. Check its meaning in a dictionary, and then write a short A/B conversation, like the ones above, which uses it.

54 Before she left school// she started her own business
Dividing prepared speech into units (1)

In most contexts, when we speak we are making up what we say as we go along. However, many people at times need to plan and prepare speech more formally, and read this aloud from a written text or develop it from notes. For example, students and academics may have to give presentations or lectures in class or at a conference; business people may have to give reports at meetings; teachers or broadcasters may need to read text aloud to their pupils or their audience. In Units 54 to 60, we will look at some of the features of pronunciation that tend to be found in the *prepared speech* produced in situations like these.

A D44 In prepared speech, we tend to put speech unit boundaries, often marked with a pause, at clause boundaries (see also Unit 32) although they can go elsewhere, too. In this example, from a presentation, speech units are marked with //. The ones at clause boundaries are marked with //:

We have a great opportunity// at the moment// to encourage awareness of science// among the public.// A recent opinion poll// which was conducted earlier this year// revealed that// 80% of the population// is interested in science.// In addition//, it shows// a growing trust in scientists// who make an important contribution// to society.// However//, the poll also showed// that few people// felt they know enough// about science.// To develop understanding of science// we need more public debate// and we should be making science// more interesting// in school.

When written text is read aloud, speech unit boundaries are often placed at punctuation marks (commas, full stops, etc.). However, speech unit boundaries may also be put in other places.

B D45 In particular, we tend to put speech unit boundaries –

- between two clauses linked by *and* or *but*:
  We have cut costs substantially// and will continue to invest.
  This is only one view// but it's supported by recent research.
- before and after an adverbial clause (i.e. a clause that gives more information about how, where, when, why, etc.):
  Before she left school// she started her own business.
  We'll be meeting at eight// to get to the airport by ten.
- after a clause which is the subject of a sentence (see also Unit 42):
  What they will do next// is unclear.
  How the process works// will be explained in the next lecture.
- before and after a non-defining relative clause (i.e. a clause that gives more information about a noun or noun phrase before it):
  The head of the police force// who is to retire next year// has criticised the new law.
  I would like to thank the conference organisers// who have worked very hard.

But notice that *defining* relative clauses are less likely to be separated from the noun they refer to by a speech unit boundary:

The number of people who are emigrating// is increasing steadily.
rather than: The number of people// who are emigrating// is increasing steadily.
We objected// to the recommendation that was put forward.
rather than: We objected// to the recommendation// that was put forward.

Note: There may not be a speech unit boundary between clauses which are short:
We'll leave when we can. (rather than: We'll leave// when we can.)

Exercises

54.1 In each sentence, two possible speech unit boundaries are marked with //. Underline the one that is more likely.

EXAMPLE The only college // that teaches medical statistics // is to close next year.

1 The ship was launched // in September 1942 // and destroyed a month later.
2 Property prices will increase // as long as interest rates // remain low.
3 The bird is often heard // but seldom // seen in the wild.
4 They took what they could carry // and left the rest // of their belongings behind.
5 Why students drop out // of university // is a complex issue.
6 Thieves made off // with the painting // despite security guards in the building.
7 Most people also speak French // which is taught // from the age of six.
8 Who gave the order // to shoot // is to be investigated further.
9 Women // who are pregnant // should avoid alcohol.
10 He claimed // he was innocent // but the jury disagreed.

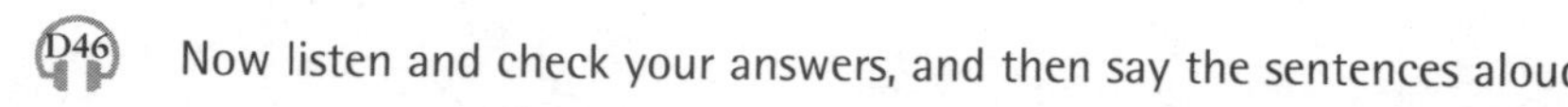
Now listen and check your answers, and then say the sentences aloud.

54.2 Prepare to read aloud this extract from a talk about complementary therapy. Think about where you will put speech unit boundaries and mark these with //. Use the information in **A** and **B** to help you. Read the extract aloud and, if possible, record and listen to yourself.

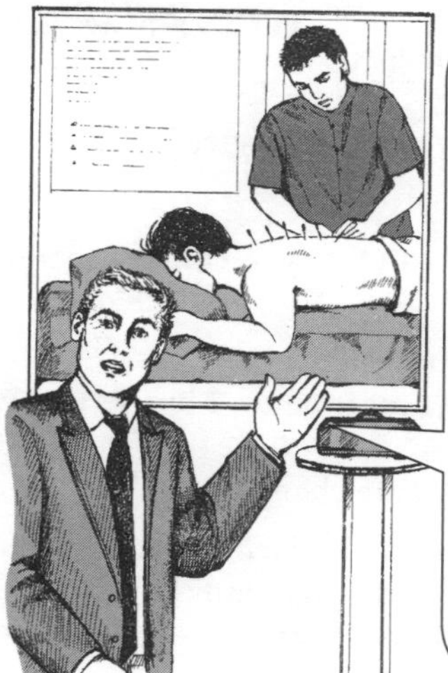

Complementary therapy, // which focuses on the whole person, // is becoming more widely used. It considers a patient's physical symptoms and also takes lifestyle into account.

Most practitioners believe that the body seeks a state of balance. What complementary therapy does is help people achieve this balance. Treatment not only relieves the disease but also promotes general wellbeing.

How complementary therapy works is still not entirely clear. Recent research has compared it with traditional medicine. In one study conducted in Canada a group of patients who had severe back pain were treated either with complementary or traditional treatments. Patients who had complementary treatments showed faster rates of improvement.

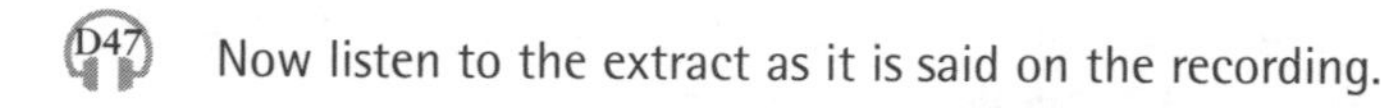

Now listen to the extract as it is said on the recording.

Follow up: Record a short section (about 30 seconds) of a radio news broadcast in English. (See Unit 4 for possible online sources.) Listen as many times as you need to and write out what is said. Try to mark the speech units with //. Which of these are at clause boundaries?

55 One of the paintings// he left to his sister Dividing prepared speech into units (2)

A (D48) In Unit 54, we saw that in prepared speech we usually place a speech unit boundary at the end of a clause. Speech unit boundaries also typically go before and after certain grammatical units *within* clauses. These are marked with // in the following example. Other speech unit boundaries are marked with //.

> Surprisingly// rates of heart disease// are rising again//. One of the most likely reasons// for this increase// is excessive eating//. As a result// levels of obesity// are going up// and people are taking less exercise//. In many parts of the country// this is becoming// a major// concern.

B (D49) In particular, we tend to put speech unit boundaries –

(a) before and after adverbials which refer to a whole clause:
  Unusually for that time of year// there was deep snow.
  The president's son has been named// unofficially// as his successor.

(b) between the subject of a clause and the verb when the subject is long:
  The last ten years of her life// were spent in France.
  Some of the rarest birds in the world// can be found on the island.

(c) before and after 'reduced clauses' that have a conjunction or adjective, but no verb:
  Wherever possible// the road will avoid existing settlements.
  (= wherever it is possible)
  The two villages// although only a few miles apart// were very different.
  (= although they are only a few miles apart)

(d) after elements that are put at the front of a clause other than the subject (the usual first element of a clause). These include –

  (i) adverbial phrases giving information about time and place:
  The train line will be closed for two weeks. // In the meantime// a bus service will be operating.
  All over the world// people are concerned about climate change.

  (ii) linking adverbs showing the connection between what you have said and what follows, such as: *furthermore, in the same way* (making an additional point); *alternatively, even so, on the other hand* (indicating contrasts); *consequently, as a result, therefore* (indicating consequences):
  There are clear limitations in the research. // Even so// the findings are valuable.
  Demand in Europe has declined. // Consequently// our profits have fallen.

  (iii) words and phrases indicating the stage of what they are saying, such as: *first(ly), second(ly), finally, in conclusion, to conclude, in summary, to sum up*:
  Secondly// waiting times need to be shortened.
  In summary// our report recommends relocating the factory overseas.

  (iv) objects that are placed before the verb:
  One of the paintings// he left to his sister. // The other// he left to me.
  A number of the experiments// we conducted in Antarctica.

C 

We also tend to put a speech unit boundary, usually with a pause, before information that we want listeners to focus particular attention on (see also Unit 60). For example:

> In today's talk, I want to introduce an important concept in language study …
> // discourse analysis.

Exercises

55.1 Mark with // the most likely place(s) to put a speech unit boundary in the green parts of these sentences. (Note that commas have been left out.)

EXAMPLE On the other hand // patients have little control over events in hospital. (see **B** (d) (ii))

1 The whole basis of Goldberg's analysis has been called into question.
2 Most of her money she left to children's charities.
3 In the first half of this year our sales have fallen by 25 per cent.
4 As a result women are having fewer children than in the 1990s.
5 Collectively the members of the organisation were known as 'The Followers'.
6 Unhappily for his family he was never seen again.
7 To conclude all these factors suggest the need for job cuts.
8 The two companies although in competition have agreed to cooperate on the project.

D51 Now listen and check your answers, and then say the sentences aloud. The Key gives further information about the answers.

55.2 Listen and notice how attention is focused on the part in **bold**.

D52
1 Only one group benefited from the change in the law ... **landowners.**
2 And the name for this process is **electrolysis.**
3 Today we're going to look at a rapidly changing area of the media ... **electronic publishing.**
4 I'd like you to note particularly the spelling of the word **'definitive'**.

Read the sentences aloud and focus attention on the part in bold in the same way.

55.3 Use the information in Units 54 and 55 to prepare to read this text aloud. It is the first part of a conference talk on climate change. Think about where you will put speech unit boundaries and mark these with //. Read the text aloud and, if possible, record and listen to yourself. Make sure that words within speech units are run together smoothly.

Ever since the industrial revolution we have dumped waste into the air. Consequently, atmospheric carbon dioxide levels are now a third higher than in pre-industrial time. The process may, it has to be said, have started long before, when we first burnt down trees to make way for agriculture. However, over the last few decades the rate of increase has grown rapidly. Although its precise nature is unclear there is an obvious relationship between levels of carbon dioxide in the atmosphere and higher global surface temperatures.

The impact of higher temperatures is difficult to assess, but there will certainly be a different world as humans and other living organisms try to adapt to change. These changes, which will affect us all, include drought and extreme weather. Southern Europe, for example, already has long periods without rainfall. And in the Americas and Asia powerful hurricanes and typhoons have recently killed more people than in several decades.

Of course, some scientists dispute the evidence. But these people, as we all know, represent industries having vested interests – their business, they believe, would be damaged by limits on carbon emissions. But among the wider scientific community the argument is about the speed of change, not whether change is taking place.

Now listen to the talk as it is said on the recording.

Follow up: Listen to the talk in Exercise 55.3 again and take notes. A few days later, record yourself giving the talk from your notes. Listen to the recording and identify any places where you might have improved the division of your speech into units.

56 Lima – as I'm sure you know – is the capital of Peru
Pronunciation of inserts

A D54 In writing we sometimes put dashes or brackets before and after words that add information to a sentence but could be left out. Here we will call these *inserts*.

For example:

> The impact on the region – in environmental terms – will be enormous.
> When the time for action comes (as it surely will), we will be ready.

In prepared speech, these inserts are often said in a separate speech unit, with a pause on either side and with a fall-rising tone:

> The main aim of this lecture// as I said EARlier //
> is to discuss the causes of the First World War.
>
> The new camera in our product range// to be aVAIlable in sepTEMber //
> will be aimed at the professional photographer.

B D55 Listen to these examples from lectures, business presentations and speeches. They show some of the main uses of inserts:

- saying how the talk is organised
  The figures I've presented so far – and will go ON to present – show that the company is in a strong financial position.
- giving examples
  Some of our major exports – COFfee for example – would be hit badly by climate change.
- limiting what you are saying
  Learning about pronunciation – in particular ENglish pronunciation – can be a difficult job.
- giving more detail
  Professor David Campbell – the FAmous hiSTOrian – will be giving next week's lecture.
- giving your opinion
  Lima – as I'm SURE you KNOW – is the capital of Peru.

Notice that there is more variety in the pronunciation of longer inserts:

> If a complaint is made – and there is no CERtainty at the MOment that this WILL be the case – we will take it seriously.

Exercises

56.1 Here are some extracts from lectures. Put // before and after the section you think will be presented as an insert, and underline the syllable where the fall-rising tone is most likely to start.

EXAMPLE There were three larger pyramids // which I'll come back to <u>la</u>ter // built in Giza at the beginning of the Old Kingdom.

1 In a number of countries New Zealand for instance attempts are being made to harness geothermal energy.
2 The city of Chester originally a Roman settlement was a major military stronghold by the time of the English Civil War in the 17th century.
3 At the top of the hill are the Three Witches as they used to be called which is a curious rock formation.
4 A large group of protestors nearly three thousand were in the audience when the president began his last speech.
5 Gregor's final novel by far his most entertaining was written when he was in his nineties.

D56 Now listen to the recording and check your answers. Then say the extracts aloud, making sure you pronounce the insert as a separate speech unit with a fall-rising tone.

56.2 Choose an insert from the box to add to each of these extracts from a business presentation and indicate its appropriate position with a line (/).

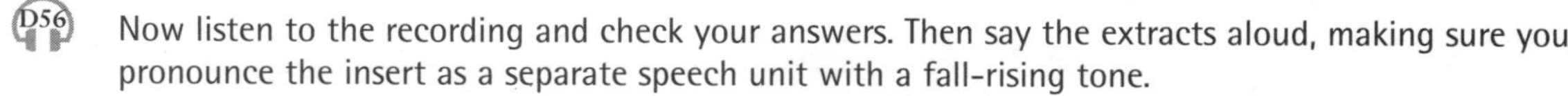
with the exception of France ~~as you can see from this graph~~
to be based in Dublin from our German sister company the DC6

as you can see from this graph
EXAMPLE Our Malaysian subsidiary / has increased sales enormously over the last year.

1 Karl Huzel will be talking to us after my presentation.

2 The countries of the European Union have all approved the new regulations on working conditions.

3 Our latest model was released in April this year.

4 The new research and development unit will be opened later this year.

D57 Now say the extracts aloud using a fall-rising tone for the inserts. Then listen and check your answers.

Follow up: Imagine that you are going to give a formal talk about a subject that interests you or that you study. Write down three pieces of information you might present, and then add extra information to each in the form of an insert. Say the sentences aloud, if possible recording them and checking the inserts.

57 We expected profits to drop, but they ↑rose
Step-ups – contrasts and new topics

A Contrasts

We can use a step-up (see Unit 47) to a relatively high pitch to show that information contrasts with previous information or what was expected. The step-up is in the first prominent word of a speech unit (see Unit 32) which includes the contrasting information. In these examples step-ups are marked with ↑:

We expected profits to drop this quarter, // but they ↑ROSE by a THIRD//. ← a contrast between an expected drop and an actual rise

Patients are now encouraged // to ↑EXercise// instead of rest after their operations. ← a contrast between the past encouragement to rest and the new practice of encouraging exercise

Although many people think of ants as a nuisance, they play // a ↑VItal ROLE// in many ecosystems. ← a contrast between the common belief that they are a nuisance and their actual vital role

We know that vegetarians have low rates of heart disease, // but we ↑DON'T fully understand WHY//. ← a contrast between what we know to be the case and our lack of understanding

Rather than wait for the authorities to solve the problem, // we should ↑ACT NOW//. ← a contrast between waiting and acting now

B New topics

Step-ups are also used, particularly in prepared speech, to show that we are starting a new topic. Here is the beginning of a speech made by a senior manager from the car company Rovoda to a conference of scientists discussing environmental problems. Notice how step-ups are used at the beginning of new topics:

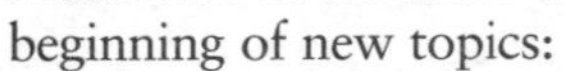

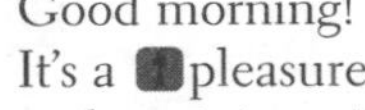

Good morning!
It's a ↑pleasure to be here to represent Rovoda and participate in this valuable discussion.
↑One of the things I enjoy about working for Rovoda is that the company recognises the importance of balancing the needs of business and society. As a car manufacturer, we know that we are part of the environmental problem, and need to be part of the solution. With ↑that in mind, I'd like to propose that the mission for all of us, starting with this meeting, is to find ways that people can continue to enjoy the freedom and lifestyles they do now, but by running cars that won't damage the planet. I realize that is a huge task, but it's not an impossible dream.
↑Think of the talent, creativity and influence we have at this meeting. If we, together with governments, decide to move forward together, a solution can be found.

Exercises

57.1 Put a ↑ before the word in each sentence you think is most likely to have a step-up signalling a contrast.

EXAMPLE We didn't think the bid would be successful, but it's been ↑accepted.

1 She always said it was her best film, although the critics hated it.
2 Rather than a military solution, we should be looking for a political one.
3 Some plastics are easy to produce, but difficult to dispose of.
4 Instead of a quick resolution to the war, their tactics prolonged it.
5 Most people think he's French, but in fact he's from Canada.
6 The model weighs only four kilos, whereas the full-scale version will weigh four thousand.
7 Despite the President's personal popularity, his party lost the election.
8 The novel was all his own work – or he claimed it was.
9 The area is a popular tourist attraction, and yet completely unspoilt.
10 Unlike most of our competitors, we've actually made a profit this year.

Now listen and check your predictions. (Also see the notes in the Key.) Then read the sentences aloud, putting a step-up in the same word as on the recording.

57.2 A history teacher is telling his students about Napoleon Bonaparte. Here is part of his lesson. Listen and put a ↑ before the word where he uses a step-up to introduce a new topic.

In ↑this lesson, we're going to look further at the life of Napoleon. As you'll remember, Napoleon was probably one of the greatest military leaders in history. In the class last week, we studied his earlier life, until about 1808, and now we'll look at events from about 1808 until his death. By 1808, you'll recall, Napoleon had crowned himself Emperor of the first French Empire. By this time he was in control of much of Europe, including Austria, Italy, Spain and Sweden. However, in 1809, Spain and Austria rose up against the French. Although the French army defeated them, thousands of men were lost. And in 1812, ignoring repeated advice against it, Napoleon began his invasion of Russia. In this campaign, over half a million soldiers in his army were killed, and by 1814 Paris had fallen and Napoleon had abdicated. Now what I'd like this half of the class to do is read the account of the battle near Vienna in 1809 in your textbooks starting on page 82. The other half should study the maps and pictures of the 1812 invasion on the handout, and write a brief account of what you have observed.

Now check your answers in the Key. Then read the text aloud, putting a step-up in the same places as on the recording.

Follow up: Prepare notes for a short talk on a historical subject that you are familiar with. Think about the places where you want to mark a new topic. Give your talk, using step-ups to mark new topics. If possible, record it and listen.

58 The headteacher, Mr ↓ Lee, will be talking to parents
Step-downs – adding information and ending topics

A D62 Adding information

When we use a noun phrase to add information about the previous noun phrase (and both refer to the same person or thing), we often step down and say the second noun phrase with a relatively low pitch in its own speech unit. The step-down is in the first prominent word of this speech unit. In these examples, step-downs are marked with ↓:

> The headTEAcher ↘// Mr ↓LEE ↘// will be talking to parents.
>
> The report is published // by the WHO ↘// the ↓WORLD HEALTH organisation ↘//.
>
> The reSEARCH team ↘↗// ↓SCIentists from the University of LEEDS ↘↗// will be spending six months in the Arctic.

We can also add information in a whole clause beginning with a step-down:

> A mySTErious arc of LIGHT ↘// ↓KNOWN as the LYNX Arc ↘// has been found to be the biggest star-forming region ever seen in space.

Note: The noun phrases (the main information and the added information) have a falling tone if they are 'news' and a rising or fall-rising tone if they are 'not news'; that is, the speaker assumes the hearer already knows the information (see Unit 39).

Notice that the same tone is usually used in the first noun phrase and in the stepped-down speech unit. However, this is not always the case:

> The AusTRAlian author PEter THOMas ↘// ↓ NOW based in New YORK ↘↗// is this year's Brook Prize winner.

here the speaker 'tells' hearers that she is talking about Peter Thomas, but 'reminds' them that Peter Thomas lives in New York – this is information she assumes hearers already know

B D63 Ending topics

Step-downs are also used, particularly in prepared speech, to show that we are ending a topic. Here is part of a conference talk given on the subject of education. Notice that step-downs are often followed by step-ups marking new topics (see Unit 57).

> In my talk I want to outline three ways of improving school students' attainment, behaviour and ↓aTTENDance. The ↑FIRST is to raise teaching quality through continuing professional development and the opportunity to observe outstanding teachers working in difficult ↓CLASSrooms. We also need greater flexibility in the subjects available to students, particularly offering students who are less able academically the option of taking work-related ↓COURSes. ↑FINally, there should be increased opportunities outside the classroom, ensuring that children from all socio-economic backgrounds have opportunities for sport and arts-related ↓acTIVities. I will now go on to talk about each of these in ↓DEtail. ↑EXcellent teaching is the key to motivating students …

Exercises

58.1 Listen to these extracts from news broadcasts as many times as you need and:

D64

(i) put a ↓ before the first prominent word with a step-down
(ii) put either ↘ (for falling tone) or ↘↗ (for fall-rising tone) in the box for the tone starting on each word in **bold**.

EXAMPLE The city of **Krakow** [↘], the ↓former capital of **Poland** [↘], has some of the best art collections in Europe.

1 Michael **Watson** [ ], the reigning **champion** [ ], has been knocked out of the French Open.
2 Whitedown **Hill** [ ], above the Trant **Valley** [ ], is to be the location of a new wind farm.
3 Two sisters from **France** [ ], both in their **seventies** [ ], have become the oldest people to swim the English Channel.
4 A black **woodpecker** [ ], a rare visitor to **Britain** [ ], has been spotted on the east coast.
5 The head of NATO in **Europe** [ ], Major Peter **Alvin** [ ], has warned that its military equipment is becoming seriously outdated.

58.2 Choose a noun phrase from the box to add to each of these news extracts and indicate its appropriate position with a line (/).

employing over three thousand people	a former communist	previously Leningrad
almost a tenth of the population	~~one of the poorest in Asia~~	inventor of the jet engine

EXAMPLE Large areas of the country / have been hit by drought. *(one of the poorest in Asia)*

1 Mr Abram Ivanich has been elected president of Novistan.

2 The Nisota car factory in Perth is to close next year.

3 A statue of Sir Frank Whittle has been unveiled in his home town.

4 Over fifty thousand people are now thought to have been infected with influenza.

5 The city of St Petersburg is encouraging people to use public transport.

D65

Now listen and check your answers. Then say the sentences aloud. Make sure you use a step-down at the beginning of the added information and the same tone (either falling or fall-rising) in the added information and the previous noun phrase.

58.3 A tour guide in Prague is explaining to tourists what they can see on their trip down the Vltava River. Here is part of what she says. Listen and put a ↑ before a word with a step-up marking a new topic and a ↓ before a word with a step-down ending a topic.

D66

On your ↑right we're passing the beautiful National Theatre, built in the mid 1800s and one of the most important Czech cultural institutions. If you want to see opera or ballet in Prague, that's the place to go. We're now passing under one of the best-known bridges in the world, the Charles Bridge. It was built in the 13th century, and has 75 statues along its sides. Over on the left, up on the hill, is Prague Castle, the home of Czech kings throughout the ages and now the seat of the President of the Czech Republic. You can also see the spires of Saint Vitus Cathedral, where most of the Czech kings are buried. To your right now is the Rudolfinum, a concert hall…

Now check your answers in the Key.

59 Small, medium, and large
Tones in a series of similar items

A D67 In prepared speech, when we give a series of three or more similar items, each item is typically said in a separate speech unit. Very often, all the items have a rising tone (or they all have a fall-rising tone) except the last, which has a falling tone. Using the same tone for each item, except the last, indicates that they are in some way equivalent. A falling tone on the last item signals the end of the series:

> Many governments fail to focus on policies which require sustained effort over years or decades – // to imPROVE eduCAtional standards // eRADicate diSEASE // MODernise the TRANSport system // and reDUCE levels of polLUtion //
>
> The only seats left are priced at// TWENty euros // THIRty euros // and FIFty euros //

⚠ **Note:** In spontaneous conversation there is more variability. For example, a speech unit may include more than one item, or a series may be incomplete:

> I've got // YELlow Orange or PINK // Which one would you like?
>
> A: She's been away a lot recently – // PARis // OSlo // MaDRID //...
> B: And is she back home now?

(the incomplete series suggests that she has been to other places, too)

B D68 Words within items in a series are usually non-prominent if they are repeated or don't provide new information:

> The meeting includes// NATional politicians // LOcal politicians // and EuroPEan politicians //

C D69 In lists that are often repeated or are part of a routine, each item is often said with a level tone (although a rising tone may also be used), except the last, which has a falling tone:

> There are three sizes available, // SMALL // MEdium // and LARGE //
>
> When I raise my hand like this I want you // to STOP TALKing // STAND up STRAIGHT // CONcentrate on ME // and get READy to SING //

D D70 Less commonly, all items may have a falling tone, particularly if we want to emphasise each item as separate and important:

> Please write the following dates down in your notebooks. The first examination // will be on MONday the SIXTH // the SECond on WEDnesday the EIGHTH // and the LAST on TUESday the fourTEENTH //

Exercises

59.1 D71 The last item in the series of similar items in each of these sentences has a falling tone. Listen and decide whether the other items have a falling tone (put ↘ in the box), rising tone (↗), fall-rising tone (↘↗), or level tone (→).

EXAMPLE This year we have opened new stores in London, New York and Moscow.

1 Make sure you give three pieces of information on each page – your name, your student number and the date.
2 When I was learning to drive my instructor made me say 'mirror, signal, manoeuvre' every time I drove away.
3 Attempts on the mountain have been made this year by Japanese climbers, Swiss climbers and Brazilian climbers.
4 You'll remember that Trollope's first three novels in his Barsetshire Chronicles were *The Warden*, *Barchester Towers* and *Doctor Thorne*.
5 I want you to paint the squares the colours of the rainbow – red, orange, yellow and so on.

Now check your answers in the Key. Then say the sentences aloud using the same tones.

59.2 D72 The series of similar items in each of these sentences is highlighted. Listen as many times as you need and in each part in green:
(i) mark the speech unit boundaries with //
(ii) underline the word in each speech unit where the main tone starts
(iii) put ↘, ↗, ↘↗, or → above this word to show the tone used.

EXAMPLE The book is set in three different periods and locations – // New Orleans in the ↗nineteenth century //, Haiti in the ↗twentieth century//, and San Francisco ↘today//.

1 She had a number of jobs in Berlin – as a waitress, bookseller, music teacher – but still found time to develop her career in the theatre.
2 Note that the last enrolment dates are the 15th of July, the 30th of July and the 30th of August.
3 A copy of the contract, signed, sealed and delivered, will be on your desk tomorrow.
4 Don't forget that for this experiment you'll need safety glasses, protective clothing and rubber gloves.
5 To get to the bookshop go down this street, turn left at the traffic lights and then cross the square.

Now check your answers in the Key. Then say the sentences aloud using the same tones.

Follow up: Go to the website http://www.historyplace.com/speeches/previous.htm and find US President John F. Kennedy's inaugural address from January 20th 1961. Listen to the following extract from the speech and decide what tones he used in the speech units marked:

> Let every nation know, whether it wishes us well or ill, // that we shall pay any price//, bear any burden//, meet any hardship//, support any friend//, oppose any foe//, to assure the survival and the success of liberty//.

Now do the same for the speech units marked in this extract from US President Richard M. Nixon's 'resigning the presidency' speech from August 8th 1974:

> In passing this office to the Vice President, I also do so with the profound sense of the weight of responsibility that will fall on his shoulders tomorrow and, therefore, // of the understanding//, the patience//, the cooperation// he will need from all Americans//.

60 'Politicians are the same all over...' Level tone in quoting and building suspense

A D73 Quotation

When we include a quotation of someone else's words in what we say, we often choose to use level tones and then a falling tone for the final speech unit in the quotation. This shows that we are simply reporting the words as they were spoken, and not giving a paraphrase of what was said:

> At this point it is worth remembering the words of Nikita Khrushchev:
> '// poliTICians ➡// are the SAME ➡// ALL Over ↘//. They PROMise ➡//
> // to BUILD a BRIDGE ➡// where there is NO RIVer ↘//.'

B D74 Preparing for quotation

Level tone is also commonly used on a reporting verb (e.g. *say*, *claim*, *argue*) which comes before a quotation. Typically, there is also a step up to a relatively high pitch on this verb, a pause, and then the first word of the quotation is also said relatively high. This marks clearly that what comes next is a quotation rather than a paraphrase:

> A headline in today's paper ↑SAYS ➡ ... : '↑TEAcher thrown out of classroom by students'.
>
> Just before the war began, a government minister ↑CLAIMED ➡... : '↑ONly by attacking now can we defend our country'.
>
> A leading group of economists have ↑ARGUED ➡ ... : '↑EURopean development aid should double in the next five years'.

C D75 Building suspense

We can also use a step-up, level tone and a pause in order to build anticipation or suspense, so that listeners focus particular attention on what comes next (see also Unit 55C). Notice that what comes after the pause may start high, mid or low:

> And the term we use for this phenomenon ↑IS ➡ ... entropy. ('entropy' is high)
>
> Much to our surprise, our research ↑SHOWED ➡ ... a sharp fall in average sea temperatures. ('sharp' is mid)
>
> If the radio signals are not from the ↑EARTH ➡ ... where do they come from? ('where' is low)

Exercises

60.1 Choose quotations from the box to complete the reports of what people said. (You may need to make minor changes at the beginning of the quotations.)

> It's a worrying and potentially damaging development.
> Painting is just another way of keeping a diary.
> ~~They're the best rock band of the twentieth century~~
> It's the most significant electronic consumer device ever invented.
> I'm an environmental status assessment consultant.

EXAMPLE They were introduced as: 'The best rock band of the twentieth century'.

1 She said that she was employed as:
'...'.

2 The managing director described the rise in oil prices as:
'...'.

3 Apparently it was Picasso who said:
'...'.

4 The book describes the mobile phone as:
'...'.

Now read the sentences aloud. Quote the people's words using level tones and a final falling tone. Then listen and compare what you said with the recording.

60.2 D77 Listen to these extracts from a news broadcast. In which do you think the highlighted part is a quotation, and in which do you think it is a paraphrase of what the original speaker said? Underline 'Quotation' or 'Paraphrase'.

EXAMPLE The Foreign Office has been accused of breaking its promises on support for refugees by a senior United Nations official. *<u>Quotation</u> / Paraphrase*

1 After a fifth shooting in the city in a week, the people of Dublin have been urged to remain alert but stay calm. *Quotation / Paraphrase*

2 In a speech yesterday, Professor Ken Sun of the Climate Research Institute claimed that there is now no doubt that global warming is producing climate change. *Quotation / Paraphrase*

3 Hurricane Katrina has been described as the worst natural disaster to hit the United States in living memory by a US government spokesperson. *Quotation / Paraphrase*

4 The Prime Minister has said that universities must train more scientists in order to meet the country's needs over the next few decades. *Quotation / Paraphrase*

60.3 D78 Think of a possible ending for each of these sentences from talks by scientists, and write it in the space. Then read the sentences aloud, using pause and intonation as described in C in order to build suspense. (Examples are given on the recording.)

EXAMPLE On the photos from Mars, much to our surprise we found … lakes of ice.

1 We've developed a computer programme that can actually …
2 The number of overweight people in the country has risen to an incredible …
3 Using the new treatment, the number of people missing work due to backaches …

Follow up: Record yourself reading the extracts in 60.2, first as if each highlighted part is a quotation, and then as if it is a paraphrase. Listen to the recording. Can you hear the difference between the two?

E1 The phonemic alphabet: Practice

Phonemic symbols for vowels

See page 192 for a list of phonemic and other symbols used in this book.

1 Short vowels /æ/ /e/ /ɪ/ /ɒ/ /ʌ/ /ʊ/ /ə/

Write the correct phonemic symbol for the underlined vowel in each word.

EXAMPLE rich ....ɪ....

1 month ....
2 gone ....
3 bank ....
4 ago ....
5 sugar ....
6 met ....
7 sung ....
8 symbol ....
9 cinema ....
10 any ....
11 would ....
12 watch ....

2 Short vowels /æ/ /e/ /ɪ/ /ɒ/ /ʌ/ /ʊ/ /ə/

Complete each word with the correct short vowel(s).

EXAMPLE The cinema was f ..ʊ.. l. (fʊl = full)

1 The kl.......k had stopped.
2 There was bl.......d on the knife.
3 st.......nd over there.
4 I hurt my h.......nd.
5 k.......d you give me a lift?
6 Do you want b.......t....... on your bread?
7 She sl.......pt on the ice.
8 The t.......st was difficult.
9 Jack's their eldest s.......n.
10 I had to g.......s the answer.
11 Don't worry, I'll pr.......t....... kt you.
12 The car didn't st.......p.

3 Long vowels /ɑː/ /ɜː/ /iː/ /ɔː/ /uː/

Underline *all* the vowel sounds that can be put into the gaps to make correct words.

EXAMPLE r.......d iː / ɜː / ɔː (riːd = read; rɔːd = roared)

1 h.......m iː / ɑː / ɜː
2 b.......t iː / uː / ɔː
3 p.......s ɜː / iː / uː
4 f.......d ɑː / uː / ɔː
5 t.......k ɔː / ɑː / uː
6 w.......m ɑː / iː / ɔː
7 h.......t ɑː / ɜː / uː
8 t.......n ɜː / ɔː / uː
9 k.......n iː / ɑː / ɜː
10 p.......t ɔː / uː /ɑː
11 k.......l uː / ɜː /ɔː
12 h.......b ɜː / ɑː / iː

4 Long vowels /ɑː/ /ɜː/ /iː/ /ɔː/ /uː/

Complete the middle of each word square with one of the long vowels, to make two correct words.

EXAMPLE

	w	
m	iː	t
	k	

Makes → meet/ meat; ↓ weak/ week

1

	d	
g		l
	t	

3

	n	
t		l
	n	

5

	h	
v		b
	t	

7

	k	
w		n
	t	

9

	r	
h		m
	d	

2

	f	
v		z
	m	

4

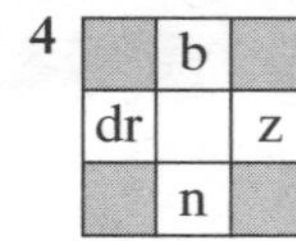

	b	
dr		z
	n	

6

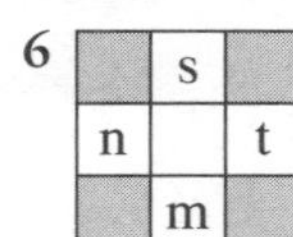

	s	
n		t
	m	

8

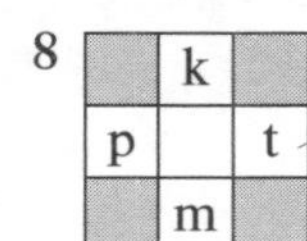

	k	
p		t
	m	

10

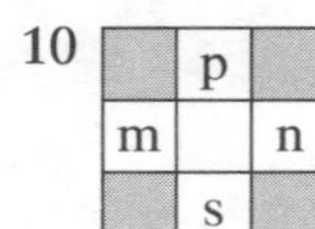

	p	
m		n
	s	

5 Short and long vowels

Underline the correct phonemic spelling of these words.

EXAMPLE deep /diːp/ – /dɪp/

1 pin /pen/ – /pɪn/
2 had /hɪd/ – /hæd/
3 send /send/ – /sænd/
4 golf /gʌlf/ – /gɒlf/
5 took /tʊk/ – /tʌk/
6 pot /pɒt/ – /pʊt/
7 part /pæt/ – /pɑːt/
8 farm /fɜːm/ – /fɑːm/
9 full /fuːl/ – /fʊl/
10 hurt /hɜːt/ – /hʊt/
11 order /ɒdə/ – /ɔːdə/
12 walked /wɔːkt/ – /wɜːkt/
13 fur /fɑː/ – /fɜː/
14 who /hiː/ – /huː/

Check your answers.
Do you know what word the *other* phonemic spelling represents in each case?

EXAMPLE /dɪp/ = dip

6 Short and long vowels

Underline the word represented by the phonemic spelling.

EXAMPLE /stɔː/ star – store

1 /spɔːt/ sport – spot
2 /kʌt/ cut – cot
3 /tiː/ tea – tow
4 /fɪt/ fat – fit
5 /hɜːt/ hut – hurt
6 /hɪt/ hit – heat
7 /bʊks/ books – box
8 /hɑːd/ heard – hard
9 /mæn/ man – men
10 /rest/ wrist – rest
11 /bɜːd/ bird – bored
12 /puːl/ pull – pool
13 /lʌk/ look – luck
14 /hɑːt/ heart – hat

Check your answers.
Can you write out the phonemic spelling of the *other* word in each case?

EXAMPLE star = /stɑː/

7 Diphthongs

Put these words into the correct square in the table. Some squares will be empty.
~~sigh~~, ~~ray~~, ~~fear~~, row (= move through water), pie, bow (= weapon), may, hoe, boy, day, hair, rare, pier, foe, hay, die, bear, tie, sow (= female pig), how, dear, tour, tear (= water from the eye), pear, mere, bow (= bend), pay, my, poor, gear, beer, say, buy, fair, rear, toy, high, tear (= pull apart), go, dare, bay, guy, soy, dough, sow (= to plant seeds), here, gay, mare, toe, row (= argument), rye, mow

	eə	ɪə	aɪ	eɪ	ɔɪ	əʊ	aʊ	ʊə
b								
d								
f		fear						
g								
h								
m								
p								
r				ray				
s			sigh					
t								

Phonemic symbols for consonants

8 Write one of the two phonemic symbols in the space to complete the word.

EXAMPLE thanks θ æŋks ʒ / θ

1 feather	ˈfe.......ə	θ / ð
2 special	ˈspe.......ᵊl	ʃ / dʒ
3 hunger	ˈhʌ.......gə	dʒ / ŋ
4 injury	ˈɪn.......ᵊri	dʒ / j
5 beach	biː.......	tʃ / dʒ
6 drink	drɪ.......k	ʒ / ŋ
7 cash	kæ.......	j / ʃ
8 seizure	ˈsiː.......ə	ʒ / ð
9 bath	bɑː.......	θ / ð
10 yes	.......es	ʃ / j
11 there	.......eə	θ / ð
12 treasure	ˈtre.......ə	ʒ / dʒ
13 sing	sɪ.......	ŋ / n
14 dangerous	ˈdeɪn.......ᵊrəs	dʒ / ð
15 feature	ˈfiː.......ə	ʃ / tʃ
16 dictionary	ˈdɪk.......ᵊnᵊri	ʒ / ʃ
17 although	ɔːlˈ.......əʊ	ð / ʒ
18 yellow	ˈ.......eləʊ	j / dʒ
19 author	ˈɔː.......ə	tʃ / θ
20 young	.......ʌŋ	ʒ / j
21 usual	ˈjuː.......ᵊl	ʃ / ʒ
22 soldier	ˈsəʊl.......ə	dʒ / ʒ

9 Underline the correct phonemic spelling to complete the sentence.

EXAMPLE I don't like it mʌtʃ / mʌʃ.

1 He works at the ˌdʒuːnɪˈvɜːsəti / ˌjuːnɪˈvɜːsəti.
2 Are these shoes made of ˈleθə / ˈleðə?
3 He was involved in a car kræʃ / kræʒ.
4 She's a really good ˈsɪndʒə / ˈsɪŋə.
5 He's the one wearing ʒiːnz / dʒiːnz.
6 Don't wake her, she's ˈsliːpɪŋ / ˈsliːpɪn.
7 What do you θɪŋk / ðɪŋk of it?
8 It's even too hot in the ʃeɪd / dʒeɪd.
9 You'll need a longer ruler to ˈmeʃə / ˈmeʒə them.
10 After a while I got ʒuːst / juːst to it.
11 I can't riːtʃ / riːdʒ it.
12 It's a small town in the ˌsaʊθˈiːst / ˌsaʊtʃˈiːst.
13 What's on ˈtelɪvɪdʒᵊn / ˈtelɪvɪʒᵊn?
14 Have you met my ˈbrʌθə / ˈbrʌðə?

Vowels and consonants

10 Find phonemic spellings for seventeen different animals in the wordsearch. The words are horizontal → or vertical ↓. Use all the letters.

e	l	ɪ	f	ə	n	t	r
d	l	f	tʃ	m	ʃ	g	æ
ɪə	aɪ	ɒ	iː	ʌ	iː	əʊ	b
h	ə	k	t	ŋ	p	t	ɪ
ɔː	n	s	ə	k	t	w	t
s	k	æ	t	i	ɜː	ʊ	d
t	aɪ	g	ə	b	t	l	ɒ
s	n	eɪ	k	eə	l	f	g

11 Match each country with its capital city.

Country	Capital city
1 'tʃaɪnə	a 'lɪzbən
2 æl'dʒɪəriə	b ˌsænti'ɑːgəʊ
3 'pəʊlənd	c ˌkwɑːlə'lʊmpʊə[r]
4 'swiːd[ə]n	d æl'dʒɪəz
5 'tʃɪli	e lɪ'lɒŋweɪ
6 mə'leɪziə	f 'wɔːsɔː
7 'pɔːtʃəg[ə]l	g beɪ'dʒɪŋ
8 'swɪts[ə]lənd	h bɜːn
9 æl'beɪniə	i tɪ'rɑːnə
10 mə'lɑːwi	j 'stɒkhəʊm

E2 Consonant clusters: Further practice

Consonant clusters at the beginning of words

1 E2 /bl-/, /br-/ and /b-/

browse – blouse	brink – blink
blue – brew	bland – brand
breeze – bees	broad – bored
blank – bank	blend – bend

Listen and repeat the words in the box.

Listen. The speaker will say two words from the box.
If you hear the same word twice, write S (same).
If you hear two different words, write D (different).

1 .... 2 .... 3 .... 4 .... 5 .... 6 .... 7 .... 8 ....

Listen. Underline the word you hear.

9 The cat's *black/back*.
10 a new *bloom/ broom*
11 She looked at her untidy hair and *blushed/brushed*.
12 Have you made the *bread/bed* yet?
13 a terrible *blow/bow*
14 I *brought/bought* it from town.

2 E3 /pl-/, /pr-/ and /p-/

proud – ploughed	please – peas
plank – prank	preach – peach
pretty – pity	plane – pain
plod – prod	praise – plays

Listen and repeat the words in the box.

Listen. The speaker will say two words from the box.
If you hear the same word twice, write S (same).
If you hear two different words, write D (different).

1 .... 2 .... 3 .... 4 .... 5 .... 6 .... 7 .... 8 ....

Listen. Underline the word you hear.

9 I didn't know what the *plan/pan* was for.
10 a small *plot/pot*
11 There were only two *prawns/pawns* left.
12 the first *pies/prize*
13 She wanted to *play/pray*.
14 All the children were *present/pleasant*.

3 E4 /kl-/, /kr-/ and /k-/

cloud – crowd	clash – cash
clown – crown	came – claim
croak – cloak	crane – cane
clutch – crutch	cost – crossed

Listen and repeat the words in the box.

Listen. The speaker will say two words from the box.
If you hear the same word twice, write S (same).
If you hear two different words, write D (different).

1 .... 2 .... 3 .... 4 .... 5 .... 6 .... 7 .... 8 ....

Listen. Underline the word you hear.

9 I think he's a *crook/cook*.
10 the main *clause/cause*
11 The captain didn't have a *crew/clue*.
12 The *climb/crime* was terrible.
13 They're very *clean/keen*.
14 They're really *cool/cruel*.

4 E5 /gl-/, /gr-/ and /g-/

great – gate	gave – grave
green – glean	gory – glory
grammar – glamour	glide – guide
glade – grade	gloom – groom

Listen and repeat the words in the box.

Listen. The speaker will say two words from the box.
If you hear the same word twice, write S (same).
If you hear two different words, write D (different).

1 .... 2 .... 3 .... 4 .... 5 .... 6 .... 7 .... 8 ....

Listen. Underline the word you hear.

9 The cows were all *grazing/gazing* over by the lake.
10 We *grew/glue* them together.
11 I hurt myself while I was cutting the *glass/grass*.
12 She *gasped/grasped* at it.
13 It just stopped *going/growing*.
14 Her cheeks started to *go/glow* red.

5 E6 /fl-/, /fr-/ and /f-/

frog – fog	fraud – ford
flagrant – fragrant	flee – free
flame – frame	four – floor
fee – flee	fresh – flesh

Listen and repeat the words in the box.

Listen. The speaker will say two words from the box.
If you hear the same word twice, write S (same).
If you hear two different words, write D (different).

1 .... 2 .... 3 .... 4 .... 5 .... 6 .... 7 .... 8 ....

Listen. Underline the word you hear.

9 It's *flatter/fatter* in the middle.
10 He stood there with the *fruit/flute* in his hand.
11 It *froze/flows* through the north of the country.
12 I *flavour/favour* plain food.
13 Have you tried *flying/frying* it?
14 a terrible *flight/fright*

6 E7 /tr-/and /t-/; /dr-/and /d-/

drip – dip	down – drown
tied – tried	truth – tooth
drain – train	tread – dread
dug – drug	tea – tree

Listen and repeat the words in the box.

Listen. The speaker will say two words from the box.
If you hear the same word twice, write S (same).
If you hear two different words, write D (different).

1 .... 2 .... 3 .... 4 .... 5 .... 6 .... 7 .... 8 ....

Listen. Underline the word you hear.

9 It can't be *two/true*.
10 I thought it was a *tap/trap*.
11 She's taking *diving/driving* lessons.
12 The *door/drawer* was open.
13 Why don't you *dry/try* it?
14 It *died/dried* during the night.

Consonant clusters at the end of words

7 E8 Final clusters starting with /-m-/ and /-n-/ (/-mp/, /-nd/, etc.)

pitch – pinch	concerned – concern
warmth – warm	bet – bent
thumb – thump	arm – armed
bomb – bombs	fringe – fridge

Listen and repeat the words in the box.

Listen. The speaker will say two words from the box.
If you hear the same word twice, write S (same).
If you hear two different words, write D (different).

1 .... 2 .... 3 .... 4 .... 5 .... 6 .... 7 .... 8 ....

Listen. Underline the word you hear.

9 I *blame/blamed* it on the cold weather.
10 We had to *change/chain* it.
11 The police weren't able to *fine/find* her.
12 The *rooms/room* can be booked in advance.
13 a company that makes *trays/trains*
14 We could see the *flames/flame* in the window.

8 E9 Final clusters starting with /-l-/ (/-lk/, /-lf/, etc.)

well – wealth	gull – gulf
cold – coal	kiln – kill
wool – wolf	hole – hold
built – build	sale – sales

Listen and repeat the words in the box.

Listen. The speaker will say two words from the box.
If you hear the same word twice, write S (same).
If you hear two different words, write D (different).

1 .... 2 .... 3 .... 4 .... 5 .... 6 .... 7 .... 8 ....

Listen. Underline the word you hear.

9 She suddenly *fell/felt* ill.
10 The use of smokeless *fuels/fuel* is compulsory.
11 We *call/called* our cat 'Sparky'.
12 We *help/held* them out.
13 I decided to *fill/film* it.
14 I dropped a *shelf/shell* on the floor.

9 E10 Final clusters ending with /-t/ (/-pt/, /-kt/ etc.)

left – let	eat – east
felt – fell	pain – paint
past – pass	fact – fat
hunt – hut	pack – packed

Listen and repeat the words in the box.

Listen. The speaker will say two words from the box.
If you hear the same word twice, write S (same).
If you hear two different words, write D (different).

1 .... 2 .... 3 .... 4 .... 5 .... 6 .... 7 .... 8 ....

Listen. Underline the word you hear.

9 just a *guest/guess*
10 He *bit/built* it.
11 I was sure I saw a *ghost/goat* in the house.
12 She was carrying a *bell/belt* in her hand.
13 We *meant/met* to discuss it.
14 when they *abolished/abolish* hunting

10 E11 Final clusters ending with /-d/ (/-md/, /-zd/, etc.)

phone – phoned	goal – gold
bombed – bond	devised – divide
harmed – hard	raced – raised
lend – led	bed – begged

Listen and repeat the words in the box.

Listen. The speaker will say two words from the box.
If you hear the same word twice, write S (same).
If you hear two different words, write D (different).

1 .... 2 .... 3 .... 4 .... 5 .... 6 .... 7 .... 8 ....

Listen. Underline the word you hear.

9 The *wind/win* was unexpected.
10 I eventually *sold/sewed* it.
11 His last film was surprisingly *bad/banned*.
12 We've *tied/timed* it better this time.
13 It was very *wild/wide*.
14 They *describe/described* it as their second home.

11 E12 Final clusters ending with /-s/ (/-ps/, /-ks/, etc.)

gaps – gas	licks – lips
base – bakes	cakes – case
once – won	clips – clicks
cats – caps	checks – chess

Listen and repeat the words in the box.

Listen. The speaker will say two words from the box.
If you hear the same word twice, write S (same).
If you hear two different words, write D (different).

1 .... 2 .... 3 .... 4 .... 5 .... 6 .... 7 .... 8 ....

Listen. Underline the word you hear.

9 He drew some *graphs/grass* on the board.
10 a quick *glass/glance*
11 They couldn't explain the *deaths/debts*.
12 She said she was *six/sick*.
13 covered in *moss/moths*
14 I went to buy some *maps/mats*.

12 E13 Final clusters ending with /-z/ (/-vz/, /-nz/, etc.)

lives – lies	youths – use
raise – rains	stars – starves
bags – bangs	size – sides
rise – rides	calls – cause

Listen and repeat the words in the box.

Listen. The speaker will say two words from the box.
If you hear the same word twice, write S (same).
If you hear two different words, write D (different).

1 .... 2 .... 3 .... 4 .... 5 .... 6 .... 7 .... 8 ....

Listen. Underline the word you hear.

9 Her *cries/crimes* were ignored.
10 The bright red *robes/rose* lay on the floor.
11 The *lawns/laws* were added later.
12 She *says/sells* a lot, doesn't she?
13 All the black *cards/cars* were to the left.
14 The *size/signs* looked good.

E3 Word stress: Further practice

This section gives further practice of suffixes covered in Units 11 and 12.

1 The suffixes *-able*, *-age* and *-al*

Write the following words in the table according to their stress pattern:

~~advisable~~ arrival assemblage changeable desirable emotional
enjoyable functional original patronage percentage pilgrimage

Ooo	oOo	oOoo
		advisable

Now listen, check your answers and repeat the words after the recording.

Most words with the suffixes *-able*, *-age*, and *-al* have stress on the same syllable as their root word. However, there are exceptions. Can you find the one exception in the words you have written in the table?

See **Word stress 7** for words ending *-ial.*

2 The suffixes *-ful*, *-less* and *-ness*

Write the following words in the table according to their stress pattern:

~~abrasiveness~~ alertness assertiveness awkwardness characterless colourless
deviousness directionless disgraceful eventful powerful regardless

Ooo	oOo	Oooo	oOoo
			abrasiveness

Now listen, check your answers and repeat the words after the recording.

Words with the suffixes *-ful*, *-less*, and *-ness* have stress on the same syllable as their root word.

3 The suffixes *-ous*, *-fy* and *-er*

Write the following words in the table according to their stress pattern:

~~announcer~~ anomalous beautify beginner borrower calamitous
dangerous diversify intensify marvellous simplify solidify

Ooo	oOo	oOoo
	announcer	

Now listen, check your answers and repeat the words after the recording.

Words with the suffixes *-ous*, *-fy*, and *-er* usually have stress on the same syllable as their root word. However, there are exceptions. Can you find the one exception in the words you have written in the table?

See **Word stress 4** for words ending *-ious* and **Word stress 5** for words ending *-ulous*, *-orous* and *-eous.*

4 The suffix *-ious*

Write the following words in the table according to their stress pattern:

~~ambitious~~ anxious cautious industrious laborious luxurious
mysterious pretentious rebellious religious spacious suspicious

Oo	oOo	oOoo
	ambitious	

The suffix *-ious* is sometimes said as one syllable (as in the words in the first two columns), and in others it is normally said as two syllables (as in the words in the last column).

Now listen, check your answers and repeat the words after the recording.

In words with the suffix *-ious*, main stress is usually on the syllable before the suffix.

See **Word stress 5** for words ending *-ulous*, *-orous* and *-eous*, and **Word stress 3** for other words ending *-ous*.

5 The suffixes *-ulous*, *-orous* and *-eous*

Write the following words in the table according to their stress pattern:

~~carnivorous~~ courageous glamorous herbivorous humorous incredulous
insectivorous miraculous miscellaneous outrageous simultaneous tremulous

Ooo	oOo	oOoo	ooOoo
		carnivorous	

Now listen, check your answers and repeat the words after the recording.

In words with the suffixes *-ulous*, *-orous*, and *-eous*, main stress is usually on the syllable before the suffix.

See **Word stress 4** for words ending *-ious*, and **Word stress 3** for other words ending *-ous*.

6 The suffixes *-ee*, *-eer*, *-ese* and *-ette*

Write the following words in the table according to their stress pattern:

~~auctioneer~~ Chinese cohabitee detainee divorcee evacuee
examinee interviewee journalese laundrette Taiwanese trainee

oO	ooO	oooO
	auctioneer	

Now listen, check your answers and repeat the words after the recording.

In words with the suffixes *-ee*, *-eer*, *-ese* and *-ette*, main stress is usually on the suffix itself.

7 E20 The suffix *-ial*

Write the following words in the table according to their stress pattern:

~~adverbial~~ ceremonial differential editorial industrial influential
managerial presidential provincial remedial substantial torrential

oOo	ooOo	oOoo	ooOoo
		adverbial	

In some words *-ial* is normally said as one syllable (as in the words in the first two columns), and in others it is normally said as two syllables (as in the words in the last two columns).

Now listen, check your answers and repeat the words after the recording.

In words with the suffix *-ial*, main stress is usually on the syllable immediately before the suffix.

See **Word stress 1** for other words ending *-al*.

8 E21 The suffixes *-ion*, *-ity* and *-ic*

Write the following words in the table according to their stress pattern:

~~abbreviation~~ accusation addiction authenticity characteristic diplomatic
elasticity ethnicity extremity formulaic location musicality

oOo	oOoo	ooOo	ooOoo	oooOo
				abbreviation

Now listen, check your answers and repeat the words after the recording.

In words with the suffixes *-ion*, *-ity* and *-ic*, main stress is on the syllable immediately before the suffix.

9 E22 The suffix *-ive*

Write the following words in the table according to their stress pattern:

~~apprehensive~~ constructive exploitative explosive illustrative impulsive
inconclusive indicative innovative interactive progressive reproductive

Ooo	oOoo	ooOo	Oooo
		apprehensive	

Now listen, check your answers and repeat the words after the recording.

In words with the suffix *-ive*, main stress is usually on the syllable immediately before the suffix. In words ending *-ative*, main stress is usually on the same syllable as the root word. However, there are exceptions. Can you find the one exception in the *-ative* words you have written in the table?

10 The suffixes *-ant*, *-ent*, *-ance*, and *-ence* (1)

Write the following words in the table according to their stress pattern:

~~coherent~~ experience hesitant ignorance inhabitant inheritance magnificent negligence pollutant resident significant tolerant

Ooo	oOo	oOoo
	coherent	

Now listen, check your answers and repeat the words after the recording.

In words with the suffixes *-ant*, *-ent*, *-ance*, and *-ence*, main stress depends on the spelling of the pre-suffix syllable (i.e. the syllable before the suffix). If the pre-suffix syllable ends in a vowel (V) or vowel plus consonant (VC) – as in the words above – stress usually goes on the syllable before the pre-suffix syllable. However, there are exceptions. Can you find two exceptions in the words you have written in the table?

For words with the suffix *-ment*, see **Word Stress 12**.

11 The suffixes *-ant*, *-ent*, *-ance*, and *-ence* (2)

Write the following words in the table according to their stress pattern:

~~appliance~~ compliance correspondent defiant deterrent independence observance obsolescence occurrence resemblance resistant triumphant

oOo	ooOo
appliance	

Now listen, check your answers and repeat the words after the recording.

In words with the suffixes *-ant*, *-ent*, *-ance*, and *-ence*, main stress depends on the spelling of the pre-suffix syllable (i.e. the syllable before the suffix). Stress usually goes on the pre-suffix syllable: (i) if this syllable ends with the letter *i* and the corresponding root word ends with the letter *y* in a stressed syllable; or (ii) if the pre-suffix syllable ends with anything *other* than V or VC (see **Word stress 10**).

For words with the suffix *-ment*, see **Word Stress 12**.

12 The suffix *-ment*

Write the following words in the table according to their stress pattern:

~~accomplishment~~ achievement development disappointment embarrassment entertainment government investment measurement recruitment retirement settlement

Ooo	oOo	oOoo	ooOo
		accomplishment	

Now listen, check your answers and repeat the words after the recording.

In words with the suffix *-ment*, stress is usually on the same syllable as in their root word.

E4 Glossary

auxiliary verb The verbs *be*, *have* and *do* are auxiliary verbs when they are used with a main verb to form questions, negatives, tenses, and passive forms, etc.

cleft sentence A cleft sentence is one in which focus is given to either the subject or object using a pattern beginning 'It…' (e.g. It was my father who gave it to me) or 'What..' (e.g. What I want is a holiday).

compound adjective A compound adjective consists of two or more words together used as an adjective, for example, *well-behaved*.

compound noun A compound noun consists of two or more words together used as a noun, for example, *language school*.

consonant A consonant sound is a sound produced by blocking the air flow from the mouth with the teeth, tongue or lips. A consonant letter is a letter that represents a consonant sound.

consonant cluster A consonant cluster is a sequence of consonant sounds that come together, for example in *spray* /spr/, *jumped* /mpt/, *electric shock* /ktr/ and /kʃ/.

contraction (or contracted form) A contraction is a shortened form of an auxiliary verb written as part of the previous word. For example, *have* is contracted to *ve* in *they've*.

ellipsis / near ellipsis Ellipsis in speech or writing is the omission of words that can be understood from the context. For example, if a speaker says 'Must go', we understand that 'I' is missed out. In speech, a short sound from the omitted word sometimes remains. In this book this is referred to as near ellipsis, for example, in *'s that you?* ('Is that you?').

function word (or grammatical word) / content word A function word expresses a grammatical meaning, for example, *this*, *but*, *on*. Function words can be contrasted with content words, for example, *car*, *blue*, *slowly*.

glottal stop A glottal stop is made by closing the vocal folds. If you cough gently you can feel the vocal folds closing just before you 'release' the cough. The phonetic symbol for a glottal stop is ʔ. In some accents of English a glottal stop replaces a /t/ sound: /fʊʔbɔːl/ for /fʊtbɔːl/ (*football*). (For more details, see Unit 29.)

idiom An idiom is a group of words in a particular order with a meaning that is different from the meanings of each word used on its own.

imperative sentences Imperative sentences do not have a subject and use the bare infinitive form of the verb (without any endings), for example, *Come here*, *Put it over there*.

International Phonetic Alphabet (IPA) The IPA is the most widely used set of symbols for showing the sounds of a language. The IPA is used in this book, *Cambridge Advanced Learner's Dictionary (CALD)* and *Cambridge English Pronouncing Dictionary (CEPD)*.

main stress (or primary stress) In a word with more than one syllable, the syllable with main stress stands out more than any other. In most dictionaries the symbol ' is placed before the syllable with main stress, for example, /'hʌndrəd/ (or 'hundred), /pə'hæps/ (or per'haps). (Compare secondary stress.)

one-stress word / two-stress word   A one-stress word has one stressed syllable (e.g /kəm'pliːt/ *complete*). A two-stress word has one syllable with main stress and another with secondary stress (e.g. /ˌdɪsə'griː/ *disagree*).

one-stress phrasal verb / two-stress phrasal verb   A one-stress phrasal verb has only one stressed syllable, in the verb, for example, *'fall for* (= to fall in love with someone). A two-stress phrasal verb has secondary stress in the verb and main stress in the particle, for example, *ˌfall 'in* (= collapse).

particle   (See phrasal verb.)

phonemic symbol   A phonemic symbol is a character that represents a sound. A list of phonemic symbols is given on page 192.

phrasal verb   A phrasal verb is a verb together with one or two following particles (a preposition or an adverb) that has a single meaning. A two-word phrasal verb (e.g. *care for*) has a verb and one particle and a three-word phrasal verb (e.g. *look up to*) has a verb and two particles.

pitch   Pitch is the level of the voice. It can be compared with notes played on a musical instrument: a high pitch corresponds to high notes and a low pitch corresponds to low notes.

prefix   A prefix is a letter or group of letters added to the beginning of a word to make a new word. Examples include *dis-*, *co-*, *super-*.

prominent   A prominent word stands out from other words around it. Prominent words are shown in capital letters and non-prominent words in lower case letters. For example, in the phrase // one of my FRIENDS//, *friends* is prominent and the other words non-prominent. If a word has more than one syllable, it is only necessary to make one syllable prominent (the prominent syllable) in order to make the whole word stand out. For example, in // it's your responsiBILity//, -BIL- is the prominent syllable and *responsibility* the prominent word.

question tag   Question tags are short phrases such as *isn't it*, *aren't they*, *do you*, *are we* added at the end of a sentence to check information, ask if someone agrees, etc.

reflexive pronoun   The reflexive pronouns are the words *myself*, *yourself*, *himself*, *herself*, *itself*, *ourselves*, *yourselves*, and *themselves*.

root   The root is the form of a word when all the prefixes and suffixes are taken away. For example, the root of the word *disagreement* is *agree*.

secondary stress   In some words with more than one syllable, a syllable with secondary stress stands out less than the syllable with main stress, but more than the remaining syllables. In most dictionaries the symbol ˌ is placed before the secondary stressed syllable, for example, /ˌaʊt'stændɪŋ/ (or ˌout'standing), /'hæmˌbɜːgəʳ/ (or 'hamˌburger).

speech unit (or tone unit)   When we speak we divide what we say into speech units. Words within speech units are usually run together without pauses, although there is often a pause between speech units. In each speech unit there is one main tone. Speech unit boundaries are indicated by //.

step-down   A step-down happens when the voice moves down to a noticeably lower pitch than it was at before. In this book, the symbol ■ is used to show a step-down.

step-up A step-up happens when the voice moves up to a noticeably higher pitch than it was at before. In this book, the symbol ⬛ is used to show a step-up.

stress In a word with more than one syllable, syllables that stand out more than others are stressed. (See also main stress and secondary stress.) An unstressed syllable is one that does not stand out.

stress shift When a word which has main stress and secondary stress is used in conversation, the syllable with main stress is usually made prominent. However, if this word is followed by another prominent word, particularly if it begins with a prominent syllable, prominence may move to an earlier syllable with secondary stress. This change is called stress shift. It happens because the rhythm of English prefers prominent syllables to be separated by non-prominent syllables where possible. In *CEPD*, words which commonly have stress shift are shown with an example: /ˌsekəndˈhænd/ *stress shift*: ˌsecondhand ˈbooks.

strong form / weak form Some function words have two pronunciations: a strong form and a weak form. For example, *but* can be pronounced /bʌt/ (strong form) or /bət/ (weak form). The weak form is the usual pronunciation of these words.

suffix A suffix is a letter or group of letters added to the end of a word to make a new word. Examples include *-ive*, *-ment*, *-eer*.

syllable A syllable is a word or part of a word that contains a vowel. (For an exception, see syllabic consonant.) The vowel may have consonants before or after it. For example, the word *abolish* has three syllables: *a-* /ə/, *-bol-* /bɒl/, *-ish* /ɪʃ/.

syllabic consonant A syllabic consonant is a consonant (mainly /l/ or /n/) that is pronounced as a syllable. For example, there are syllabic consonants at the end of the words *bottle* and *happen*. Dictionaries show syllabic consonants either with a ˌ symbol under the consonant (bottle - /bɒtl̩/) or use the symbol ə to show that the vowel before the syllabic consonant can be left out (happen - /hæpən/).

tail A tail is a word or short phrase added to the end of a sentence to emphasise or make clearer what we have just said, for example: It's a nice town, *Buxton*; It's really expensive, *that is*.

tone In each speech unit there is one main movement of the voice up or down, starting on the last prominent word of the speech unit. English has four main tones: falling tone ⬛, rising tone ⬛, fall-rising tone ⬛, and rise-falling tone ⬛. In addition, there may be little or no movement of the voice in the speech unit, and we refer to this as level tone ⬛.

vowel A vowel sound is a sound produced without blocking the air flow from the mouth with our teeth, tongue or lips. A vowel letter is a letter that represents a vowel sound.

E5 Further reading

Reference works

For a detailed work on the pronunciation of British English:

Cruttenden, A. (ed.) (2001) *Gimson's Pronunciation of English*, 6th edn. London: Hodder Arnold.

For more on English phonetics and phonology:

Roach, P. (2000) *English Phonetics and Phonology: A Practical Course*, 3rd edn. Cambridge: Cambridge University Press.

For a dictionary of pronunciation:

Jones, D. (2006) *Cambridge English Pronouncing Dictionary*, 17th edn. Edited by P. Roach, J. Setter and J. Hartman. Cambridge: Cambridge University Press.

For more on the pronunciation of national and regional varieties of English:

Gramley, S. and Pätzold, K.-M. (2004) *A Survey of Modern English*, 2nd edn. London: Routledge.

For more on differences between North American and British English pronunciation:

Celce-Murcia, M., Brinton, D. M. and Goodwin, J. M. (1996) *Teaching Pronunciation: A Reference for Teachers of English to Speakers of Other Languages*. Cambridge: Cambridge University Press. (See in particular Appendix 1.)

For more on the pronunciation of English as an 'international' language (see Unit 2):

Jenkins, J. (2000) *The Phonology of English as an International Language: New Models, New Norms, New Goals*. Oxford: Oxford University Press.

For more on 'tails' (see Unit 40):

Carter, R. and McCarthy, M. (1997) *Exploring Spoken English*. Cambridge: Cambridge University Press.

For more on phrasal verbs (see Units 19 and 20):

Cambridge Phrasal Verbs Dictionary (2006) 2nd edn. Cambridge: Cambridge University Press.

For information on the pronunciation problems of particular first language speakers:

Swan, M. and Smith, B. (eds.) (2001) *Learner English: A Teacher's Guide to Interference and Other Problems*, 2nd edn. Cambridge: Cambridge University Press.

Material for further practice

Bradford, B. (1998) *Intonation in Context: Intonation Practice for Upper-Intermediate and Advanced Learners of English*. Cambridge: Cambridge University Press.

Brazil, D. (1994) *Pronunciation for Advanced Learners of English*. Cambridge: Cambridge University Press.

Cauldwell, R. (2002) *Streaming Speech: Listening and Pronunciation for Advanced Learners of English*. (British/ Irish version). Birmingham: Speechinaction. (American/ Canadian version, 2005).

Cauldwell, R (2005) *Listening to Accents of the British Isles*. Birmingham: Speechinaction.

Gilbert, J. (2004) *Clear Speech*, 3rd edn. Cambridge: Cambridge University Press. (North American English)

Hahn, L. D. and Dickerson, W. B. (1999) *Speechcraft: Discourse Pronunciation for Advanced Learners*. Ann Arbor: The University of Michigan Press. (North American English)

Vaughan-Rees, M. (2002) *Test Your Pronunciation*. Harlow: Pearson.

Other books in the *English Pronunciation in Use* series

Hancock, M. (2003) *English Pronunciation in Use Intermediate*. Cambridge: Cambridge University Press.

Marks, J. (2007) *English Pronunciation in Use Elementary*. Cambridge: Cambridge University Press.

Key

On the recording you will mostly hear speakers of BBC English (see page 10). Where other speakers are recorded, the country or region of Britain they come from is noted.

Unit 1

1.1 **Speaker 1**
I don't get a lot of time to myself these days, but if I have a couple of hours to spare then I go down to the tennis club. I've just joined a tennis club near me and we've moved to a new house and er the tennis courts are right outside the back of my garden, so I just literally walk down and go through the gate and spend a couple of hours knocking balls about.

Speaker 2 (United States)
When I've got some free time um I like to read. Usually I avoid the latest fiction and look for novels or novelists that I've always known about and wanted to read. But occasionally I just stroll through a bookshop and sometimes it's just the cover of a book that makes me grab it and take it home.

Speaker 3 (Canada)
When I've got spare time I like to go to the lake. It's about a twenty minute drive and when I get there I go water skiing. I just love water skiing when the weather's good. And afterward if I've got enough energy, I pick Saskatoon berries on the lane behind the cabin. And later on in the week I make some pies.

Speaker 4 (Australia)
My favourite thing to do on a sunny day is to go to the beach. It takes about an hour from my house. I have to get the train and a bus, but it's worth it. Lots of my friends live near the beach, so it's always the perfect way to catch up and enjoy the sunshine.

Speaker 5 (South Africa)
One of my favourite things to do when I've got a bit of spare time is to go fishing with my friends. Er we get a bit of tackle together, the fishing rods, pile it all into the back of a four-by-four and we head up into the mountains. There's some wonderful streams up there, well stocked with trout, and carp, and bream. We normally take a bit of a picnic up, you know, some bread rolls, and some ham and cheese, and it's just a nice day out.

1.2 Here are some of the things you might have noticed:

	British (Br) *vs* American (US)
magazine	The stress is different: on the 3rd syllable (maga'zine) in Br and on the 1st syllable ('magazine) in US.
common	The first vowel is different: /ɒ/ (as in 'hot') in Br and /ɑː/ (as in 'car') in US.
research	The stress is different: on the 2nd syllable (re'search) in Br and on the 1st syllable ('research) in US.
over	There is a sound close to /r/ at the end of the word in US, but in Br it ends with a vowel.
forty	The 't' is 'flapped' in US so that it sounds like 'd'.
overweight	(See 'over' above.)
survey	There is a sound close to /r/ before /v/ in US, but not in Br.
walk	The vowel is different: /ɔː/ (as in 'door') in Br and /ɑː/ (as in 'car') in US.
better	The 't' is 'flapped' in US so that it sounds like 'd'.
leisure	The first vowel is different: /e/ (as in 'ten') in Br and /iː/ (as in 'see') in US.
understandable	There is a sound close to /r/ before '-stand-' in US, but not in Br.
exercise	There is a sound close to /r/ before '-cise' in US, but not in Br.
schedule	The first consonant is different: /ʃ/ (as in 'she') in Br and /sk/ in US. (Although note that some speakers of Br say /sk/ at the beginning of 'schedule'.)

1.3 **1 (northern England)**

When I get a day off, I like to go up into the Yorkshire Dales. These are sort of hills, er about twenty miles from where I live. And I'll er walk through the day. I'll set off while it's still dark and walk for about eight hours. And at the end of that finish up in a village somewhere and have a nice meal.

Here are some of the differences you may have noticed between this accent and BBC English:

- the vowel in 'I', 'like', 'nice' (/aɪ/ in BBC English) is more 'open', beginning with a sound close to /ɑː/ (as in 'car')
- the vowel in 'walk' (/ɔː/ in BBC English) is said almost as two vowels /ɔː/ + /ə/
- the 'r' sound in 'fo<u>r</u> about' is said with a slight tap of the tongue behind the top teeth

2 (Scotland)

I live in the country and I'm I'm quite lucky because where I live is sort of on the top of um a range of low, flat hills. So it's quite windy. On good days, I like to take my children out and we go and fly kites. The children have got little kites, because obviously if it's too windy and with a big kite it would be really too, too much for them, they couldn't control it. Um but they they thoroughly enjoy being out just just in the fresh air.

Here are some of the differences you may have noticed between this accent and BBC English:

- 'r' is pronounced where it would not be in BBC English (in 'sort', 'for then', 'air') and said with a flap of the tongue
- the vowel in 'like', 'fly', 'kite', etc. (/aɪ/ in BBC English) begins with a sound close to 'ee' (/iː/)
- the vowel in 'low', 'so', 'go' (/əʊ/ in BBC English) is pronounced more like a simple vowel, close to /ɔː/

3 (Wales)

In my spare time I really like visiting gardens. Usually, the gardens of big houses. And at every time of the year there's something different to see. The spring, of course, is the best time, when everything's coming into bud, and then later in the summer into full flower. It's really wonderful. And even when it's raining, you can still get great pleasure visiting gardens.

Here are some of the differences you may have noticed between this accent and BBC English:

- the vowel in 'year' (/ɪə/ in BBC English) is pronounced with more rounded lips
- the vowel in 'gardens' (/ɑː/ in BBC English) is more 'open', beginning with a sound close to /æ/ (as in 'cat')
- the /r/ in 'raining' and 'really' is said with a flap of the tongue

4 (Northern Ireland)

Usually, 'cause erm I'm working during the week er and sometimes on a Saturday as well the only day off that I have would be a Sunday. Er and on Sunday we like to get up early, make a big breakfast and if the weather's good er I take my kids for a long walk in the country. Erm we go off er with our little fishing rods and sometimes er go down to the local stream and with a net and try and er catch a few tiddlers or something like that.

(Note: A tiddler is a very small fish.)

Here are some of the differences you may have noticed between this accent and BBC English:

- the vowel in '<u>u</u>sually' and 'd<u>u</u>ring' (/uː/ in BBC English) is pronounced rather like the vowel in 'good' (/ʊ/)
- the vowel in 'off' (/ɒ/ in BBC English) is pronounced with more rounded lips
- the vowel in 'stream' (/iː/ in BBC English) is pronounced almost as two vowels /iː/ + /ə/

Unit 2

2.1 Speaker 1 is from Spain. Speaker 2 is from India. Speaker 3 is from China.
Speaker 4 is from Poland. Speaker 5 is from Japan.

Speaker 1 (Spain)
I have one brother and one sister. My brother is thirty years old. Er he's married. He has two children er three and five. He works as a teacher in a local school. My sister is twenty-five and she's just finished her degree and she has decided to go round the world travelling, so that was a bit of a shock for my parents.

Speaker 2 (India)
I have er only one sister. She is older than me and er she is getting married, actually, next year, which is very exciting for all of us. And we are very busy preparing for the wedding. Erm but I am married myself all two years now. Er I had a lovely wedding and it is my anniversary next week.

Speaker 3 (China)
There are four people in my family, my parents and my brother and me. My brother is two years younger than me, and he's married with a kid. And my father, er both my parents are retired now, but my father is still going to senior citizen university, where he's doing photography, whereas my mum is interested in cooking.

Speaker 4 (Poland)
I have one brother, he's two years older than I am. He's a dentist. He's married and he has two kids. Erm they are aged twenty and eighteen. The older one is already at the university. He studies archaeology, and er the younger one er is going to take his 'A' levels very soon.

Speaker 5 (Japan)
I am er thirty-two years old and I have a sister um who is twenty-eight. And I have older brother, er thirty-four. And my sister is now married and lives in America, and my brother is a lawyer. And erm I am married er myself and erm my wife er is from Germany. And er we're living happily together.

2.2

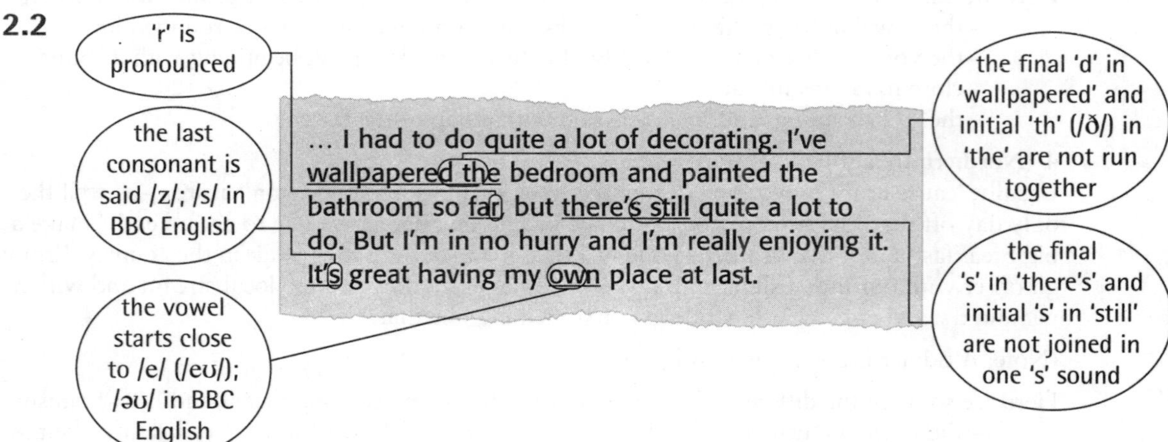

Full transcription:
I've had to buy some really expensive things for the kitchen – a fridge, a dishwasher and a cooker. I already had cutlery and cups and saucers, and my brother gave me some new plates and bowls. I had to get quite a lot of furniture, too. I didn't need a new bed, but I bought a nice old wooden table and some chairs for the sitting room. I had to do quite a lot of decorating. I've wallpapered the bedroom and painted the bathroom so far, but there's still quite a lot to do. But I'm in no hurry and I'm really enjoying it. It's great having my own place at last.

Unit 3

3.1

1 a=ii; b=i	4 a=ii; b=i	7 a=i; b=ii	10 a=i; b=ii	13 a=i; b=ii	16 a=ii; b=i
2 a=i; b=ii	5 a=i; b=ii	8 a=i; b=ii	11 a=ii; b=i	14 a=i; b=ii	17 a=ii; b=i
3 a=ii; b=i	6 a=ii; b=i	9 a=ii; b=i	12 a=i; b=ii	15 a=i; b=ii	18 a=ii; b=i

3.2

1 tortuous
2 methylated spirits
3 flabbergasted
4 symbiosis
5 subterranean
6 decompression chamber
7 pistachio
8 glitterati
9 debutante
10 repetitive strain injury
11 rotisserie
12 idiolect

Follow-up
Beauchamp /ˈbiːtʃəm/
McFadzean /məkˈfædiən/
Mousehole /ˈmaʊzᵊl/ (Note that ᵊ means that the vowel /ə/ might be left out.)
Towcester /ˈtəʊstəʳ/ (Note that ʳ means that a /r/ sound may be added if the next word begins with a vowel.)
isogloss /ˈaɪsəʊglɒs/ (isogloss is a line on a map giving information about dialects)
ozokerite /əʊˈzəʊkᵊrɪt/ (ozokerite is a mineral. Note that ᵊ means that the vowel /ə/ might be left out.)

Unit 4

4.3 These words have the same pronunciation in British and American English:
belligerent (/bəˈlɪdʒᵊrənt/), continuum (/kənˈtɪnjuəm/), precinct (/ˈpriːsɪŋkt/), sepia (/ˈsiːpiə/).

These words have different pronunciations in British and American English:
charade (/ʃəˈrɑːd/ (Br); /ʃəˈreɪd/ (US)), felafel (/fəˈlæfᵊl/ (Br); /fəˈlɑːfᵊl/ (US)), vitamin (/ˈvɪtəmɪn/ (Br); /ˈvaɪtəmɪn/ (US)), wrath (/rɒθ/ (Br); /rɑːθ/ (US)).

Follow up
Here are some example search results:
Key search words 'pronunciation guide stars':
http://www.earthsky.org/skywatching/pronunciation.php (North American pronunciation)
Key search words 'pronunciation guide fashion':
http://fashion.about.com/cs/designers/l/blpronounce.htm
Key search words 'pronunciation guide geography':
http://www.brookscole.com/earthscience_d/templates/student_resources/0030339669_salter/geo2_pronunciation/geoApp2.html# (North American pronunciation)

Unit 5

5.1 Slow speech is more likely in situations 1, 3 and 4.

5.2
(Australia) 1 I didn't know whether they were leaving or not.
(South Africa) 2 She said she'd never seen anything like it before.
3 They don't seem to be getting on too well.
(Australia) 4 As long as you don't mind us coming in late.
(South Africa) 5 We should be able to get there in a couple of hours.

5.3 (Speaker C = Canada)
A: So why did you go for Jensens// to supply the machines//
B: Well// at the time// I thought they were the best available//
C: And we've done business with them before//
A: But that was years ago//
B: Yes// but the management hasn't changed at all//
C: And they've still got a pretty good reputation//
A: But you now feel// that the product isn't up to scratch//
B: No// they've been pretty poor// to be honest//
A: So you think// we ought to be looking for a different supplier//
B: Yes// I do// And for compensation from Jensens//
C: Shall I contact the lawyers about it//
A: Yes, please// We'll leave that to you//

5.4
1 // but that was <u>years</u> ago//
2 // but the <u>management</u> hasn't <u>changed</u> at all//
3 // to be <u>honest</u>//
4 // we ought to be <u>looking</u> for a different <u>supplier</u>//
5 // we'll <u>leave</u> that to <u>you</u>//

Unit 6

⚠ Remember that in Section C you can find detailed description and additional practice of the pronunciation features of fast speech introduced in Units 5 and 6.

6.1

together pronounced 'zee' /ziː/ — pronounced /jə/

1 <u>Has he</u> <u>been</u> to see <u>you</u> <u>since Saturday</u>?

pronounced 'bin' /bɪn/ — together pronounced 'sinsaturday'; the two /s/ sounds are merged

pronounced 'aster' /ɑːstə/; /k/ and /h/ are missed out — /t/ is missed out — /d/ is missed out — /t/ is pronounced as a glottal stop /ʔ/

2 I <u>asked her</u> for the <u>best</u> tickets <u>they'd</u> <u>got</u> left.

together pronounced 'jer' /dʒə/ — /t/ is pronounced as a glottal stop /ʔ/

3 <u>Do you</u> <u>mind moving</u> along a <u>bit</u>?

together pronounced 'mymoving'; /d/ is missed out, /n/ pronounced like /m/, and the two /m/ sounds then merged

6.2

neglec~~t~~s ~~h~~er

1 A: Rick doesn't take one bit of interest. He neglects her .

soun~~d~~s — together pronounced 'zee' /ziː/

A: That sounds terrible. Why <u>does he</u> do that?

~~h~~e's — ~~be~~cause — doin~~g~~

B: Maybe he's jealous because she's doing so well.

together pronounced /dʒə/ ~~wh~~o's
2 A: Do you know who's coming?

~~ex~~cep~~t~~
B: Everyone except Cathy.

'll
A: What time will they be here?

~~a~~bout
B: About six.

/ə/ /jə/ /fər/; a /r/ sound is added before the vowel
3 A: Are you coming out for a walk?

'll jus~~t~~ /t/ is pronounced like /p/ before /m/
B: Okay. I'll just get my coat.

together pronounced /ændʒə/ together pronounced /niːdʒə/
A: And your hat. And you'll need your gloves, too.
together pronounced /əndʒəl/

Unit 7

7.1 **(United States)**
1 (a piece of thin cord) string
2 (a woman who rules a country) queen
3 (an injury to a muscle) strain
4 (a country in southern Europe) Spain
5 (a poor area in a city) slum
6 (a feeling when you have been hurt) pain
7 (to drink a small amount) sip
8 (done with great speed) quick
9 (to make someone frightened) scare
10 (a hard transparent material) glass

7.2 **(Canada)**
1 (grow) to increase in size (NOT glow)
2 (quake) to shake with fear (NOT cake)
3 (swim) to move through water (NOT slim)
4 (store) another word for shop (NOT straw)
5 (spit) watery liquid in your mouth (NOT split)
6 (pay) to give money for something (NOT play)
7 (flame) burning gas (NOT frame)
8 (pure) not mixed (NOT poor)

7.3
1 Just cross the road.
2 The cat was following its trail.
3 Before that I had to ride a motorbike.
4 It's Michael's twin.
5 He fell into a deeper sleep.
6 I thought it was a terrible sight.
7 Just below your nose.
8 This one is a pear.

Unit 8

8.1 Number of final consonant sounds

1 final consonant sound	catch /tʃ/ ears /z/ earth /θ/ ledge /dʒ/
2 final consonant sounds	axe /ks/ laughed /ft/ touched /tʃt/
3 final consonant sounds	accents /nts/ against /nst/ aspects /kts/ diamonds /ndz/ grasped /spt/ next /kst/ risked /skt/ stamps /mps/
4 final consonant sounds	attempts /mpts/ contexts /ksts/ sculpts /lpts/ tempts /mpts/

8.2
1 next (no simplification)
2 accents ~~t~~
3 stamps (no simplification)
4 against (no simplification)
5 aspects ~~t~~
6 diamonds ~~d~~
7 context (no simplification)
8 grasped (no simplification)

8.3 **(Australia)**
1 paint 2 designers 3 faster 4 trains 5 ridged 6 exports

8.4 The police **think** the **roads** on the south **coast** will be **packed** when the **seventh** Felton Pop Festival **begins next** weekend. **Last** year more than 10,000 pop **fans packed** into the **field** where the festival was **held**. There is **simple** accommodation on a nearby farm, but most people will **camp** in small **tents**.

Follow-up
English has longer consonant clusters and a wider range of possible combinations of consonants in word-final clusters than many other languages. For example, in Greek, words that end in more than one consonant sound are rare apart from words borrowed from other languages. In Greek, the most common word-final consonant sound is /s/ and less frequently /n/.

Unit 9

9.1 When I started playing badminton, I was sixty and I hadn't done any strenuous (/ˈstrenjuəs/) exercise (/ˈeksəsaɪz/) for almost twenty years. But after just a few months I'd won the over-fifties national championship and an international competition. My husband thinks I'm crazy and that I'll injure myself. But I've found a number of advantages in taking up a sport. I feel much healthier, and it's important to be active at my age. And meeting new people has improved my social life. So I'll carry on playing until I get too old.

9.2
1 // she's a freelance translator// (no simplification)
2 // the president spoke next// (/t/ is shortened)
3 // she wore a silk dress// (/k/ is shortened)
4 // it looked green to me// (/t/ is left out)
5 // it's on the first floor// (/t/ is left out)
6 // he speaks three languages// (no simplification)
7 // lift your arms slowly// ('…s s…' make one lengthened /s/ sound)
8 // there was a cold breeze// (/d/ is left out)
9 // what's that unpleasant smell// (/t/ is left out)
10 // it's huge// (no simplification)

9.3 The most likely answers are:

direct speech	(/t/ is left out)
general strike	(no simplification)
golf club	(no simplification)
lamp shade	(no simplification)
first class	(/t/ is left out)
passive smoking	(no simplification)
rock music	(/k/ is shortened)
lost property	(/t/ is left out)
speech therapist	(no simplification)
time travel	(no simplification)
tourist trap	(/t/ is left out)

Follow-up
Here are some examples of compounds which have consonant clusters across word boundaries taken from the field of physics: chaos theory, electron microscope, focal point, jet propulsion, tensile strength, surface tension.

Unit 10

10.1
1 occasional (1)
2 supplement(1)
3 temperamental (2)
4 cosmopolitan (2)
5 pedestrian (1)
6 incoherent (2)
7 electronic (2)
8 spectacular (1)
9 documentary (2)

10.2 *indicates stress shift.
1 pronunciation
2 routine *
3 propaganda
4 Mediterranean *
5 sixteen
6 satisfactory *
7 independent
8 Mediterranean
9 sixteen *
10 propaganda
11 routine
12 independent *
13 satisfactory
14 pronunciation

The words which do not have stress shift are 'pronunciation' and 'propaganda'.

10.3 concise disarming footbridge lifelike paintbox subjective tablecloth

(Speaker A = South Africa)
1 concise
2 handbag
3 lifelike
4 subjective
5 tablecloth
6 paintbox
7 disarming

Follow-up
(i) In Indian English, for example, stress often comes on the next to last syllable of a word regardless of where it comes in the word in other varieties. For example, 'event, 'refer in Indian English compared with e'vent, re'fer in British English.
(ii) Here are some words stressed differently in British and American English: 'adult, 'brochure, 'debris, mou'stache (in British English); a'dult, bro'chure, de'bris, 'moustache (in American English).

Unit 11

11.1 **(United States)** Note that this speaker of American English pronounces 'herb' /ɛːrb/; in British English it is usually pronounced /hɜːb/.
(Example: Note also that 'medicine' is usually pronounced with 2 syllables /'medsᵊn/, but may be pronounced with three in slow, careful speech /'medɪsᵊn/.)

1 di'saster – di'sastrous
2 'outrage – out'rageous
3 Re'gardless – re'gard
4 'industry – in'dustrious
5 per'centage – per'cent
6 my'sterious – 'mystery
7 agri'cultural – 'agriculture

11.2 **(Jamaica)**
Words with the same stress pattern as their root:
de'pendable (de'pend) re'liable (re'ly) pro'fessional (pro'fession)
me'chanical (me'chanic) ac'ceptable (ac'cept) de'batable (de'bate)

Words with a different stress pattern from their root:
uni'versal ('universe) 'reputable (re'pute) acci'dental ('accident)

11.3 * indicates stress shift.
1 <u>ab</u>sentee * 2 <u>vol</u>unteer * 3 Canton<u>ese</u> 4 rou<u>lette</u> 5 <u>Su</u>danese *

Follow-up
Here are some more nationality adjectives ending *-ese*: Beninese, Chinese, Congolese, Guyanese, Lebanese, Maltese, Portuguese, Senegalese, Sudanese, Taiwanese, Tongolese, Vietnamese. Said on their own, they all have main stress on *-ese*; said in the context of 'the .... people', they are all likely to have stress shift with main stress in the first syllable.

Unit 12

12.1 **(Canada)**
1 (being hostile to something) hostility
2 (when someone is prosecuted) prosecution
3 (being willing to cooperate) cooperative
4 (a newspaper article giving the editor's opinion) editorial
5 (when people speculate to make a profit) speculation
6 (acting on impulse) impulsive
7 (being familiar with something) familiarity
8 (to do with photography) photographic

The word with a suffix which is an exception to the rule given at the beginning of **A** is 'co'operative'. (It doesn't have stress on the syllable immediately before *-ive*.)

12.2

/tʃən/ (e.g. sugges<u>tion</u>)	/ʃən/ (e.g. educa<u>tion</u>)	/ʒən/ (e.g. deci<u>sion</u>)
combustion congestion digestion exhaustion	accommodation celebration comprehension depression expression suspension	erosion explosion invasion revision

12.3 resident, performance, defiant, convergence, reference
excellence, correspondent, assistant, maintenance, applicant
coincidence, informant, acceptance, insistence, significance

The exception is ''excellence'. The syllable before the suffix *-ence* ends in 'ell' (VCC) and so stress would be on this syllable if the second rule in **B** were followed. (Note that ''excellent' is also an exception.)

12.4 The words with the same (S) stress pattern as their root are:
de'fiant (de'fy)
con'vergence (con'verge)
ˌcorre'spondent (ˌcorre'spond)
as'sistant (as'sist)
in'formant (in'form)
ac'ceptance (ac'cept)
in'sistence (in'sist)

The words with a different (D) stress pattern from their root are:
'reference (re'fer)
'excellence (ex'cel)
'maintenance (main'tain)
'applicant (ap'ply)
co'incidence (coin'cide)
sig'nificance ('signify)

Follow-up
Here are some examples from the field of medicine:

/tʃən/ (e.g. suggestion)	/ʃən/ (e.g. education)	/ʒən/ (e.g. decision)
indigestion	addiction hypertension concussion	vision

Unit 13

13.1 **(Australia)**
inter'vention = S (inter'vene)
se'curity = S (se'cure)
advan'tageous = D (ad'vantage)
Ca'nadian = D ('Canada)
con'sumption = S (con'sume)
ma'turity = S (ma'ture)
stu'pidity = D ('stupid)
appli'cation = D (a'pply)
'sanity = S (sane)
nor'mality = D ('normal)
de'livery = S (de'liver)
pre'cision = S (pre'cise)
'preference = D (pre'fer)
sin'cerity = S (sin'cere)
di'version = S (di'vert)

13.2 The words with a different vowel sound from their root are:
intervention /e/ (intervene /iː/)
consumption /ʌ/ (consume /uː/)
sanity /æ/ (sane /eɪ/)
precision /ɪ/ (precise /aɪ/)
sincerity /e/ (sincere /ɪə/)

The words with the same vowel sound as their root are:
familiarise /ɪ/ (familiar /ɪ/)
security /ʊə/ (secure /ʊə/)
maturity /ʊə/ (mature /ʊə/)
delivery /ɪ/ (deliver /ɪ/)
diversion /ɜː/ (divert /ɜː/)

13.3 1 a divide b division
2 a competitive b compete
3 a collision b collide
4 a example b exemplary
5 a national b nation

13.4

Vowel sound in main stressed syllable of root	/ɒ/ (as in stop)	/ɪ/ (as in sit)	/aɪ/ (as in drive)	/æ/ (as in black)	/e/ (as in pen)
	commercial (commerce) evolution (evolve) modernity (modern)	symbolic (symbol) historic (history) influential (influence)	applicant (apply) financial (finance) decision (decide)	accidental (accident) calculation (calculate) magnetic (magnet)	speciality (special) demonstration (demonstrate) medicinal (medicine)

Unit 14

14.1 1 unwise 2 unpack 3 discourage 4 illegal

14.2 (Speaker A = Spain)
1 replace 2 illegal 3 unpack 4 discourage

14.3

/diː-/	/dɪ-/	/riː-/	/rɪ-/
debug deregulate destabilise devalue	deflate deform delineate demote descend	reapply recharge reconsider resit restructure	reflect refresh relapse replace review

14.4 (South Africa)
1 a recover /rɪˈkʌvə/ (= get well) b re-cover /ˌriːˈkʌvə/ (= cover again)
2 a re-sign /ˌriːˈsaɪn/ (= sign again) b resign /rɪˈzaɪn/ (= give up a job)
3 a re-count /ˌriːˈkaʊnt/ (= count again) b recount /rɪˈkaʊnt/ (= describe)

Unit 15

15.1 (United States)
1 co-education
2 subconscious
3 interface
4 underachievers; subtitles
5 Superstars; counteroffensive (counteroffensive is also possible)
6 supernatural; undercurrents
7 co-writers; hypertext
8 international; counterparts

15.2 2 g (oooOo) 3 d (ooOoo) 4 f (Ooo) 5 a (oOo) 6 e (Oooo) 7 b (ooOo)

15.3 *indicates stress shift
1 impractical
2 review
3 impolite*
4 misplaced*
5 dishonest
6 dehydrated*
7 undressed

Follow-up

Here are some more *sub-* and *super-* words with their main stressed syllable underlined:
subgroup, suborbital, superhuman, subeditor, superglue, subculture, superbug

Unit 16

16.1

1 chemical formula (*adjective + noun*)
2 bank account (*noun + noun*)
3 American football (*adjective + noun*)
4 artificial intelligence (*adjective + noun*)
5 coffee shop (*noun + noun*)
6 best man (*adjective + noun*)
7 mobile phone (*adjective + noun*)
8 flight attendant (*noun + noun*)
9 sofa bed (*noun + noun*)
10 magnetic field (*adjective + noun*)
11 tea strainer (*noun + noun*)
12 space station (*noun + noun*)

16.2 **(Canada)**

1 voicemail
2 a paper towel
3 a civil war
4 a greenhouse
5 an ice rink
6 distance learning
7 a loudspeaker
8 a hot potato
9 a claim form
10 house-hunting
11 a town hall
12 a pay phone
13 a defining moment
14 orange juice
15 lipstick
16 boiling point
17 a search party
18 a shop assistant
19 dental floss
20 a rubber band

'Greenhouse', 'town hall', 'defining moment', 'dental floss' and 'orange juice' are all exceptions to the rules in **B** and **C**. They are all mentioned in the reference page.

Follow-up

Here are ten examples from the field of music with main stressed syllables underlined.
barbershop disc jockey grand piano tuning fork heavy metal mouthpiece musical instrument bluegrass French horn soundtrack

Unit 17

17.1

1 homesick
2 far-fetched
3 spine-chilling
4 mind-blowing
5 armour-plated
6 cinemagoing
7 gift-wrapped
8 well-meaning
9 empty-handed
10 fireproof
11 self-financing
12 machine-readable

The exception is 'ˌarmour-ˈplated'. Most noun + past participle compound adjectives have main stress on the *first* part.

17.2 **(Australia)**

* indicates compounds which have stress shift

bad-tempered
public-spirited
time-consuming
good-looking
close-cropped*
short-sighted
high-flying*
world-famous
hard-working
ground-breaking
well-dressed
loose-fitting*
eye-catching
tongue-tied
camera-shy
long-term*
fat-free
well-earned*

17.3 Definitions of abbreviations:
CEO = chief executive officer DVD = digital versatile disc or digital video disc
AOB = any other business PC = personal computer
OHP = overhead projector NHS = National Health Service (the British state health care system)
ATM = automated teller machine (a machine, often outside a bank, where you can get money from your account using a bank card)
RP = received pronunciation (an accent of British English considered to have no regional features)
AGM = annual general meeting
RSI = repetitive strain injury (a medical condition causing pain in the hand, wrists, etc., especially in people who use computers a lot)
TLC = tender loving care (being looked after carefully and gently) VAT = value added tax
UFO = unidentified flying object WHO = World Health Organisation
EU = European Union RSVP = répondez s'il vous plaît (= please reply)
CV = curriculum vitae ETA = estimated time of arrival
CD = compact disc IT = information technology
CND = Campaign for Nuclear Disarmament (a British organisation opposing nuclear weapons)
DIY = do-it-yourself (decorating or repairing your home rather than paying someone else to do it)
GMT = Greenwich Mean Time HGV = heavy goods vehicle (a large truck used for transporting goods)

The letter with main stress is underlined and * indicates stress shift.

1 CEO
2 PC*
3 NHS
4 RP
5 AGM*
6 TLC
7 WHO*
8 EU*
9 ETA
10 CD*
11 DIY
12 GMT

Unit 18

18.1 **(South Africa)**

main stress on the first part	main stress on the second part	main stress on the third part
pinball machine	left-luggage office	first-time buyer
aircraft carrier	headed notepaper	downhill skiing
nail varnish remover	car boot sale	bullet-proof vest
payback period	level playing field	two-way mirror
	cooling-off period	right-hand drive
		household name

18.2 The syllables with main stress are underlined. The correct answer is given first.
Example: washing-up liquid (peanut butter)

1 grant-maintained school (teacher-training college)
2 old-people's home (semi-detached house)
3 air traffic controller (travelling salesman)
4 windscreen wipers (rear-view mirror)
5 baseball cap (shoulder-length hair)

18.3

1 double-decker bus
2 bullet-proof vest
3 four-leaf clover
4 hot-water bottle
5 three-piece suit
6 right-angled triangle

The exception is 'hot-water bottle' which has main stress on the second part, 'water'.

Follow-up

Here are some things you might see. The syllables with main stress are underlined.
bedside lamp walk-in wardrobe four-poster bed drop-leaf table
wide-screen television radio-cassette player table-tennis bat built-in wardrobe

Unit 19

19.1 **(United States)**

1 1 2 2 3 2 4 1 5 2 6 1 7 1 8 1

19.2 **(Speaker A = Spain)**

Prominent syllables in the parts in **bold** are given in capitals.
1 What are you **DRIVing** at?
2 I thought she'd **disapPROVE of them.**
3 I said I think it will **reSULT IN** climate change. (The particle is made prominent for contrast.)
4 Yes, I **READ about it.**
5 Where does she **COME from?**
6 But I don't know what to **AIM AT**. (The particle is made prominent for special emphasis.)
7 Yes, it's **TEEMing with them.**

19.3 **(Speaker A = India)**

Prominent syllables in the parts in **bold** are given in capitals.
1 Yes, when you're next in town, why don't you **COME BY**? (ˌcome ˈby = visit)
2 Well, at this time of year fresh vegetables are difficult to **COME by.** (ˈcome by = obtain)
3 I was stroking Susan's cat when it just **TURNED on me.** (ˈturn on = attack)
4 Yes, he certainly knows how to **TURN it ON.** (ˌturn ˈon = to show a particular quality)

Follow-up

For example, you could note stress in phrasal verbs like this:
one-stress: ˈsettle for ˈhint at
two-stress: ˌglaze ˈover ˌset ˈoff

Unit 20

20.1

1 handed your homework in (The particle is non-prominent as the object, 'your homework', is between it and the verb and is prominent.)
2 turn it off
3 rolled my trousers up (The particle is non-prominent as the object, 'my trousers', is between it and the verb and is prominent.)
4 get by
5 get along
6 pointing out
7 fell off the wall (The particle is non-prominent as the object, 'the wall', is after it but still in the same clause.)
8 send them on

20.2 **(Speaker A = Poland)**
Prominent syllables in the parts in **bold** are given in capitals.
1 A: Did you lend Ellen your mobile? B: No, she just **WALKED OFF with it.**
2 A: Do you think you'll buy the house? B: If I can **COME up with the MONey.** ('… COME UP with the MONey' would also be possible)
3 A: You don't really want the job, do you? B: No, but I don't know how I'm going to **GET OUT of it.**
4 A: Have the holiday brochures arrived yet? B: I've only just **SENT aWAY for them.**
5 A: Steve's working really hard at the moment. B: Yes, I think he's hoping to **PUT in for a proMOtion.** ('… PUT IN for a proMOtion' would also be possible)
6 A: So how do you suggest improving education in the country? B: Well, first, we should **DO aWAY with PRIvate SCHOOLS.** ('… DO away with PRIvate SCHOOLS' would also be possible)

20.3 1 **a** check it in **b** check-in
2 **a** gets together **b** get-together
3 **a** back them up **b** backup
4 **a** follow it up **b** follow-up

Follow-up
Here are some examples from the area of business. Main and secondary stressed syllables are marked in the example phrasal verbs and compound nouns. Prominent syllables are marked in the example sentences.

Phrasal verb:	ˌwalk ˈout	The 200 striking workers WALKED OUT last week.
Compound noun:	ˈwalkout	There's been a WALKout at the factory.
Phrasal verb:	ˌmark ˈup	Prices have been MARKED UP since last week.
Compound noun:	ˈmark-up	The MARK-up on the products is over 100 per cent.

Unit 21

21.2 **(Speaker A = Japan)**
The reason why some function words are in the strong form is given in brackets.
Example **a** S (word is at end of sentence) **b** W
1 **a** W **b** S ('would' is used as a content word rather than a function word)
2 **a** W **b** S ('were' is contrasted with 'weren't')
3 **a** W **b** S ('from' is contrasted with 'for')
4 **a** S ('your' is used as a content word rather than a function word) **b** W
5 **a** S (word is at end of sentence) **b** W

21.3

1 2 – 2	They were waiting for their brother.
2 3 – 2	I knew that she was going to be late again.
3 2 – 3	Would you take her to the swimming pool?
4 4 – 3	I thought we were at the station already, but I was wrong.
5 2 – 4	Shall we go to the zoo, or have you been before?
6 3 – 3	There are some more books here that he could have.
7 3 – 2 – 3	He asked me for some money and I lent it to him.
8 6	She told me that we would have been better off going by bus.

Unit 22

22.1 Words in **bold** which are prominent are underlined.

1 A: **Do** you know of **any** good restaurants in Brockhurst?
B: Well, I haven't been for **some** years, but there used to be **some** very good ones. *The Oyster* was **the** place to eat seafood.
A: Mmm. I **do** like seafood.
B: But I'm sure **any** of **the** restaurants there will be good.

2 A: Try turning the tap off.
B: I **have** tried turning it, but it's stuck.
A: **Did you** ask **anyone** for help?
B: No. Look, why don't **you** try?
A: Okay. Hmmm. There must be **some** way of doing it.
B: I **did** tell you it was stuck.
A: There. It just needed **some** strength! **Anyone** could **have** done it.

22.2 **(Speaker A = Jamaica)**
Prominent words are in capitals.

1 is THAT IT?
2 OH, IS it?
3 YES, THIS is IT.
4 YES, THAT'S IT.
5 THAT'S it.
6 THIS is IT, then.
7 WHAT IS it?
8 i CAN'T. THAT'S just IT.

22.3 **(Speaker A = China)**
Prominent words in the parts in **bold** are in capitals.

1 A: I couldn't understand a word he said. B: **WHERE was he FROM?**
2 A: Can I book a table for tonight, please? B: **HOW many is it FOR?**
3 A: While I was out, someone left these flowers outside my house. B: **WHO could it have BEEN?**
4 A: That woman you were talking to seemed nice. B: Yes, but I don't know **WHO she WAS.**
5 A: Couldn't you have helped him at all? B: There was nothing **we could have DONE.**
6 A: You just sit and relax. B: But isn't there anything **i can DO?**

Follow-up

Here is an extract from a conversation between two people talking about computers. Notice how Speaker 2 (S2) uses 'This is it' to mean something like: 'I agree. You have done a lot of work on it and you don't want to lose the information'.

S1 I've got it on the hard disk and I've got it on an A drive. But I wanted to have it on two just in case I lose – er you know – the floppy – or er – you know anything happens. It's best to – isn't it?
S2 Oh right. Yeah. Yeah. Yeah.
S1 I've done a hell of a lot of work on that.
S2 **This is it.** Yeah.
S1 I don't want to lose it.

Unit 23

23.1
1 NC
2 C (director /aɪ/ – director /ə/)
3 C (December /ɪ/ – December /ə/)
4 NC
5 C (ambulance /ʊ/ – ambulance /ə/)
6 NC
7 NC
8 C (vocabulary /əʊ/ – vocabulary /ə/)
9 NC
10 C (corridor /ɔː/ – corridor /ə/)
11 C (consent /ɒ/ – consent /ə/)
12 NC

23.2 **(First speaker = India; second speaker = Scotland)**
The definitions on the recording are given before each answer. The symbol . shows syllable divisions.
1 A wish to learn about something. curiosity /ˌkjʊə.ri'ɒs.ɪ.ti/
2 Very much like a particular thing. virtual /'vɜːr.tʃu.əl/
3 To do with countries that were once colonies. colonial /kə'ləʊ.ni.əl/
4 One of the things used to make something. ingredient /ɪŋ'griː.di.ənt/
5 Someone who is famous. celebrity /sɪ'leb.rɪ.ti/
6 Very angry. furious /'fjʊə.ri.əs/
7 The force that makes things fall to the ground. gravity /'græv.ɪ.ti/
8 The larger part of something. majority /mə'dʒɒ.rɪ.ti/
9 A phrase that acts like an adverb. adverbial /æd'vɜːr.bi.əl/
10 Describes someone who spends a long time studying. studious /'stjuː.di.əs/

(Note: The second speaker (from Scotland) pronounces 'r' in virtual and adverbial, where these would not be pronounced in BBC English.)

23.3 The symbol . shows syllable divisions.
1 furious /'fjʊə.rjəs/
2 studious /'stjuː.dʒəs/
3 celebrity /sə'leb.rə.ti/
4 colonial /kə'ləʊ.njəl/
5 majority /mə'dʒɒ.rə.ti/
6 adverbial /əd'vɜː.bjəl/
7 ingredient /ɪŋ'griː.dʒənt/
8 curiosity /ˌkjʊə.ri'ɒs.ə.ti/
9 gravity /'græv.ə.ti/
10 virtual /'vɜː.tʃəl/

Unit 24

24.1
1 My cousin lives in a mansion with a huge garden.
2 He took out a little bottle full of poison and poured it into her tea.
3 Eleven people were injured in the collision.
4 When she got on the bicycle and began to pedal she started to wobble.
5 Since she started playing the violin, her ambition has been to be a classical musician.
6 I burnt my knuckle on a candle and had to go to hospital.
7 He wrote an article about a famous politician who was sent to prison.

24.2 **(Speaker A = Canada)**

24.3
… religions – Buddhism and Hinduism
… political systems – capitalism and communism
… things to avoid when appointing someone to a job – ageism and favouritism
… good qualities for someone to have in a job – enthusiasm and professionalism (or optimism)
… feelings you might have about a situation – optimism and pessimism (or enthusiasm)

Follow-up
The Channel Tunnel is the tunnel under the English Channel connecting England and France.

Unit 25

25 A faux pas (*noun*) a socially embarrassing mistake
joie de vivre (*noun*) great enjoyment of life
déjà vu (*noun*) the feeling that you have already experienced what is happening now
fait accompli (*noun*) something that has happened and can't be changed
carte blanche (*noun*) complete freedom to take whatever action you want
entre nous (*adj/adv*) used to say that something should be a secret 'between ourselves'
en route (*adv*) on the way to or from somewhere
nuance (*noun*) a very small difference in meaning, appearance, etc.

25 B doppelgänger (*noun*) a person who looks exactly like you but is not related to you
realpolitik (*noun*) practical politics, decided by immediate needs rather than by principle
wanderlust (*noun*) the wish to travel far and to many different places

25 C incommunicado (*adj*) not communicating with anyone
mañana (*adv*) some time in the future
El Nino or El Niño (*noun*) an unusual current in the Pacific Ocean that temporarily changes world weather patterns

25 D cognoscente (*noun*) a person who has a lot of specialist knowledge, particularly of the arts – plural: cognoscenti
prima donna (*noun*) someone who thinks they are special and should be treated in a special way

25 E bonsai (*noun*) a very small tree that has been stopped from growing to its full size
kimono (*noun*) a loose piece of outer clothing with side sleeves
origami (*noun*) making decorative objects by folding paper

25 F feng shui (*noun*) an ancient Chinese belief that the way your house is built and the way that you arrange objects affects success, health and happiness
lychee (*noun*) a fruit with a rough brown shell and sweet white flesh
typhoon (*noun*) a violent wind which has a circular motion, found in the West Pacific Ocean

25.1 *French:*
denouement /deɪ'nuːmɑ̃ːŋ/ (*noun*) the end of a book or play where everything is explained
nouvelle cuisine /ˌnuːvelkwɪ'ziːn/ (*noun*) a style of cooking in which a small amount of food is served in an attractive pattern on the plate

Chinese:
gingseng /'dʒɪnseŋ/ (*noun*) the root of a tropical plant used to improve health
kumquat /'kʌmkwɒt/ (*noun*) a small, oval orange-coloured fruit

Italian:
diva /'diːvə/ (*noun*) a famous female singer
sotto voce /ˌsɒtəʊ'vəʊtʃeɪ/ (*adjective*) said in a very quiet voice

German:
ersatz /'eəsæts/ or /'eəzɑːts/ (*adjective*) describes something used instead of something else because the original is rare or too expensive
schadenfreude /'ʃɑːdᵊnˌfrɔɪdə/ (*noun*) a feeling of pleasure you get when something bad happens to someone else

Japanese:
haiku /'haɪkuː/ (*noun*) a poem made up of 17 syllables only
ninja /'nɪndʒə/ (*noun*) a Japanese sword-carrying fighter

Spanish:
macho /'mætʃəʊ/ (*adjective*) behaving forcefully and without emotion in a way that was thought typical of a man
pronto /'prɒntəʊ/ (*adjective*) quickly and at once

25.2

1 d /ˌbetˈnwɑːʳ/
2 g /ˌkɔːzselˈebrə/
3 a /dərɪˈgɜːʳ/
4 f /ˌkliːɑ̃ːnˈtel/
5 c /ˈkɒntrətɑ̃ːŋ/
6 h /ˌɑ̃ːnˈswiːt/
7 b /ˌnɔ̃ːndəˈpluːm/
8 e /ˌsævwɑːˈfeəʳ/

25.3

glasnost /ˈglæsnɒst/ (*noun*) a policy of making government more open and accountable to its people
intelligentsia /ɪnˌtelɪˈdʒentsiə/ (*noun*) the highly educated people in a society who are interested in arts and politics
politburo /ˈpɒlɪtˌbjʊərəʊ/ (*noun*) the main governing group in a Communist country
samovar /ˈsæməvɑːʳ/ (*noun*) a large metal container used to heat water for tea
troika /ˈtrɔɪkə/ (*noun*) a group of three powerful politicians

Unit 26

26.1 (Speaker A = Spain)

1	A: Where are you going?	6	B: By‿air. /j/
2	A: When?	8	B: Yes, I grew‿up there. /w/
3	A: Why?	11	B: Yes, a new‿umbrella. /w/
4	A: Who is he?	12	B: He‿asked me for one. /j/
5	A: Have you got cousins there, too?	2	B: Tomorrow‿afternoon. /w/
6	A: How will you get there?	9	B: I'll stay‿a week. /j/
7	A: How long will it take?	1	B: To‿Austria. /w/
8	A: Have you been there before?	5	B: No, they‿all live in France. /j/
9	A: How long will you be there?	10	B: It's too‿expensive. /w/
10	A: Why don't you stay longer?	3	B: To see‿Adam. /j/
11	A: Will you take Adam a present?	7	B: A few‿hours. /w/
12	A: Why an umbrella?	4	B: My‿uncle. /j/

26.2 Possible /r/ links are marked.

1 He's got a finger‿in every pie. (= be involved in and have influence over many different activities; usually used in a disapproving way)
2 It's in the nature‿of things. (= usual and expected)
3 She's without a care‿in the world. (= without any worries)
4 It's as clear‿as mud. (= difficult to understand; usually used in humorous way)
5 It's the law‿of the jungle. (= the idea that people who care only about themselves will be most likely to succeed in a society or organisation)
6 Let's focus on the matter‿in hand. (= the subject or situation being discussed)
7 Is that your‿idea‿of a joke? (= what you consider to be a joke)
8 He's a creature of habit. (= he always does the same thing in the same way)
9 Pride comes before a fall. (= if you are too confident about your abilities, something bad will happen showing that you are not as good as you think)
10 Get your‿act together! (= organise yourself more effectively)

26.3 The answers and the sentences on the recording are given.

1 lock / lot back / bat
The house is a lot safer now we've got a new back door.

2 play / played park / part
We played tennis in the park near my home last weekend.

3 hit / hid trick / trip
First he hit David on the head and then tried to trick Maggie into giving him money.

4 like / light planned / plan
The room is painted a light green, but I plan to change it soon.

5 right / ride road / robe
We took a right turn, and went along the road by the sea.

Follow-up

Mr Brookes would probably have disapproved of 'It's the law‿of the jungle.' and 'Is that your idea‿of a joke?' People who have strong feelings that language should be used 'correctly' often see the insertion of a /r/ sound in contexts like this as an example of 'lazy' speech. However, the majority of people don't disapprove.

Unit 27

1	A: He's leaving now.	4	B: Let's ask the farmer.
2	A: We're arriving at ten.	1	B: I thought he'd gone already.
3	A: I haven't got any money on me.	6	B: Yes, I think it's ridiculous.
4	A: Do you think it'd be okay to camp here?	2	B: It'll be good to see you.
5	A: You should've taken the job.	7	B: Well, let's eat now.
6	A: I suppose you've heard Kathy's idea?	3	B: Don't worry. I've got my credit card.
7	A: I'm starving.	5	B: You're right. I should.

27.2 **(Australia)**

1 My feet'**ll** get wet because my shoes'**ve** got holes in.
2 There's no butter, but this'**ll** do instead.
3 I'**m** sure Ann'**d** help if she could.
4 How'**d** they know we'**d** be there? (Note that 'did' in 'How did …' is less likely to be contracted than other words in this exercise.)
5 Adam'**s** phoned to say he is**n't** ready to go yet, but he'**ll** call again when he is.
6 There'**ve** been four parcels delivered for you while you'**ve** been away.
7 What'**ll** you do if Tom'**s** already gone?

27.3

1 **I'd've** bought some more coffee if **I'd** known **we'd** run out. (= I would have; I had; we had)
2 The film **won't've** started yet, so **we've** got lots of time. (= will not have; we have)
3 I suppose **they'll've** closed by now, so **we better** come back tomorrow. (= they will have; we had better)
4 **I wouldn't've** gone if **there'd** been anything good on TV. (= I would not have; there had)
5 A: **I shouldn't've** had that last slice of pizza.
B: I told you **it'd** make you feel sick! (= I should not have; it would)

Follow-up

As well as the usual contracted forms, others found in song lyrics include: gonna (= going to), kinda (= kind of), sorta (= sort of), wanna (= want to).

Unit 28

28.1 Pronunciation of the sections in **bold** is given in brackets.
A: **What are you** making? NE (/wɒtʃə/)
B: **It's a cake** for Richard's birthday. E (/əkeɪk/)
A: **It's amazing**, isn't it? E (/əmeɪzɪŋ/)
B: **Do you think** he'll like it? NE (/dʒθɪŋk/)
A: **I'm sure** he will, although **he's a bit** fussy about food, isn't he? E (/ʃɔː^{r}/) / NE (/zəbɪt/)
B: **Have you seen** this? E (/siːn/)
A: Wow! **Is that** a real flower? NE (/zðæt/)
B: No, **it's made** from sugar. NE (/tsmeɪd/)
A: **When does it** have to be ready? NE (/wenzɪt/)
B: **It's his** birthday tomorrow. **Do you know** where he is now? NE (/tsɪz/) / NE (/dʒnəʊ/)
A: **I've no** idea. E (/nəʊ/)

28.2 **(Speaker A = Poland)**
12 A 'dibber' is a small hand-held tool used by gardeners for making holes in soil into which seeds can be dropped.
14 A 'brown-bag lunch' is a phrase mainly used in North American English. It is food bought or prepared at home to be eaten during a lunch break at work, often carried in a brown paper bag. In British English we would be more likely to talk about a 'packed lunch'.

Unit 29

29.1
1 He wrote it.
2 A published article.
3 It's in firs~~t~~ gear.
4 It was just him.
5 Take a lef~~t~~ turn.
6 They kep~~t~~ quiet.
7 It look~~ed~~ good.
8 We reach~~ed~~ Berlin.
9 We crossed over.
10 I'll contact Ann.
11 He finish~~ed~~ first.
12 I slep~~t~~ badly.

29.2

A No change to /t/	B /t/ left out	C /t/ replaced with glottal stop	D /t/ + /j/ said as /tʃ/
3, 8, 11, 15	1, 5, 9, 12	4, 6, 14, 16	2, 7, 10, 13

29.3 The letters in black show what happens to /t/ on the recording, but other changes are possible and these are shown in green. For example, in 'What you', /t/ and /j/ are said as /tʃ/ (D), but /t/ could also be replaced by a glottal stop (C).

A: What (D/C) you got (C) there?

B: It (A)'s Don Simpson's latest (A, B) novel. Have you read it (C/A)?

A: Bought (A) it (C) just (B) the other day.

B: I don't (C) think it (A)'s as good as his first (A).

A: Don't (D/C) you? But (C) then that (C) was really tremendous (A).

Follow-up
For example, go to the BBC's 'Voices' website (http://www.bbc.co.uk/voices/) and listen to speakers who live in and around London. Many very often replace /t/ with a glottal stop.

Unit 30

30.1

1 She's worl~~d~~ champion.
2 We sailed slowly.
3 She change~~d~~ clothes.
4 I'll send Lucy.
5 I was pleased with it.
6 She arrive~~d~~ there.
7 Can you hold it?
8 I understan~~d~~ that.
9 We climbed over.
10 It move~~d~~ towards us.
11 They're second hand.
12 He turned round.

30.2

1 A: He wasn't at home.
B: No, I think ~~h~~e's on holiday.

2 A: It says here, the President's coming.
B: Where?
A: Here.
B: I really hope we'll get to see ~~h~~er.

3 A: How's Tom these days?
B: Haven't you heard about ~~h~~is heart attack?

4 A: Kate says she left ~~h~~er handbag here.
Have you seen it?
B: This one? But Judy says it's hers.

30.3

ʔ
A: Have you **got** much work on **jus~~t~~** now?

ʔ ʔ
B: Dr Thomas **~~h~~as** given us a very hard essay, but I **mustn't get** a low mark this time.

ʔ
A: I had an **argument** with my tutor **las~~t~~** week.

ʔ
B: **What** happened?

ʔ /ə/
A: Well, I **couldn't fin~~d~~** my coursework, so I **as~~ked~~** for a couple **of** days extra.

ʔ /n/ ʔ
She **got** really annoyed with me **and** complained I was **a~~l~~ways late** for lectures.

/ə/
Anyway, I told **~~h~~er** I thought **~~h~~er** course was a waste **of** time.

/dʒ/ (/d/+/j/) ʔ ʔ ʔ ʔ
B: **Did** you? Well, **at leas~~t~~** Dr Thomas **doesn't** shout at us, **a~~l~~though** I'm **not** very **confident** that I'll pass **~~h~~is** exam.

Unit 31

31.1

1 int~~e~~rest – traditi~~o~~nal
2 consid~~e~~rable – diff~~e~~rence
3 mis~~e~~rable – second~~a~~ry
4 fright~~e~~ning – discov~~e~~ry
5 pris~~o~~ner – myst~~e~~ry
6 caref~~u~~lly – direct~~o~~ry
7 thankf~~u~~lly – batt~~e~~ry
8 accident~~a~~lly – deaf~~e~~ning

31.2

loyally 3
machinery 4
geometrically 5
suppose 2
technically 3
perhaps 2
anniversary 5
delivery 4
historically 4
police 2
medicine 3
nursery 3

31.3

1 3/S
2 1/D (s~~u~~ppose)
3 4/D (annivers~~a~~ry)
4 1/D (p~~o~~lice)
5 4/S
6 3/S
7 3/D (deliv~~e~~ry)
8 2/D (med~~i~~cine)
9 5/S
10 1/D (p~~e~~rhaps)
11 4/S
12 2/D (nurs~~e~~ry)

31.4 Left-hand extract from *Popcorn* by Ben Elton.
Middle extract from *The Scholar. A West-side story* by Courttia Newland.
Right-hand extract from *The Echo* by Minette Walters.

Follow-up
They might want to get your attention or be asking you to get out of the way. It is a common way of saying 'excuse me'. In informal speech it is sometimes reduced even more to 'scuse' /skjuːz/.

Unit 32

32.1 1 that's the main thing// and then// if you've got any questions afterwards// hopefully// we'll still have time// to go through a few of them// is that okay
2 she'd left// when she had a baby// and then// decided not to go back// although the job had been kept open for her
3 Tom dear// where's the advert// for this calculator// because I don't know the address// and I don't know// who I've got to make the cheque payable to

32.2 **(United States)**
1 when I woke up // I didn't even realise // what time it was
2 of course // it's written in a language // that hardly anyone can understand
3 I was working late // because they want it done // as quickly as possible
4 because he was ill // I didn't expect him // to come to work
5 if I get some time // I'll be over on the weekend // to see you both
6 luckily // we haven't had any rain // since the day we arrived
7 it should never have been built // in my opinion // this new office building

(Note: In 5, speakers of British English would usually say '*at* the weekend'.)

Unit 33

33.1 Prominent words are underlined and the prominent syllable in these words is in capital letters.
1 // MOST of the time// we ADvertise jobs// in national NEWSpapers// and on our WEBsite// occCAsionally however// we might apPROACH someone// to see if they're INterested// someone we might REAlly want//
2 **(Canada)**
// when we ran out of MONey// we WORKED for a bit// and then got a TRAIN// somewhere ELSE// and eVENtually we ended up// in a little VILlage// in the ANdes// WAY up high//

33.2 Speech unit divisions are marked with //. Prominent words are underlined and the prominent syllable in these words is in capital letters.
1 should the GOVernment pay// for HEALTH care// or do you THINK it's// the indiVIDual's responsibility// to SAVE money// for when they need TREATment// my PERsonal view// is that we should pay for our OWN treatment
2 **(Canada)**
I'm imPRESSED// with your COOKing Annie// that was VERy nice// I parTICularly liked// how you did the RICE// I'd really like the RECipe sometime// if you could write it DOWN for me

33.3 Prominent words are underlined and the prominent syllable in these words is in capital letters.
1 // we've had WONderful weather// for the LAST two WEEKS// but ADam and Emma // have been up in SCOTland// where they've had HEAvy RAIN// and even FLOODing// in the WESTern parts of the country//

2 **(Canada)**
// I was THINKing of buying// a SECond-hand CAR// from this garAGE// but because I DON'T know anything aBOUT cars// I PAID for the AA// to inSPECT it// and they FOUND all KINDS of things wrong// so of COURSE// I didn't BUY it//

(Note: In 2, speakers of British English would usually say 'GARage'; the AA = the Automobile Association, a British motoring organisation which gives help and advice to its members.)

Unit 34

34.1 **(Female speaker = Australia)**
1a + (ii), **1b** + (i); **2a** + (ii), **2b** + (i); **3a** + (i), **3b** + (ii); **4a** + (ii), **4b** + (i)

34.2 (Speaker A = Spain)
The words most likely to be prominent are underlined. Prominent syllables in these words are in capital letters. These versions are on the recording.

1 She's got three SISters.
2 I'm going NEXT week.
3 It's in EAST Newtown.
4 We live at fifty-NINE.
5 I said I'd be there LAter.
6 It was a BIG mistake.
7 But I work at HOME on Fridays.
8 You should have taken the first on the RIGHT.

34.3 The words most likely to be prominent are underlined. Prominent syllables in these words are in capital letters. These versions are on the recording.
In an OLD house by the RIVer.
It's only a SHORT walk from the STAtion.
It's FIVE minutes from the BUS stop.
The FIRST house on the LEFT.

Follow-up
Possibilities include:
A: He says he's a friend of yours. B: // ɪ've never SEEN him before//
A: Do you know everyone here? B: // ɪ've never seen HIM before//

Unit 35

35 A a race against time = trying to do something quickly because there is only a short time in which to finish it
could barely hear myself think = there was so much noise that it was almost impossible to hear anything

35.1 The incorrect speech unit divisions are crossed out, and the fixed phrases and idioms are in **bold**, with explanations below.
hi Maggie// got your message// and your question about car repairs// sorry// but **I haven't got~~//~~ a clue**// the best person to contact is …// oh// **it was on the tip~~//~~ of my tongue**// and **my mind just~~//~~ went blank**// Peter Thomas// that was it// **he's a mine~~//~~ of information**// about that sort of thing// anyway// I'll be over to see you// when I can// as soon as the doctor's given me// **a clean bill~~//~~ of health**// the new medication// is **doing me~~//~~ a power of good**// so I'm hoping **to be up~~//~~ and about**// in the next week or so// speak to you soon//

I haven't got a clue = I have no information about it
it was on the tip of my tongue = I know the information and should be able to remember it soon
my mind went blank = I couldn't think of what to say
he's a mine of information = he knows a lot
a clean bill of health = after a medical examination, saying that someone is healthy
doing me a power of good = making me feel better
to be up and about = well enough to be out of bed and moving around after an illness

35.2 1 Don't jump to conclusions.
2 They're putting a brave face on it.
3 He's had a change of heart.
4 You can say that again.
5 You may well ask.
6 He took them in his stride.

35.3 **(Speaker A = Poland)**
A: How did Nick get on in his exams last week?
B: He took them in his stride.
A: Didn't get nervous?
B: (1) Not in the slightest.
A: I suppose he'll be off to university next year?
B: (2) Don't jump to conclusions.
A: But I thought he wanted to be a doctor.
B: (3) He's had a change of heart.
A: He'd be crazy not to go to university.
B: (4) You can say that again.
A: His parents must be really annoyed.
B: (5) They're putting a brave face on it.
A: So what does he want to do now?
B: (6) You may well ask.

not in the slightest = not at all
don't jump to conclusions = don't guess the facts about a situation without having enough information
they're putting a brave face on it = acting as if they are happy when they are not
a change of heart = a change in opinion
you can say that again = I completely agree with what you have just said
you may well ask = it would be interesting to know the answer
he took them in his stride = he dealt with something difficult in a calm way without letting it affect what he was doing

Unit 36

36.1 Prominent words are underlined and the prominent syllables in these words are in capital letters.
1 // But you KNOW I can't drive//
2 // I'm not INterested in cricket//
3 // But you haven't even apPLIED for the job yet//
4 // there were HUNdreds of people waiting//

36.2 The most likely answers are given.
1 to drink
2 went off
3 going
4 in my soup
5 from there
6 she's holding
7 from now
8 place
9 you're reading
10 in here

36.3 **(Speaker A = India)**

1	A: Still no word from Dan.	4	B: I'm sure he'll have a whale of a time.
2	A: Tim has raised some objections to your proposals.	3	B: You'll really have your work cut out for you.
3	A: I'm looking after my two nephews this weekend.	1	B: Oh, well, I suppose no news is good news.
4	A: He's working in Barcelona for the summer.	6	B: I bet that wiped the smile off her face.
5	A: These cakes are great. Can I have another one?	5	B: Sure, there's plenty more where that came from.
6	A: Paula didn't get the promotion she'd been expecting.	2	B: Trust him to throw a spanner in the works.

Unit 37

37.1 1 or anything 2 or wherever 3 the place 4 the things 5 or someone

37.2 Vague expressions are underlined, and prominent words before these vague expressions are circled.

A: You've just got back from Italy, haven't you? The Amalfi coast or somewhere.
B: That's right. We stayed in Positano. Do you know it?
A: Yes, I went there twenty years ago or something. But I don't remember much about the place. A good holiday?
B: Well, we had some problems at first. They lost our luggage at the airport – it got put on the wrong plane or something like that. So the first night we didn't have a change of clothes or toothbrushes or whatever. It turned up the following day, though.
A: So how did you spend your time there?
B: We just relaxed, walked around, sat on the beach and that sort of thing. And we looked around the shops and places.
A: Did you buy a lot of stuff?
B: No, just a few presents and things.

37.3
1 … and that.
2 … or so.
3 … the thing.
4 … or something.
5 … or whenever.
6 … or anything like that.

Unit 38

38.1
1 She was killing herself laughing.
2 We had to do all the cooking ourselves.
3 They blame themselves for it.
4 He didn't know what to do with himself.
5 Take care of yourself.
6 He made it all himself.
7 I'm going to get myself a bike.
8 They made fools of themselves.
9 I picked them myself.
10 Speak for yourself.
11 I just burned myself.
12 Take one for yourself, too.

38.2
1 What did you do to yourself?
2 I fell asleep on the train and found myself in Cardiff.
3 The city centre itself is quite interesting.
4 She went for a walk by herself.
5 He's got himself a new car.
6 Have a good time. Enjoy yourselves.
7 Do they bake the bread themselves?
8 I'm keeping myself warm.
9 I grew all the vegetables myself.
10 She tried to defend herself.

38.3
A: I've made you a cake.
B: Is that it?
A: Yes, help yourself.
B: Er, you have some first.
A: But I didn't make it for me.
B: I can't eat it all myself. Marco would like it. Why not give some to him?
A: But I made it for you. You don't like it, do you?
B: Well, it's not the cake itself. It's the icing…
A: And I was feeling so pleased with myself.

Follow-up
'DIY' stands for 'do-it-yourself', referring to decorating or repairing your home for yourself rather than paying someone else to do it for you. The last word is usually prominent: DO it yourSELF. Note also that when the abbreviation is said, the last letter is usually prominent, e.g. He's a DIY enthusiast.

Unit 39

39.1 Prominent words are underlined and the prominent syllables in these words are in capital letters.

1 Was she REALly?
2 I supPOSE so.
3 I've ALways lived around here.
4 It's broken down aGAIN.
5 Shall I have a go?
6 You remember PABlo.
7 I gave it to my SON.
8 Can we GO now?
9 One MOment, please.
10 There was DUST all over the place.

39.2 **(Speaker A = Wales)**

The last prominent syllable in each speech unit (where the falling or rising tone starts) is in capital letters.

1 A: What time shall we leave?
B: // we could go NOW // as you're READy //
2 A: What time did David get back?
B: // I heard him come IN // at about THREE //
3 A: I'm not sure his plan would work very well.
B: // I thought his sugGEStion // was riDICulous //
4 A: The hall was packed, wasn't it?
B: // I HATE it // when it's so CROWded //
5 A: Do you want a drink?
B: // I wouldn't mind some Orange juice // if you've GOT any //
6 A: When did they tell you it would get here?
B: // They SAID it would be delivered // by YESterday //
7 A: Have you heard *Trio Gitano* play before?
B: // I FIRST saw them perform // a couple of YEARS ago //
8 A: I could move that easily.
B: // well why don't you TRY // if you think you're so STRONG //

Follow-up

Example: // I came aCROSS it (already introduced in 'where did you find it')// in an anTIQUE shop (giving A the information he asked for)//

1 // we could go NOW (giving A the information he asked for)// as you're READy (apparent to both A and B)//
2 // I heard him come IN (already introduced in 'what time did David get back?')// at about THREE (giving A the information he asked for)//
3 // I thought his sugGEStion (already introduced in 'his plan')// was riDICulous (B tells A his opinion)//
4 // I HATE it (B tells A his opinion)// when it's so CROWded (already introduced in 'the hall was packed')//
5 // I wouldn't mind some Orange juice (B tells A what kind of drink he wants)// if you've GOT any (the fact that A has drinks to offer is implied in the question; a falling tone here would seem to question whether A, in fact, had any drinks to offer)//
6 // they SAID it would be delivered (already introduced in 'tell … get here')// by YESterday (giving A the information he asked for)//
7 // I FIRST saw them perform (already introduced in 'heard … play before') // a couple of YEARS ago (giving A the information he asked for)//
8 // well why don't you TRY (making a new suggestion) // if you think you're so STRONG (implied in A's claim that he could move it easily)//

Unit 40

40.1
1 It's so boring ■, tennis ■.
2 I think it's gone off ■, this cream ■.
3 I took them myself ■, most of these photos ■.
4 That's my coat ■, the one with the fur collar ■.
5 They're a bit unfriendly ■, our neighbours ■.
6 It's really annoying ■, that dripping tap ■.
7 They're quite similar ■, those two shirts ■.
8 She was the first one in our family to go to university ■, my sister ■.

40.2 Note: Remember that most tails have a rising tone, but where they follow a *wh-* question, they usually have a falling tone.
1 Where's it being held, Friday's concert? ■
2 What's it like, this cheese? ■
3 It can be dangerous, skiing. ■
4 It's made from Thai silk, Vicky's dress. ■
5 When are they coming, Frank and Gill? ■
6 How much did you pay for them, these tickets? ■
7 It's not a great day for us to meet, Sunday. ■

40.3
A: *They're fascinating* ↘, *these things* ↗.
B: Careful, *it's sharp* ↘, *that knife* ↗.
A: Looks old, too.
B: *They've been in my family for over a hundred years* ↘, *most of those things* ↗.
A: *Amazing* ↘, *that* ↗.
B: *(He) Brought them back from Nepal* ↘, *my grandfather did* ↗.
A: *That's/It's somewhere I'd really like to go* ↘, *Nepal* ↗.
B: Me, too. But I'd have to go by plane, and *I hate it* ↘, *flying* ↗.

Follow-up
Here are some example criticisms:
They're a bit worn out, those carpets.
It's broken, this window.
It's very cold, the bathroom.
Here are some example compliments:
It's fantastic, the view from this window.
It's very reasonable, the price.
I really like it, the dining room.

Unit 41

41.1 A: Wonderful view from up here, isn't it?
B: Great.
A: I said it would be worth the effort, didn't I?
B: Hmm.
A: You're not tired, are you?
B: Exhausted. Give me some water, will you?
A: Not very fit, are you? Still, not much further.
B: But we're at the top, aren't we?
A: Just another kilometre to go. We can't turn round now, can we?
B: Of course we can. Let's go back now, shall we? Please.

41.2 **(Speaker A = Japan)**
1 2 3 4 5 6 7

41.3 **(Speaker A = Jamaica)**
The most likely tag with the more likely tone is given. These are used on the recording.
1 aren't they (is also possible, but less likely)
2 wasn't it
3 will there (is also possible, but less likely)
4 are you
5 could (or can/will/would) you

Follow-up
Examples of question tags in other languages are *n'est-ce pas?* (French) and *eller hur?* (Swedish).

Unit 42

42.1 **(Speaker A = Northern Ireland)**
The last prominent syllable in each question, where the falling or rising tone starts, is in capital letters.
5 what you should DO is write and comPLAIN .
6 what we WANT is some RAIN .
7 All they had LEFT were these SAUSages .
8 All I can SEE is a block of FLATS .

42.2 3 coffee and TOAST is what I USually have .
4 A new comPUter is what I'm HOPing for .
5 write and comPLAIN is what you should DO .
6 some RAIN is what we WANT .
7 These SAUSages were all they had LEFT .
8 A block of FLATS is all I can SEE .

42.3 **(Speaker A = China)**
The most likely patterns of intonation are given.
1 It was his brother who went to Australia.
2 It was my back that was aching.
3 It was the Democrats who won the election.

Follow-up
Here are some beginnings of *what-* and *it-* clefts that might be useful in conversation:
What I want to do first is …
What I don't understand is why …
It was my brother who suggested …
What I think is nice is …
It was only last week that I …
It was the bad weather that stopped me from …

Unit 43

43.1 The last prominent syllable in each question, where the falling or rising tone starts, is in capital letters.

1 Were the poLICE involved? *making sure*
2 Are you feeling oKAY now? *finding out*
3 Don't we turn LEFT here? *making sure*
4 Why didn't you phone me EARlier? *finding out*
5 Have you discussed it with your PArents yet? *finding out*
6 How do you get the TOP off? *making sure*
7 Did I see you in TOWN on Saturday? *making sure*
8 What happened after THAT? *finding out*

43.2 The most likely tones, and those used on the recording, are given. However, other tones are possible. The last prominent syllable in each question, where the falling or rising tone starts, is in capital letters.

Are you aWAKE?
I wonder what TIME it is?
When did you book the TAxi for?
Which terminal does the plane LEAVE from?
You don't KNOW?
Doesn't PHILip work at the airport?
Are you SURE?
WHAT time is it again?
Would you mind if I put the RAdio on?
WHEN'S the taxi coming?

43.3 The last prominent syllable in each question, where the falling or rising tone starts, is in capital letters.

Example: Is it oKAY to park here?
1 Can I get you another DRINK?
2 Have you been here beFORE?
3 Wasn't DON at the meal?
4 Can you see it more CLEARly now?
5 Would you like me to FETCH it for you?

Follow-up

Here are the first ten questions in an episode of a radio soap opera. The last prominent syllable is in capital letters, and the tone starting on this syllable is indicated.

1 Do you want a HAND, sally ? (an offer of help; see C note)
2 well, how ELSE can I look at it ? (a finding out question; see **A**)
3 Great, WEREN'T they ? (the speaker expects the hearer to agree; see Unit 41**A**)
4 so, what are we DOing this year ? (a finding out question; see **A**)
5 what time's LUNCH ? (a finding out question; see **A**)
6 And you think that's oKAY ? (If we take 'And you think that's okay' to be a statement, then we might have expected a rising tone [see **C**]. However, if we take it to mean 'And do you think that's okay?' with 'do you' left out, then this would be a *yes–no* question intended to find out; see A)
7 And this is BETter ? (a statement; see **C**)
8 Not this afterNOON ? (Unit 41 doesn't deal with intonation in this type of question directly. However, it seems to be like a statement, and rising tone is usual; see **C**)
9 HAPpy ? (a reduced form of the *yes–no*, making sure question 'Are you happy?)
10 what aBOUT ? (By using a rising tone here, the speaker seems to mean 'Remind me what (it's) about'; in other words, the question is checking something that the speaker implies they have temporarily forgotten; see **B**)

Unit 44

44.1 **(Speaker A = Australia)**

1 2 3 4 5 6 7 8 9 10

44.2 **(Speaker B = Spain)**

The last prominent syllable in each part, where the falling or fall-rising tone starts on the recording, is given in capital letters.

1 when are they supposed to be BACK ? This EVEning ?
2 where's she LIVing now ? with her PArents ?
3 How many of your cousins have you inVIted ? ALL of them ?
4 why did you do such a silly THING ? Because your friends TOLD you to ?
5 How much of the assignment have you written so FAR ? ANy of it ?
6 what's wrong with your MOTHer ? Nothing SErious ?
7 which doctor did you want to SEE ? Dr IREland ?

Follow-up

what FOR ? (= why e.g. A: I want you to come with me. B: What for?)
How COME ? (used to ask why something has happened e.g. A: We had to get a taxi. B: How come?)
why NOT ? (used to agree to a suggestion e.g. A: Shall we go out for a curry? B: Why not?)
what's UP ? (= what is happening or what is wrong? e.g. A: What's up? B: I'm stuck!)
so WHAT ? (= it's not important or I don't care e.g. A: Your parents won't be happy. B: So what?)

Unit 45

45.1 (Speaker A = India)

1 HOW much ?
2 WHEN do you need it ?
3 HOW old is it ?
4 You did WHAT ?
5 HOW far is it ?
6 HOW many ?
7 WHAT were you looking for ? (Note: A spatula is a tool used in cooking, particularly for lifting food out of a pan. It is wide and flat at the end, and not sharp.)
8 WHERE ?
9 WHICH one's yours ?
10 She's doing WHAT ? (Note: Abseiling is going down a very steep slope by holding on to a rope. The rope is fastened at the top of the slope.)

45.2 (Speaker A = Poland)

The last prominent syllable in each question, where the falling or rising tone starts, is given in capital letters.

1 WHAT did you say?
2 How can you TELL?
3 WHAT sort do you want?
4 WHY doesn't he want to go?
5 WHAT is?
6 How many were THERE?
7 WHO did you buy it for?

Follow-up

1 WHAT did you say?
3 WHAT sort do you want?
4 WHY doesn't he want to go?
7 WHO did you buy it for?

Unit 46

46.1 **(speaker A = Japan)**
The syllable where the falling or fall-rising tone starts is given in capital letters.
Example: They're really quite COMfortable ↘, even though they're TIGHT ↘↗.
1 I PHONED him ↘↗, but there was no ANswer ↘.
2 I didn't get to SPEAK to him ↘, though everyone ELSE seemed to ↘↗.
3 My DAD was asleep ↘↗, but my Mum was waiting UP for me ↘.
4 I used to live on EXmoor ↘, not DARTmoor ↘↗.
5 Although he's overWEIGHT ↘↗, he's actually quite FIT ↘.
6 You'd be better off travelling on Saturday MORning ↘, rather than Friday NIGHT ↘↗.

46.2 **(Speaker A = Northern Ireland)**
The syllable where the falling or rising tone starts is given in capital letters.
Example I actually liked her FIRST one ↘ more than her SECond ↗.
1 But it's easier to talk face-to-FACE ↘ than on the PHONE ↗.
2 You either need smaller FINgers ↗ or new GLASses ↘.
3 Much as we'd LIKE to go ↗, we can't afFORD it ↘.
4 She's going to Perth in SCOTland ↘, not Perth in AusTRAlia ↗.
5 It's not a NOVel exactly ↗, more a short STOry ↘.
6 Instead of going by BOAT ↗, we went by HELicopter ↘.

Follow-up
Examples
46.1, 1 There was no ANswer ↘ when I PHONED him ↘↗.
46.1, 2 Though everyone ELSE seemed to ↘↗ I didn't get to SPEAK to him ↘.
46.2, 3 We can't afFORD it ↘, much as we'd LIKE to go ↗.
46.2, 4 She's not going to Perth in AusTRAlia ↗, she's going to Perth in SCOTland ↘.

Unit 47

47.2 **(Speaker A = Jamaica)**

1 **a** No, three <u>spoonfuls</u> of sugar.
2 **a** No, they've <u>bought</u> me a car.
3 **a** No, I'm not going to <u>school</u> today.
4 **a** But I took it to <u>work</u>.

1 **b** No, three spoonfuls of <u>sugar</u>.
2 **b** No, they've bought me a <u>car</u>.
3 **b** No, I'm not <u>going</u> to school today.
4 **b** But I <u>took</u> it to work.

47.3 **(Speaker A = China)**

1 <u>soft</u>ware
2 <u>in</u>doors
3 <u>in</u>flate
4 <u>un</u>wound
5 post<u>code</u>
6 <u>sea</u>sick

Follow-up
The speaker presumably wanted to contrast the government's promise that it *would* happen and the fact that it is not happening *now*. Saying '… it's not ↑HAPPening ↘' would not have done this in this context, but highlighting '… ing' in the way he did successfully focuses our attention on the timing of the event (now) rather than the event itself. He could, of course, have achieved the same effect by saying '… it's not happening ↑NOW ↘'.

Unit 48

48.1

1 You couldn't do me a favour?
2 Do you want to borrow my umbrella?
3 I'd rather meet at ten, if you can make it.
4 Couldn't you come another day?
5 Will you be able to write a reference for me?
6 Can I open the door for you?
7 Can you get something for me from town while you're there?

Numbers 2 and 6 would probably sound more polite or sincere with a falling (rather than a fall-rising) tone, as they are offers.

48.2 (Speaker A = Spain)

1	A: Mr Brown's an excellent dentist.	3	B: His later ones were.
2	A: I've put on a lot of weight recently.	6	B: I wanted to come.
3	A: Dali's paintings were so strange.	1	B: He's very good with children.
4	A: You're very good at chess, aren't you?	5	B: It was certainly unexpected.
5	A: Great news about Martha's new job.	4	B: Well, I used to play well.
6	A: It's a pity you couldn't come skiing with us.	2	B: You still look fit, though.

48.3 1 ii 2 ii 3 ii 4 i

Follow-up
Here are some example positive sentences about Norway and possible responses expressing reservation.
1 'The standard of living is very high.' 'But it's very exPENsive there.'
2 'The scenery is beautiful.' 'Along the COAST it is.'
3 'The winters are great for skiing.' 'The skiing's better in SWITzerland.'

Unit 49

49.1 These are the most likely tones for these attitude words and phrases in these positions, and are the ones given on the recording. However, others are possible.
1 presumably; in fact
2 naturally; of course
3 Apparently; as it happens
4 On reflection; in fairness; so to speak

49.2

1	A: Why don't you get a new job?	4	B: Yes. **Mind you**, it should at the price.
2	A: How did the workers feel about the decision?	2	B: It was unpopular, **to say the least**.
3	A: What did your mother say when you left?	5	B: You don't expect me to believe that, **surely**?
4	A: This wine tastes wonderful.	1	B: **Believe me**, I would if I could.
5	A: My dog ate my homework.	3	B: She was disappointed, **to put it mildly**.

49.3 1 outwardly 2 technically 3 politically 4 superficially

Follow-up
Here are some more examples.
I've got a food mixer. The only problem is, I can't find the instructions.
I know you think we should get a new car. The question is, do we really need one?
I've got the money to lend you. The point is I don't want to.

Unit 50

50.1 1 sadly: a = ↘ ↗ b = ↗
2 luckily: a = ↘ ↗ b = ↗
3 frankly: a = ↗ b = ↘ ↗
4 strangely enough: a = ↗ b = ↘ ↗

50.2 1 A: Basically ↘↗ B: essentially ↗
2 A: Apparently ↘↗ B: on the whole ↗
3 A: apparently ↗ B: Actually ↘↗
4 A: Presumably ↘↗ B: actually ↗

Follow-up
Here are some example incorrect statements about a friend, and possible corrections.
1 'He's a civil engineer.' 'He's a structural engineer, **actually** ↗.'
2 'He lives in Paris.' '**Actually** ↘↗, he lives in Geneva.'
3 'He's married.' 'He's divorced, **actually** ↗.'

Unit 51

51.1 (Speaker A = Scotland)
1 ↘ 2 ↗↘ (enthusiastic) 3 ↘ 4 ↘ 5 ↘ 6 ↗↘ (enthusiastic) 7 ↗↘ (enthusiastic)

51.2 (Speaker A = Japan)
1 convenient 2 horrified 3 useless 4 bizarre 5 exhausting 6 stunning

51.3 The responses on the recording are given first. Other possible responses are in brackets.
1 A: He reckons United are going to win. B: That's riDICulous ↗↘! (No WAY ↗↘! You're KIDding ↗↘!)
2 A: I crashed my car again. B: You IDiot ↗↘. (You're KIDding ↗↘!)
3 A: Go on, lend me the money. B: No WAY ↗↘! (You're KIDding ↗↘! [= I don't believe you're asking me])
4 A: Jane has left Adam. B: You're KIDding ↗↘. (No WAY ↗↘! That's riDICulous ↗↘! [both = I think you're wrong])
5 A: He's bought a Porsche. B: A PORSCHE ↗↘! (No WAY ↗↘! That's riDICulous ↗↘! [both = I think you're wrong])

51.4 1 A: Karen says she wants to be a vet. B: REALly! ↗↘
2 A: I thought the homework was easy. B: REALly? ↗
3 A: The builders say they'll be finished by tomorrow. B: REALly? ↗
4 A: Lee's going to work in Nepal. B: REALly! ↗↘
5 A: Crossing the river shouldn't be a problem. B: REALly? ↗
6 A: I passed my driving test. B: REALly! ↗↘
7 A: Paul and Nickie are getting married. B: REALly! ↗↘
8 A: My sister's planning to cycle across the country. B: REALly? ↗
9 A: I plan to lose five kilos in the next month. B: REALly? ↗
10 A: There's a fox in the garden. B: REALly! ↗↘

Follow-up
Here are some example demands from a teacher or boss, and responses expressing surprise.
1 'I want you to start work/school at 5 o' clock tomorrow.' 'FIVE ↗↘!'
2 'The whole lesson/meeting will be conducted in Spanish.' 'SPANish ↗↘!'
3 'You should answer all one hundred questions.' 'All one HUNdred ↗↘!'

Unit 52

52.3 A: So it'll go past those trees …
B: mHM.
A: … across that footpath …
B: YEAH.
A: … and down across the top of that field.
B: RIGHT, and who owns that?
A: All the fields around here are part of a big farm.
B: uHUH.
A: Belongs to the farmer who lives in that white house.
B: RIGHT.
A: Of course, he won't be happy about the plans.
B: WON'T he?
A: No, I doubt that he'll want to sell any of his land.
B: oKAY. So what'll happen then?
A: I suppose the council could force him to sell.
B: REALly?
A: But that wouldn't be popular with the local community.
B: i SEE.

Unit 53

53.1 (Speaker A = Jamaica)
1 Otherwise 2 Worse still 3 Well 4 Besides 5 In that case

53.2 (Speaker A = China)
1 By the way 2 Better still 3 Well 4 Anyway 5 by the same token

53.3 (Speaker A = Spain)
Example answers
1 In that case, I'll take a couple of days off work.
2 Incidentally, have you seen Mona recently?
3 Besides, I don't really enjoy jazz.
4 Look, I keep telling you it's not for sale.

Follow-up
'then again' (or 'there again') is usually used to add a new thought that is different or opposite to what has just been said. For example:
A: I doubt that Fran will want to walk to work.
B: **Then aGAIN**, she might be happy to get some fresh air.

Unit 54

54.1
1 The ship was launched // in September 1942 // and destroyed a month later.
2 Property prices will increase // as long as interest rates // remain low.
3 The bird is often heard // but seldom // seen in the wild.
4 They took what they could carry // and left the rest // of their belongings behind.
5 Why students drop out // of university // is a complex issue.
6 Thieves made off // with the painting // despite security guards in the building.
7 Most people also speak French // which is taught // from the age of six.
8 Who gave the order // to shoot // is to be investigated further.
9 Women // who are pregnant // should avoid alcohol.
10 He claimed // he was innocent // but the jury disagreed.

54.2 Possible speech unit boundaries are shown. These are used in the recording.
Complementary therapy,// which focuses on the whole person,// is becoming more widely used.// It considers a patient's physical symptoms// and also takes lifestyle into account.//

Most practitioners believe// that the body seeks a state of balance.// What complementary therapy does// is help people achieve this balance.// Treatment not only relieves the disease// but also promotes general wellbeing.//

How complementary therapy works// is still not entirely clear.// Recent research// has compared it with traditional medicine.// In one study conducted in Canada// a group of patients// who had severe back pain// were treated either with complementary// or traditional treatments.// Patients who had complementary treatments// showed faster rates of improvement.

Unit 55

55.1 The most likely speech unit boundaries in the green parts are given. These are used on the recording. The relevant rule from section **B** is also given.
1 The whole basis of Goldberg's analysis// has been called into question. (b)
2 Most of her money// she left to children's charities. (d) (iv)
3 In the first half of this year// our sales have fallen by 25 per cent. (d) (i)
4 As a result// women are having fewer children than in the 1990s. (d) (ii)
5 Collectively// the members of the organisation// were known as 'The Followers'. (a) and (b)
6 Unhappily for his family// he was never seen again. (a)
7 To conclude// all these factors suggest the need for job cuts. (d) (iii)
8 The two companies// although in competition// have agreed to cooperate on the project. (c)

55.3 Possible speech unit boundaries are shown. These are used in the recording.
Ever since the industrial revolution// we have dumped waste// into the air.// Consequently,// atmospheric carbon dioxide levels// are now a third higher// than in pre-industrial time.// The process may,// it has to be said,// have started long before,// when we first burnt down trees// to make way for agriculture.// However,// over the last few decades// the rate of increase// has grown rapidly.// Although its precise nature is unclear// there is an obvious relationship// between levels of carbon dioxide in the atmosphere// and higher global surface temperatures.//

The impact of higher temperatures// is difficult to assess,// but there will certainly be a different world// as humans and other living organisms// try to adapt to change.// These changes,// which will affect us all,// include drought and extreme weather.// Southern Europe,// for example,// already has long periods// without rainfall.// And in the Americas and Asia// powerful hurricanes// and typhoons// have recently killed// more people// than in several// decades.//

Of course,// some scientists dispute the evidence.// But these people,// as we all know,// represent industries// having vested interests// – their business,// they believe,// would be damaged// by limits on carbon emissions.// But among the wider scientific community// the argument is about the speed of change,// not whether change is taking place.//

Unit 56

56.1
1 In a number of countries// New Zealand for instance// attempts are being made to harness geothermal energy.
2 The city of Chester// originally a Roman settlement// was a major military stronghold by the time of the English Civil War in the 17th century.
3 At the top of the hill are the Three Witches// as they used to be called// which is a curious rock formation.
4 A large group of protestors// nearly three thousand// were in the audience when the president began his last speech.
5 Gregor's final novel// by far his most entertaining// was written when he was in his nineties.

56.2 Prominent syllables in the inserts are in capital letters.
1 Karl Huzel – from our GERman SISter company – will be talking to us after my presentation.
2 The countries of the European Union – with the exCEPtion of FRANCE – have all approved the new regulations on working conditions.
3 Our latest model – the DC6 – was released in April this year.
4 The new research and development unit – to be BASED in DUBlin — will be opened later this year.

Follow-up
Here are three examples, with inserts, from the field of astronomy.
1 The estimated total number of asteroids in the solar system – many of which are very small – is greater than half a million.
2 The science of measuring the brightness of stars – known as photometry – dates back more than 2000 years.
3 The generally accepted theory of sunspots – proposed by Babcock in 1961 – suggests that they are caused by changes in the sun's magnetic field.

Unit 57

57.1 The step-ups on the recording are marked, but other places for step-ups are possible.

1. She always said it was her best film, although the critics ↑ hated it.
   ('... ↑ critics ...' would also be possible, contrasting 'her' and 'the critics')
2. Rather than a military solution, we should be looking for a ↑ political one.
3. Some plastics are easy to produce, but ↑ difficult to dispose of.
   ('... difficult to ↑ dispose of' would also be possible, contrasting 'produce' and 'dispose of')
4. Instead of a quick resolution to the war, their tactics ↑ prolonged it.
5. Most people think he's French, but in fact he's from ↑ Canada.
   ('... in ↑ fact ...' would also be possible, contrasting what 'most people think' and 'fact')
6. The model weighs only four kilos, whereas the full-scale version will weigh four ↑ thousand.
   ('... ↑ full-scale version ...' would also be possible, contrasting the 'model' and the 'full-scale version')
7. Despite the President's personal popularity, his party ↑ lost the election.
   ('... ↑ party ...' would also be possible, contrasting 'the President' and 'his party')
8. The novel was all his own work – or he ↑ claimed it was.
9. The area is a popular tourist attraction, and yet ↑ completely unspoilt.
10. Unlike most of our competitors, we've ↑ actually made a profit this year.
    ('... a ↑ profit ...' would also be possible, contrasting 'a profit' with 'a loss', which is implied)

57.2 In ↑this lesson, we're going to look further at the life of Napoleon. As you'll remember, Napoleon was probably one of the greatest military leaders in history. In the class ↑last week, we studied his earlier life, until about 1808, and now we'll look at events from about 1808 until his death. ↑By 1808, you'll recall, Napoleon had crowned himself Emperor of the first French Empire. By this time he was in control of much of Europe, including Austria, Italy, Spain and Sweden. However, in ↑1809, Spain and Austria rose up against the French. Although the French army defeated them, thousands of men were lost. And in ↑1812, ignoring repeated advice against it, Napoleon began his invasion of Russia. In this campaign, over half a million soldiers in his army were killed, and by 1814 Paris had fallen and Napoleon had abdicated. Now ↑what I'd like this half of the class to do is read the account of the battle near Vienna in 1809 in your textbooks starting on page 82. The ↑other half should study the maps and pictures of the 1812 invasion on the handout, and write a brief account of what you have observed.

Unit 58

58.1 1 Michael **Watson** ↘↗, the ↓ reigning **champion** ↘↗, has been knocked out of the French Open.

2 Whitedown **Hill** ↘, ↓ above the Trant **Valley** ↘↗, is to be the location of a new wind farm.

3 Two sisters from **France** ↘, ↓ both in their **seventies** ↘, have become the oldest people to swim the English Channel.

4 A black **woodpecker** ↘, a ↓ rare visitor to **Britain** ↘↗, has been spotted on the east coast.

5 The head of NATO in **Europe** ↘↗, ↓ Major Peter **Alvin** ↘↗, has warned that its military equipment is becoming seriously outdated.

58.2 The tones used in the added information and the previous noun phrase are shown. These tones begin on the previous prominent syllable.
Example: Large areas of the COUNtry ↘, one of the ↓ POORest in Asia ↘, have been hit by drought.

1 Mr Abram IvANich ↘↗, a ↓ FORmer COMMunist ↘↗, has been elected president of Novistan.

2 The Nisota car factory in PERTH ↘, ↓ emPLOYing over THREE thousand PEople ↘, is to close next year.

3 A statue of Sir Frank WHIttle, ↘↗, ↓ inVENtor of the JET engine ↘↗, has been unveiled in his home town.

4 Over fifty thousand PEople ↘, almost a ↓ TENth of the popuLAtion ↘, are now thought to have been infected with influenza.

5 The city of St PEtersburg ↘↗, ↓ PREviously LENingrad ↘↗, is encouraging people to use public transport.

58.3 On your ↑ right we're passing the beautiful National Theatre, built in the mid 1800s and one of the most important Czech cultural institutions. If you want to see opera or ballet in Prague, that's the place to ↓ go. We're ↑ now passing under one of the best-known bridges in the world, the Charles Bridge. It was built in the 13th century, and has 75 statues along its ↓ sides. Over on the ↑ left, up on the hill, is Prague Castle, the home of Czech kings throughout the ages and now the seat of the President of the Czech ↓ Republic. You can ↑ also see the spires of Saint Vitus Cathedral, where most of the Czech kings are ↓ buried. To your ↑ right now is the Rudolfinum, a concert hall…

Unit 59

59.1 1 Make sure you give three pieces of information on each page – your name ↘, your student number ↘ and the date ↘.

2 When I was learning to drive my instructor made me say 'mirror →, signal →, manoeuvre ↘' every time I drove away.

3 Attempts on the mountain have been made this year by Japanese climbers ↗, Swiss climbers ↗ and Brazilian climbers ↘.

4 You'll remember that Trollope's first three novels in his Barsetshire Chronicles were *The Warden* ↘↗, *Barchester Towers* ↘↗ and *Doctor Thorne* ↘.

5 I want you to paint the squares the colours of the rainbow – red →, orange →, yellow → and so on ↘.

59.2 1 She had a number of jobs in Berlin – // as a →waitress//, →bookseller//, →music teacher// – but still found time to develop her career in the theatre.

2 Note that the last enrolment dates are // the 15th of ↘July//, the ↘30th of July// and the 30th of ↘August//.

3 A copy of the contract, // →signed//, →sealed// and ↘delivered//, will be on your desk tomorrow. [Note: 'signed, sealed, and delivered' means that it is officially signed and completed]

4 Don't forget that for this experiment you'll need // ↘↗safety glasses//, protective ↘↗clothing// and rubber ↘gloves//.

5 To get to the bookshop // go down this ↗street//, turn left at the ↗traffic lights// and then cross the ↘square//.

Follow-up

The last prominent syllable in each marked speech unit (where the tone starts) is in capital letters.
Let every nation know, whether it wishes us well or ill,// that we shall pay any PRICE ↗ //, bear any BURden ↗ //, meet any HARDship ↗ //, support any FRIEND ↗ //, oppose any FOE ↗ //, to assure the survival and the success of LIBerty ↘ //.

In passing this office to the Vice President, I also do so with the profound sense of the weight of responsibility that will fall on his shoulders tomorrow and, therefore,// of the underSTANding ↘ //, the PAtience ↘ //, the coopeRAtion ↘ // he will need from all Americans.

Unit 60

60.1 1 She said that she was employed as: 'an environmental status assessment consultant'.
2 The managing director described the rise in oil prices as: 'a worrying and potentially damaging development'.
3 Apparently it was Picasso who said: 'Painting is just another way of keeping a diary.'
4 The book describes the mobile phone as: 'the most significant electronic consumer device ever invented'.

60.2 1 Paraphrase 2 Paraphrase 3 Quotation 4 Paraphrase

60.3 Example sentences on the recording:
1 We've developed a computer programme that can actually … teach itself a new language.
2 The number of overweight people in the country has risen to an incredible … 50 million.
3 Using the new treatment, the number of people missing work due to backaches … was cut by half.

Section E1

1 1 ʌ 2 ɒ 3 æ 4 ə 5 ʊ 6 e 7 ʌ 8 ɪ 9 ə 10 e 11 ʊ 12 ɒ

2
1 klɒk = clock
2 blʌd = blood
3 stænd = stand
4 hænd = hand
5 kʊd = could
6 bʌtə = butter
7 slɪpt = slipped
8 test = test
9 sʌn = son
10 ges = guess
11 prətekt = protect
12 stɒp = stop

3

1 h _ m	iː / ɑː / ɜː	(hɑːm = harm)
2 b _ t	iː / uː / ɔː	(biːt = beat/beet; buːt = boot; bɔːt = bought)
3 p _ s	ɜː / iː / uː	(pɜːs = purse; piːs = piece/peace)
4 f _ d	ɑː / uː / ɔː	(fuːd = food; fɔːd = ford)
5 t _ k	ɔː / ɑː / uː	(tɔːk = talk/torque)
6 w _ m	ɑː / iː / ɔː	(wɔːm = warm)
7 h _ t	ɑː / ɜː / uː	(hɑːt = heart; hɜːt = hurt; huːt = hoot)
8 t _ n	ɜː /ɔː / uː	(tɜːn = turn; tɔːn = torn)
9 k _ n	iː / ɑː / ɜː	(kiːn = keen)
10 p _ t	ɔː / uː /ɑː	(pɔːt = port; pɑːt = part)
11 k _ l	uː / ɜː / ɔː	(kuːl = cool; kɜːl = curl; kɔːl = call)
12 h _ b	ɜː / ɑː / iː	(hɜːb = herb)

4

1

	d	
g	ɜː	l
	t	

→ girl ↓ dirt

3

	n	
t	uː	l
	n	

→ tool ↓ noon

5

	h	
v	ɜː	b
	t	

→ verb ↓ hurt

7

	k	
w	ɔː	n
	t	

→ warn/worn
↓ caught/court

9

	r	
h	uː	m
	d	

→ whom
↓ rude

2

	f	
v	ɑː	z
	m	

→ vase ↓ farm

4

	b	
dr	ɔː	z
	n	

→ draws/drawers
↓ born/borne

6

	s	
n	iː	t
	m	

→ neat
↓ seem/seam

8

	k	
p	ɑː	t
	m	

→ part ↓ calm

10

	p	
m	iː	n
	s	

→ mean
↓ peace/piece

5
1 /pen/ – /pɪn/
2 /hɪd/ – /hæd/
3 /send/ – /sænd/
4 /gʌlf/ – /gɒlf/
5 /tʊk/ – /tʌk/
6 /pɒt/ – /pʊt/
7 /pæt/ – /pɑːt/
8 /fɜːm/ – /fɑːm/
9 /fuːl/ – /fʊl/
10 /hɜːt/ – /hʌt/
11 /ɒdə/ – /ɔːdə/
12 /wɔːkt/ – /wɜːkt/
13 /fɑː/ – /fɜː/
14 /hiː/ – /huː/

1 /pen/ = pen
2 /hɪd/ = hid
3 /sænd/ = sand
4 /gʌlf/ = gulf
5 /tʌk/ = tuck
6 /pʊt/ = put
7 /pæt/ = pat
8 /fɜːm/ = firm
9 /fuːl/ = fool
10 /hʌt/ = hut
11 /ɒdə/ = odder
12 /wɜːkt/ = worked
13 /fɑː/ = far
14 /hiː/ = he

6

1 sport – spot
2 cut – cot
3 tea – two
4 fat – fit
5 hut – hurt
6 hit – heat
7 books – box
8 heard – hard
9 man – men
10 wrist – rest
11 bird – bored
12 pull – pool
13 look – luck
14 heart – hat

1 spot = /spɒt/
2 cot = /kɒt/
3 two = /tuː/
4 fat = /fæt/
5 hut = /hʌt/
6 heat = /hiːt/
7 box = /bɒks/
8 heard = /hɜːd/
9 men = /men/
10 wrist = /rɪst/
11 bored = /bɔːd/
12 pull = /pʊl/
13 look = /lʊk/
14 hat = /hæt/

7

	eə	ɪə	aɪ	eɪ	ɔɪ	əʊ	aʊ	ʊə
b	bear	beer	buy	bay	boy	bow (= weapon)	bow (= bend)	
d	dare	dear	die	day		dough		
f	fair	fear				foe		
g		gear	guy	gay		go		
h	hair	here	high	hay		hoe	how	
m	mare	mere	my	may		mow		
p	pear	pier	pie	pay				poor*
r	rare	rear	rye	ray		row (= move through water)	row (= argument)	
s			sigh	say	soy	sow (= to plant seeds)	sow (= a female pig)	
t	tear (= pull apart)	tear (= water from the eye)	tie		toy	toe		tour*

* 'poor' can also be pronounced /pɔː/ and 'tour' can also be pronounced /tɔː/.

8

1 ˈfeðə
2 ˈspeʃəl
3 ˈhʌŋgə
4 ˈɪndʒəri
5 biːtʃ
6 drɪŋk
7 kæʃ
8 ˈsiːʒə
9 bɑːθ
10 jes
11 ðeə
12 ˈtreʒə
13 sɪŋ
14 ˈdeɪndʒərəs
15 ˈfiːtʃə
16 ˈdɪkʃənəri
17 ɔːlˈðəʊ
18 ˈjeləʊ
19 ˈɔːθə
20 jʌŋ
21 ˈjuːʒəl
22 ˈsəʊldʒə

9

1 ˌdʒuːnɪˈvɜːsəti / ˌjuːnɪˈvɜːsəti
2 ˈleθə / ˈleðə
3 kræʃ / kræʒ
4 ˈsɪndʒə / ˈsɪŋə
5 ʒiːnz / dʒiːnz
6 ˈsliːpɪŋ / ˈsliːpɪn
7 θɪŋk / ðɪŋk
8 ʃeɪd / dʒeɪd
9 ˈmeʃə / ˈmeʒə
10 ʒuːst / juːst
11 riːtʃ / riːdʒ
12 ˌsaʊθˈiːst / ˌsaʊtʃˈiːst
13 ˈtelɪvɪdʒən / ˈtelɪvɪʒən
14 ˈbrʌθə / ˈbrʌðə

10

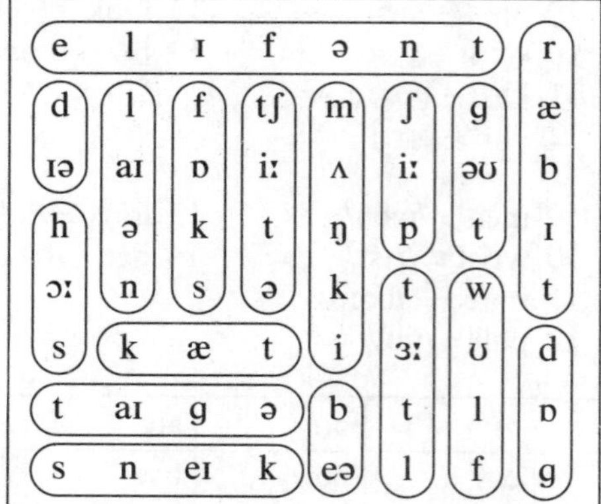

11

Country	Capital city
1 'tʃaɪnə – China	g beɪ'dʒɪŋ – Beijing
2 æl'dʒɪəriə – Algeria	d æl'dʒɪəz – Algiers
3 'pəʊlənd – Poland	f 'wɔːsɔː – Warsaw
4 'swiːdᵊn – Sweden	j 'stɒkhəʊm – Stockholm
5 'tʃɪli – Chile	b ˌsænti'ɑːgəʊ – Santiago
6 mə'leɪziə – Malaysia	c ˌkwɑːlə'lʊmpʊəʳ – Kuala Lumpur
7 'pɔːtʃəgᵊl – Portugal	a 'lɪzbən – Lisbon
8 'swɪtsᵊlənd – Switzerland	h bɜːn – Berne
9 æl'beɪniə – Albania	i tɪ'rɑːnə – Tirana
10 mə'lɑːwi – Malawi	e lɪ'lɒŋweɪ – Lilongwe

Section E2

1 1 brand – bland (D); 2 blouse – browse (D); 3 blank (S); 4 bend – blend (D); 5 brink (S); 6 breeze (S); 7 broad – bored (D); 8 brew (S); 9 black; 10 broom; 11 blushed; 12 bread; 13 bow; 14 bought

2 1 prank (S); 2 pretty (S); 3 proud (S); 4 plane – pain (D); 5 plod – prod (D); 6 peach – preach (D); 7 please (S); 8 plays – praise (D); 9 plan; 10 pot; 11 prawns; 12 pies; 13 play; 14 present

3 1 croak (S); 2 crane (S); 3 cloud – crowd (D); 4 cash – clash (D); 5 crutch (S); 6 cost – crossed (D); 7 claim – came (D); 8 clown (S); 9 cook; 10 clause; 11 crew; 12 climb; 13 keen; 14 cruel

4 1 grammar (S); 2 gory – glory (D); 3 grade – glade (D); 4 great – gate (D); 5 groom (S); 6 glean (S); 7 glide – guide (D); 8 gave (S); 9 grazing; 10 glue; 11 grass; 12 gasped; 13 going; 14 glow

5 1 fragrant – flagrant (D); 2 flame (S); 3 four – floor (D); 4 ford – fraud (D); 5 flee – free (D); 6 flesh (S); 7 flee (S); 8 frog (S); 9 flatter; 10 fruit; 11 flows; 12 favour; 13 flying; 14 fright

6 1 dug (S); 2 tree – tea (D); 3 tread – dread (D); 4 tooth (S); 5 train (S); 6 down – drown (D); 7 drip – dip (D); 8 tied – tried (D); 9 two; 10 trap; 11 diving; 12 drawer; 13 try; 14 died

7 1 warmth (S); 2 concerned – concern (D); 3 fridge (S); 4 thump (S); 5 bomb (S); 6 bet – bent (D); 7 pinch (S); 8 armed – arm (D); 9 blame; 10 change; 11 find; 12 rooms; 13 trays; 14 flame

8 1 gulf – gull (D); 2 coal (S); 3 well – wealth (D); 4 sale (S); 5 hold (S); 6 build (S); 7 wolf – wool (D); 8 kill – kiln (D); 9 fell; 10 fuels; 11 called; 12 help; 13 film; 14 shell

9 1 eat (S); 2 hunt (S); 3 fell – felt (D); 4 past – pass (D); 5 let – left (D); 6 packed – pack (D); 7 paint (S); 8 fat (S); 9 guess; 10 built; 11 goat; 12 bell; 13 meant; 14 abolished

10 1 led – lend (D); 2 devised (S); 3 bombed – bond (D); 4 led – lend (D); 5 begged – bed (D); 6 raced – raised (D); 7 harmed (S); 8 gold – goal (D); 9 wind; 10 sewed; 11 bad; 12 timed; 13 wild; 14 describe

11 1 clips – clicks (D); 2 cats – caps (D); 3 gaps (S); 4 checks (S); 5 lips (S); 6 once (S); 7 bakes – base (D); 8 case – cakes (D); 9 graphs; 10 glance; 11 deaths; 12 sick; 13 moss; 14 maps

12 1 youths (S); 2 stars (S); 3 bags (S); 4 lies – lives (D); 5 rains – raise (D); 6 rides – rise (D); 7 size – sides (D); 8 cause (S); 9 crimes; 10 robes; 11 lawns; 12 sells; 13 cars; 14 size

Section E3

1

Ooo	oOo	oOoo
changeable functional patronage pilgrimage	arrival assemblage percentage	advisable desirable emotional enjoyable original

The exception is 'original' (compare 'origin and o'riginal).

2

Ooo	oOo	Oooo	oOoo
awkwardness colourless powerful	alertness disgraceful eventful regardless	characterless deviousness	abrasiveness assertiveness directionless

3

Ooo	oOo	oOoo
beautify borrower dangerous marvellous simplify	announcer beginner	anomalous calamitous diversify intensify solidify

The exception is 'solidify' (compare 'solid and so'lidify).

4

Oo	oOo	oOoo
anxious cautious spacious	ambitious pretentious religious suspicious	industrious laborious luxurious mysterious rebellious

5

Ooo	oOo	oOoo	ooOoo
glamorous humorous tremulous	courageous outrageous	carnivorous herbivorous incredulous miraculous	insectivorous miscellaneous simultaneous

⚠ In fast speech, *-eous* in 'miscellaneous' and 'simultaneous' might be said as one syllable (/-jəs/), so would have the pattern ooOo.

6

oO	ooO	oooO
Chinese laundrette trainee	auctioneer detainee divorcee journalese Taiwanese	cohabitee evacuee examinee interviewee

7

oOo	ooOo	oOoo	ooOoo
provincial substantial torrential	differential influential presidential	adverbial industrial remedial	ceremonial editorial managerial

⚠ In fast speech, *-ial* in 'averbial', 'remedial' and 'ceremonial' might be said as one syllable (/-jəl/), so would have the patterns oOo ('adverbial' and 'remedial') and ooOo ('ceremonial').

8

oOo	oOoo	ooOo	ooOoo	oooOo
addiction location	ethnicity extremity	accusation diplomatic formulaic	authenticity elasticity musicality	abbreviation characteristic

9

oOo	oOoo	ooOo	Oooo
constructive explosive impulsive progressive	exploitative indicative	apprehensive inconclusive interactive reproductive	illustrative innovative

The exception is 'indicative' (compare 'indicate and in'dicative).

10

Ooo	oOo	oOoo
hesitant ignorance negligence resident tolerant	coherent pollutant	experience inhabitant inheritance magnificent significant

11

oOo		ooOo
appliance compliance defiant deterrent observance	occurrence resemblance resistant triumphant	correspondent independence obsolescence

12

Ooo	oOo	oOoo	ooOo
government measurement settlement	achievement investment recruitment retirement	accomplishment development embarrassment	disappointment entertainment

Key to phonemic and other symbols

Vowels

Short vowels		Long vowels		Diphthongs	
ɪ	pit, it	iː	see, eat	eɪ	day, eight
e	wet, end	ɑː	part, arm	aɪ	my, eyes
æ	cat, apple	ɔː	saw, always	ɔɪ	boy, join
ʌ	run, up	uː	too, you	əʊ	low, open
ɒ	hot, opposite	ɜː	her, early	aʊ	how, out
ʊ	put, would			ɪə	near, here
				eə	hair, where
ə	ago, doctor			ʊə	tourist, sure
i	happy, cosy				
u	influence, annual				

Consonants

b	bee, about	m	map, lamp	z	zoo, loves
d	do, side	n	nose, any	dʒ	general, age
f	fat, safe	p	pen, stop	ŋ	hang, hoping
g	go, big	r	red, around	ð	that, other
h	hat, behind	s	soon, us	θ	thin, bath
j	yet, you	t	ten, last	ʃ	ship, push
k	key, week	v	vet, live	ʒ	measure, usual
l	led, allow	w	wet, swim	tʃ	chin, catch

Other symbols used in this book

/ʔ/ a glottal stop, as in /ˈfʊʔbɑːl/ ('football'). See Section E4 *Glossary* for more information.

/^{ə}/ shows that /ə/ can be pronounced or not pronounced, as in /ˈæv^{ə}rɪdʒ/ (average).

/^{r}/ shows that in BBC English /r/ is pronounced when it is followed by a vowel sound but not when it is followed by a consonant sound, as in /ˈbrʌðə^{r}/ (brother). In some other varieties, such as North American English, /r/ is always pronounced.

/ˈ/ put before the syllable with main stress, as in /ɪˈvent/ (eˈvent).

/ˌ/ put before the syllable with secondary stress, as in /ˌætməsˈferɪk/ (ˌatmosˈpheric).

/l̩/ shows a syllabic consonant, as in /ˈbɒtl̩/ (bottle). See Section E4 *Glossary* for more information.

/./ shows syllable divisions within a word, as in /ˈdɪf.ə/ (differ).